ALSO BY LEV KOPELEV

To Be Preserved Forever (1977)
The Education of a True Believer (1980)

EASE
MY
SORROWS

EASE MY SORROWS

A MEMOIR

LEV KOPELEV

Translated from the Russian by Antonina W. Bouis

RANDOM HOUSE · NEW YORK

Library of Congress Cataloging in Publication Data

Kopelev, Lev, 1912–
  Ease my sorrows.

  "An Ardis book."
  Translation of: Utoli moïa pechali.
  Includes index.
  1. Kopelev, Lev, 1912–   —Biography.
2. Authors, Russian—20th century—Biography.
3. Political prisoners—Soviet Union—Biography.
I. Title.
PG3482.7.P4Z47513 1983   891.78′4403 [B]   83-3267
ISBN 0-394-52784-4

A NOTE ON
LEV KOPELEV
BY ROBERT G. KAISER

In America we no longer seem to have giants—people who play such large and important roles that they dwarf their fellow men. But in Russia there still are giants, and Lev Kopelev is one of them.

Alas, Kopelev is no longer in Russia. Like so many of the most gifted Russians of our time, he has been forced to leave. Astoundingly, given the cynicism of the age, Kopelev left in 1980 for another country where he is also recognized as a giant, the Federal Republic of Germany. I was with him there not long ago and watched Germans stop to stare at this towering man with the huge white beard as we walked through the streets of Cologne, where he now lives. In West Germany the mass media have made Kopelev a famous *figura*. He is actually better known there than he was in his native land.

But it was in Russia that Kopelev earned his stature as a giant. He did it by living an extraordinary life, which—over the course of seventy years —has included great foolishness, great courage, great suffering, and many great and small triumphs. Happily, this rich life goes on much as before in its new surroundings. Kopelev may be getting old by the calendar, but he has barely paused to acknowledge that fact. He is busy now writing and speaking the lessons he has learned in order to share them with all of us.

Sharing is an instinct with Kopelev, as it is with most people whom others love to be around. We all know one or two such personalities, people who are so generous, so interesting, so *big* as human beings as to be irresistible.

I first met Lev Kopelev and his wife, Raisa Orlova, in the spring of 1972. I was the Moscow correspondent of the Washington *Post*, and I had been brought to the Kopelevs' apartment on Red Army Street by another American, who had been given their address by a mutual friend. This other American was my colleague Carroll Kilpatrick, then the *Post*'s White House correspondent, who was in Moscow with Richard M. Nixon. It was an exciting time; the first hint of détente was in the air, and intellectuals like the Kopelevs allowed themselves to indulge once again the classic Russian intellectuals' hope for liberalization, a loosening up of official controls on writing, thinking, traveling, and so on.

Meeting Kopelev is one of life's memorable experiences. He is huge, 6'3" at least, broad of beam, and his beard flows in white profusion from beneath sparkling eyes and a prominent nose. He has a big voice, a big grin, a big grip, and a huge appreciation for humanity. He treats every new person like a pearl found by chance in an oyster—a great treasure, but just what you'd expect, right? It is the sort of personality I associate with the Old Testament prophets, at least the lovable ones.

That day in May 1972, the Kopelevs were delighted to have two American newspapermen in their front room, and they gave us a warm welcome. We symbolized the outside world from which they were isolated but to which they were drawn for news, for literature, for ideas. At once we disappointed them; we had failed to bring the latest American news magazines and copies of the Paris *Herald Tribune* that they craved. Then we disappointed them a second time. They launched into an account of the latest Moscow literary intrigues, expecting us both to follow all the nuances. I tried to pretend I was grasping it all (I had been in Moscow for six months and was struggling to learn all I could of such things), but Carroll made not the slightest pretext of following their story. He had heard of Solzhenitsyn but not of Aleksandr Tvardovsky, the editor who had first published Solzhenitsyn and who had died the year before, the editor who played an important part in the story they were telling. The next time I came to visit, by myself, Raya expressed her astonishment that the White House correspondent of the Washington *Post* had never heard of such a great figure as Tvardovsky.

Intellectual standards and expectations are high in the Kopelev household. My failure to achieve intimacy with the work of Thomas Mann and Bertolt Brecht—among countless other German masters—was a terrible failing in Lev's eyes, though he never criticized directly. And Raya, an expert on American literature, expected my wife and me to know all the books of all the significant modern American authors, and was taken aback when it became clear we did not. Russian intellectuals are serious about their work.

But my failure to live up to their standards did not exhaust the Kopelevs' patience. They are both natural teachers, and both were willing to devote long hours to my education about Russia. Those hours were the highlight of my years in the Soviet Union.

Now Kopelev has shared the best lessons from most of his life in three volumes of memoirs. This is the third. Together they chronicle much of an extraordinary adventure that took Kopelev through nearly all the exciting events of Soviet history, from the collectivization of agriculture in the 1920s (which Kopelev promoted personally as an ardent and naïve young Communist) through the horrors of Stalinism, the war, the post-Stalin thaw, and the exciting 1960s and 1970s, when Russia emerged from its isolation, though the hopes of Kopelev and his friends were repeatedly dashed. His has been such a full life that even three volumes could not encompass it; this volume ends in 1953, long before Kopelev became a key member of the Moscow circle of dissident intellectuals, working with

Andrei Sakharov and many others in vain pursuit of a more democratic Soviet society.

These memoirs provide fascinating evidence about twentieth-century Russia, essentially for two reasons. First, Kopelev is a gifted reporter, blessed with an astounding memory. His books are filled with miniature portraits of Soviet citizens, men and women recognizable to us as fellow humans, even as fellow members of "Western civilization" (though this similarity can be overstated, because Russia, though part of Europe, is equally part of Asia and the East), who come to life in these pages. Kopelev has always collected people; here he shares his collection.

The second reason these books are important is the author himself. Kopelev is no ordinary intellectual, and no ordinary dissident. For many years, *including* years he spent in prison after the war on ludicrous, trumped-up charges, Kopelev was a devoted, loyal Stalinist. He believed unreservedly in the promise of communism, and followed Stalin blindly. Later, when he realized how wrong he had been, Kopelev began to write these memoirs, at first without any hope of publishing them. "We wrote for our children," he explained to me later, speaking for himself and for Raya, who is also publishing her memoirs, "for our grandchildren, because we were sure that they would ask, 'How was it possible that you believed in Stalin? How was it possible that you took part in such crimes and such bad deeds?' "

The Kopelev memoirs offer many answers to those questions, though in the end a smidgeon of mystery remains. Perhaps a person who has been deeply, profoundly changed can no longer fully evoke his previous self. Kopelev can tell us what he was like as a Stalinist, but he is now such a tolerant, gentle man that I suspect some part of the portrait may be missing. Tolerance, he and Raya have both told me, was the one great lesson they learned that turned them away from their old selves. "This [Soviet] system is bad not because it is ruled by bad people, but because it lets good people do bad things," Lev said to me once. "Normal, average, good people are involved in very bad politics."

Kopelev has led a fascinating life from the time he came home from school to his middle-class Jewish family in the Ukraine wearing the red scarf of the Young Pioneers. "My father was very angry about the scarf," Kopelev recalled. "He even tried to beat me." It would be impossible to say which phase of his subsequent adventures was the most interesting, but I am most intrigued by the years he spent in a *sharashka*, or special prison camp for scientists, the period described in *Ease My Sorrows*.

Only a Stalin could have dreamt up the sharashka. It was a special facility where gifted Soviet citizens imprisoned for "political crimes" could continue to serve the motherland by conducting useful research. In some sharashkas airplanes were designed, in others radar. Kopelev was convicted of "bourgeois humanism" after World War II because, as a political officer with Soviet troops advancing on Berlin, he had tried to prevent his men from raping and pillaging their way through Prussia. He spent much of his prison term in a sharashka on the edge of Moscow—a prison, to be sure, but a relatively comfortable one. In it Kopelev and many others worked on designing electronic scramblers that could break up, then recompose the human voice so that enemies of the state could not bug official Soviet communications. (Lev was there because of his skills as a linguist.)

Kopelev's vivid portrait of the sharashka in this book is not the first time this institution has been described in print. One of Kopelev's fellow prisoners turned out to be a writer—indeed, he turned out to be the most renowned Russian writer of our time, Aleksandr Solzhenitsyn. Solzhenitsyn described the sharashka in what I consider his finest book, *The First Circle*. One of the principal characters in that novel is Lev Rubin, a gentle giant, highly intelligent, but stubbornly devoted to Stalin and communism. Rubin is Solzhenitsyn's version of Kopelev.

Solzhenitsyn's book is fiction, so he had a license to revise the reality for his own literary purposes; but the way he did so, judging by Kopelev's account here, is noteworthy. *The First Circle* begins with a vivid scene in which a Soviet diplomat makes an anonymous call from a public phone booth in Moscow to the apartment of a prominent professor of medicine warning him not to send medicine to some colleagues in France as he had promised to do, because giving something to foreigners would get him into serious trouble. In *The First Circle* this phone call was a noble, if futile, gesture. It turns out that the political police have recorded the call, and the tape is sent to this sharashka. The experts there are asked to determine whose voice is on the tape—who made the anonymous phone call. In this context it is dirty Stalinist business, tracking down a decent person who tried to do a decent thing.

There was a phone call, a tape, and an instruction to figure out who was speaking. But for Kopelev, the event had a totally different character.* The call was not a humane gesture, but a traitor's work. The voice on the tape (several tapes, actually) was calling not a professor of medicine but Western embassies in Moscow, particularly the American Embassy, to betray a Soviet intelligence operation scheduled to occur in New York City. Kopelev felt no qualms working on this assignment, because he believed he was dealing with a turncoat, who was betraying his country to the imperialists.

Why did Solzhenitsyn so alter the story? Kopelev has raised the question for future scholars and literary detectives. He also, in this volume, provides a brilliant portrait of the young Solzhenitsyn that will be invaluable to critics and future biographers of another of modern Russia's giants. Here

---

*In the new edition of *The First Circle*, included in Volume I of Solzhenitsyn's *Collected Works*, published by the YMCA Press in Paris in 1978, Solzhenitsyn has revised the treatment of this incident so that it is substantially similar to Kopelev's description of it.

is Solzhenitsyn before he has written anything of note, a man who is still looking for the posture he wants to adopt toward Soviet society.

This chance meeting of two extraordinary men in Stalin's GULag was to have much greater consequences. Solzhenitsyn was later exiled to Central Asia, where he contracted and was later cured of cancer, then was transferred in the 1950s to the small Russian town of Ryazan, where he became a schoolteacher and began writing novels. Kopelev was freed, and he returned to Moscow, where he became an active participant in the capital's intellectual life. In the early 1960s Solzhenitsyn came to the Kopelevs with a short novel he had written and asked them for help in getting it published. They took it to Aleksandr Tvardovsky, who published it in his magazine, *Novy Mir* (The New World), as *One Day in the Life of Ivan Denisovich*, a book about the life of prisoners in Stalin's camps that electrified the Soviet Union.

Kopelev's principal intellectual interests have been German literature and the German language. In Moscow he was a virtual one-man cultural exchange program with both East and West Germany. He befriended the leading writers from both countries, who came to see him on visits to the Soviet Union. His many friends among German newspaper correspondents helped make him a well-known figure in West Germany.

When the first volume of Kopelev's memoirs appeared in 1976, it caused a great sensation in Germany. In it Kopelev described both the brutal treatment the Soviet army had inflicted on Germans (just deserts, most of the Russians figured) and his own attempts to prevent the worst excesses of rape and mayhem, as well as the trials and prison terms that were *his* deserts. The book touched some responsive chord in the German psyche, perhaps because it reaffirmed the humanity of ordinary Germans caught up in the war and personified the Russian army in one particularly attractive human being. Whatever the reason, the book became a best seller in Germany. Kopelev didn't know it at the time, but this triumph turned out to be more than just a happy surprise. It also smoothed his path to a new life in West Germany.

That became suddenly desirable in 1980, when Kopelev realized that after Sakharov's forced exile to the city of Gorky, he was headed for serious trouble if he did not get out of the Soviet Union.

Even then Kopelev refused to leave on a permanent exit visa. After intervention from some of the most influential people in West Germany, the Soviets granted him a passport and permission to make a temporary trip to the Federal Republic. But soon a letter arrived from Moscow announcing that the Soviet government had stripped Lev and Raya of their citizenship—patriotism's last reward.

To lose one's country is a tragedy for anyone, but it is particularly cruel punishment for a Russian. The Kopelevs are now forever cut off from their children, their friends, and their roots. They are extraordinarily lucky by the standards of most involuntary exiles—they have a comfortable life in a country where they are respected and where Lev at least is thoroughly at home. (Raya, who speaks excellent English, is learning German also.) Still, they have lost their home.

They knew the risk they were taking when they left Moscow in 1980. They took with them a small parcel of Russian soil—"To throw on my grave in case I die while abroad," Kopelev explained to the customs agent in Moscow, an employee of the KGB. This gentleman didn't like the idea, however, and he confiscated the black earth.

CONTENTS

EASE
MY
SORROWS

1

THE
MARFINO
SHARASHKA

I absolutely must write this. So, here, listen . . .
—ALEKSEI N. TOLSTOY, "Ease My Sorrows"

October 1947. The night after the trial. In Butyrki Prison I was brought to a large overcrowded room. No fewer than fifty bodies piled on the plank beds, on the narrow benches along the table, on the floor. A heavy, foul stuffiness. I started making my way to the window, closer to the stream of frosty air.

The man lying by the window sat up like a shot. A blue-eyed knight with a short reddish beard. "Don't you dare shut it!"

"I don't intend to. On the contrary, I want to get closer."

We argued at first. But by the next day we were friends.

Dmitri Panin was a native Muscovite, an aristocrat, engineer, and theoretician of blacksmithing. He was arrested in 1940 for "conversations" and sentenced *in absentia* to five years by an OSO (secret "court" under the MGB).* And then in the camp in 1943 he was tried for "defeatist agitation" and was "given the whole spool"—ten years.

He had been brought to Butyrki Prison in Moscow from Vorkuta, near the Arctic Ocean, by a special warrant.

There were a lot like him in the room—engineers, scientific workers. It was from them that I first heard about sharashkas.†

*The Soviet secret police, which arrested criminals against the state and ran the GULag, has operated under various titles since its establishment in 1917, though it also had a prerevolutionary ancestry. It was called the Cheka (All-Russian Extraordinary Commission for the Struggle Against Counterrevolution and Sabotage) until 1922, when it was reorganized as OGPU (Unified State Political Administration). In 1934 it became the NKVD (the People's Commissariat for Internal Affairs) and carried out the purges of 1937–1938 under Nikolai Yezhov. After Yezhov's execution, Lavrentii Beria ran the NKGB (People's Commissariat of State Security), which in 1946 became the MGB (Ministry of State Security), and in 1953, the KGB (Committee for State Security).

Thus, when Kopelev began serving his sentence in 1947, the sharashkas were administered by the MGB, under Minister Viktor Abakumov. (Translator's note.)

†A sharashka is a special scientific and technical institute staffed by prisoners and free employees. "Ease My Sorrows" is the name of a church in Marfino, on the outskirts of Moscow, that was converted into a sharashka. (Translator's note.)

"They really need educated people now. They've brought entire plants and laboratories from Germany, piles of technical documents. And now they're bringing specialists from all the camps here for the sharashkas. These are special design offices or institutes in which *zeks** are the main work force. Ramzin and Tupolev† commanded sharashkas.

"Everything is set up very simply. Professors, engineers with higher degrees, inventors—they're all used to being spoiled. They get lots of money, special food rations for academics. In those circumstances one occasionally gets the urge to live it up—in a restaurant with girls or at the dacha with one's legal spouse. And take one's vacation no earlier than August, no later than September, and only on the South Shore or in Sochi-Matsesta. On the outside, your head is rarely concerned only with work. All kinds of extraneous thoughts pop up, and worries, and dreams —about bars, careers, apartments, dachas, fights with colleagues, children, relatives, friends, acquaintances.

"So, that means that on the outside an engineer can't work to his full capacity and beyond it. A worker, with the help of the Party committee and the factory committee, can be pushed without problems to Stakhano-vite status—others do his thinking for him; his duty is simply to keep his nose to the grindstone and not get in the way of the flying bullshit. And he will give as much as he's ordered to—a hundred, even two hundred, even a thousand percent. Neither a mind nor a conscience is needed for that. But for a man who has even something like a conscience—things are more complicated. And especially if he understands a lot about himself, thinks that he's smarter than his bosses.

"A person like that can be helped only by our Soviet security organs. They grab him by the scruff of the neck, drag him to Lubyanka, Lefortovo, or Sykhanovka‡—confess, bastard, who did you spy on, how did you wreck, where did you sabotage . . . They lower him once or twice into the cooler when it's freezing, when there's water in it. They'll hit him on the face, the ass, the ribs—not to kill or maim, but so that he will feel pain and shame, so that he will know that he is no longer a human being but just a nothing and that they can do whatever they want to him. The prosecutor will explain the articles to him and promise him the maximum. The investi-gator threatens to arrest his wife if he doesn't confess.

"And then, after all that, they give him a magnanimous ten years. Some weak-nerved types would see fifteen and twenty years as a gift, an unex-pected joy. And then they'll console him: work hard and you'll be able to

---

*Soviet slang for prisoner (often written *z/k*), from the Russian *zakliuchennyi* ("prisoner"). (Translator's note.)

†Leonid Konstantinovich Ramzin (1887–1948), a boiler engineer arrested in the Promparty Affair (see p. 34); the leading engineer of a sharashka and later released and highly honored.

Andrei Nikolaevich Tupolev (1888–1972), aircraft designer arrested as an "enemy of the people" in 1938; worked in a sharashka, and was released in 1943. (Translator's note.)

‡Moscow prisons of the secret police. (Translator's note.)

earn early parole and even awards. Use people like Ramzin for a model, prove that you have repented sincerely, that your knowledge and abilities are of benefit to the motherland—and all you had will be returned to you and you will receive even more.

"So they're preparing the cadres for the sharashkas. Our people are really working there, giving full value. No days off. Vacation is a foreign word. Overtime is sheer pleasure; anything's better than sleeping in the cell. You chase away thoughts of freedom, of home—they only bring on depression and despair. And work is no longer a duty but the only meaning of life, the substitute for all pleasures and all comforts. Work is medicine, work is a drug . . .

"In the camps they say: 'Labor made the ape into a man, and man into an ass.' Working in a camp means hauling, bending your back, pushing with your horns. But without kicking the bucket, 'floating off,' earning 'a wooden jacket' (coffin)—you have to goof off, shirk, pad, look like you're working, chisel, inflict wounds that will fester.

"But in the sharashka, it's just the reverse. They address you by your name and patronymic, feed you decently, better than many eat on the outside; you work in warmth, sleep on a straw mattress with a sheet. No worries—just make sure to use your brain, think, invent, perfect, advance science and technology."

Mitya Panin was the first one to tell me about the sharashkas. And it was he, either having invented it himself or repeating someone else's words, who called them the first circle of our prison-camp hell.

On his advice I wrote an application.

"You know foreign languages. Why should you go to a camp and croak at a logging site or in a mine? You won't be able to land a medic's job everywhere. And you know yourself what it's like for a decent person to deal with the inmates who land the easy jobs. Languages are precious knowledge. They can save you. Write to the fourth special section of the Ministry of Internal Affairs: 'I am fluent in German, English, French, Spanish, Dutch, Italian.' You're not too fluent? It doesn't matter, no one can check. When you get into a sharashka, you'll study there. What others do you know? Polish, Czech, Serbo-Croatian. Come on, come on, the more the better. Be sure to add: 'I have considerable experience in translating scientific and technical literature. I would like to be of use in connection with . . .' Well you know the rest. Most important, sign yourself 'Candidate of Sciences'—they appreciate that."

About two weeks later I was called in: "Travel light." (That is, without my things.)

In the small investigator's office sat two colonels. Silver epaulets and dark-blue piping. On the table before them—files with prison dossiers. The long-faced one, balding and wearing glasses, started speaking good high school German. I replied. He asked a few simple questions in English, twisting his tongue assiduously. And unconstrainedly in French.

The second colonel, broad-shouldered and coarse, asked me in Russian where I had studied, the subject of my dissertation, what I had done at the front. "You've applied here to the fourth section. How did you learn about that section? Who told you? You didn't ask his name? How can that be—you live in the same cell and you don't know his name? And you expect us to trust you! Ah, you were only in the baths with him, making random conversation?! Well, let's assume that's possible. So, we want to use you in your field. But in a department, in a unit that is completely secret. The strictest state secret. The person who blabbed to you in the bath committed a divulgence. Gab like that is subject to the severest punishment, right up to the highest measures. You will be trusted with certain matters. Perhaps even with very serious matters. But for that, things will be demanded of you. Understand?

"You may take him away."

(Later I got to know both colonels better. The long-faced intellectual was Anton Mikhailovich V., the prototype of Yakonov in Solzhenitsyn's novel *The First Circle*. The other one is mentioned there, too—Foma Fomich Zh., a veteran of the security organs. He was educated in an Odessa music workers' school. They say he was a talented bayan-accordion player. Later, having become a worker of the special section of the GPU-NKVD-MGB in charge of engineers and scientists, he received the degree of doctor of sciences.)

When Panin was called in with his things, we said good-bye—the way they usually do in prisons—forever. We made the wry joke: "Schweik set a date for six o'clock in the evening after the war. We'll meet at 'six o'clock in the evening after prison.' "

About two weeks later I was taken out of Butyrki along with several other engineers from our cell. We drove no more than forty or fifty minutes. That meant still within city limits.

We were unloaded in a large courtyard garden. Dark firs, a thick dark-gray thread of bare trees and bushes. The fence wasn't visible. It suggested itself under the dense rank of lights.

A three-story brick building of the old construction. At the far end, a tower with a cupola. A brightly lit entrance.

We were admitted by guards in MVD* uniforms, unhurriedly calm. None of the barking shouts of the camp screws, none of the hoarse threatening whispers of the prison supervisors.

"Go up to the third floor. Everything will be explained there."

The staircase belonged in the front hall of an old town house or a Gymnasium—stone steps, banisters on iron posts.

Descending toward us was Mitya Panin. He wore his old padded jacket

*Ministry of Internal Affairs. (Translator's note.)

flung over his shoulders like a hussar's cloak. He spoke in a businesslike manner, as though we had parted an hour ago. "This is the Marfino sharashka. They call it Object Number Eight or Special Prison Number Sixteen. Everything here is from the dismantled Berlin labs of the Philips Company. They're developing a 'police radio.'* We've been waiting for you for a week now. The chief here is the kind you can talk to in a human way. A young engineer captain. Phlegmatic, not malicious. And we convinced him to request you from Butyrki—famous linguist and highly experienced translator from all languages that you are. The cellars are stuffed with thousands of files, and there are both scientific and industrial descriptions of the equipment, which has never been seen here before. No one in this place understands written German. We'll set you loose on that. Who's we? My friend and I. I'll introduce you. A wonderful man! Aleksandr Isaevich Solzhenitsyn. Also from the front lines. A captain. Bright. A most noble soul. A personality! He's in charge of the technical library. I'm certain that you will come to love him, too. It was he who helped me convince the chief; he maintained that there were a lot of unexamined books and that notes about them were imperative."

A large semicircular room, composed of the lower half of a church.†

In the left half stood several desks and carrels.

The entire right half was taken up by the library. A dozen shelves and cases with books and a large desk for the librarian.

He rose to meet us. Tall, with light-brown hair, dressed in a faded army tunic. Intense light-blue eyes. Large forehead. Harsh rays of wrinkles over the bridge of his nose. One is uneven—a scar.

A firm handshake. A quick smile.

"Hello. Mitya has told me a lot of good things about you. Your desk is all prepared. Right here. We'll be neighbors. Can you type? Well, speed isn't important for now. My advice: start translating right onto the typewriter. It'll be good training. Where did you fight? Is that so."

His gaze became even more intense and seemed to grow shaded.

(Later he said: "I didn't believe you at first. It even seemed suspicious. The very same fronts.")

"I was also in the northwest."

He told me that his battery had been stationed near Molvotitsy. We recalled the road, the woods dense with land mines, where several of our soldiers had been killed. Then he had been transferred to the Kursk Salient. And on the Second Byelorussian Front he was again in the same places as I. Near Narevo, where a small house on a hill had miraculously survived

---

*The radiotelephone, or walkie-talkie, now used by militiamen on the beat, in squad cars, by taxi drivers, police spies, and so on.

†Later, when the entire sharashka building had been expanded, this room became the one described in *The First Circle*.

in the very line of fire. And he had heard my voice, naturally, while we were transmitting. (That day was easy to remember. Two German tanks rode up and down the edge of the forest and fired armor-piercing shells. They whined and howled in a loathsome way, but they were dangerous only in a direct hit. And it turned out that he was the one correcting the fire of the battery that fought off the tanks.)

"And from where did you enter Prussia? Exactly! So did I. No, when we were coming into Gross Kozlau nothing was burning yet. That means you moved later. Is that right? You also looked for Hindenburg's grave? What a coincidence! Wait, wait, what was the date when you were in Hohenstein? No, when we turned off from the highway, I don't think there were any tire marks. You noticed tracks? Right, yesterday's fellow soldiers don't need to use the formal 'you.' So, you followed in my tracks. Look how fate brings people together. When were you arrested? In April? I was nabbed back in February, on Red Army Day. First I was in Brodnitsy, in a stone cellar—a field prison. No, they didn't take me to Tukhel, they sent me to Moscow."

We began recalling guards, interrogators . . .

"Wait. There's time for that. We have long walks here. In the evening you can wander around the yard for almost two hours. But now see what you need for work—which dictionaries, reference works. I'll get them, requisition them. And tomorrow you can start first thing in the morning. I have a file all ready for you—equipment specifications—primarily in German. I tried translating them myself, but it was hard. We learned very different German in school and at the university. Newspapers? Of course we have them: *Pravda*, *Izvestia*, *Krasnaya zvezda* [*Red Star*]. I can give you the back files, too. But only to be read here. They can't be taken from the library. How far back do you want them? The whole autumn? Fine."

Later he said: "You were the first one to ask for back issues. The first one after me. When we were brought here from Noginsk—the sharashka was first planned for there, and then they transferred it here—the files were the first thing I read. Just look at that: we were at the same fronts, the same counterespionage group swept us up. And we have the same appetite for newspapers. It makes us related in a way."

That first winter in the sharashka—1947–1948—the prisoners were situated in two rooms on the third floor. On the same floor were the duty room, the medical office, and the office of the head of the prison. At the end, a short stairway led to the storeroom under the cupola. On the vaulted ceiling pale paint was still peeling: blue sky, the faces and robes of angels, scraps of Slavonic script. Beneath them hulked wooden shelves with crates and bales.

The second floor was for the main laboratories; the first, for the dining room and workshops. Two thirds of the yard was marked off by a high fence, doubled by plywood walls lined with sheet metal. That's where the construction took place. Nonpolitical prisoners worked there.

Our workday began in the morning and lasted until six in the evening. We were allowed to go for walks first thing in the morning, before and after breakfast. The workday could be extended as one wanted. The heads of all the laboratories were prisoners. They gave the daily supervisors lists of those who stayed on to work after dinner.

The evening check was made without formality. The duty supervisor looked into the laboratory. "How many of you here? Everyone in place? No one in the bathroom? Let's get to the cell no later than midnight. Don't be late."

Visits with relatives were supposed to take place every three months. And one could receive any number of letters, packages. But we could send letters only to people out of town. The prison assistant administrator, aka mailman and supply clerk, a harried, fat-faced lieutenant, explained that Muscovites could receive packages three times a month and a visit once every three months.

"But correspondence is not allowed! Wait until your meeting. You can explain everything then."

Solzhenitsyn made a suggestion. "Why don't you go ask the head of the prison—Lieutenant Colonel G., he's not one of the screws. He's a line officer, an army man. He likes military bearing and he likes people to look him in the eye. He can't stand weaklings, toadies, and obfuscators. Otherwise, I don't think he's mean. Approach him according to regulations. Maybe he'll help."

In the camps we had learned to distinguish between good superiors and bad. The criterion was simple and infallible: one forbids everything that is not specifically permitted, the other permits everything that is not specifically forbidden.

Shaving carefully, I adjusted my tunic so that there wasn't a single wrinkle in front, polished my boots and buttons. I knocked briefly, but clearly.

"Yes . . ."

Upon entering, I stamped three steps, clicked my heels, and froze at attention.

"Permission to speak?"

The lieutenant colonel was sitting at the window. He turned. A thin, broad-shouldered man, his short hair streaked with gray. He did not smile readily. Intense light eyes. "What was your rank? Where did you fight? Article? Sentence? What do you have to say?"

"I'm requesting permission to contact my family, living in Moscow, so that they will write and bring a package. Request permission as an exception. I won't get a meeting until spring, and my daughter is sick. And I need the package. I've been sick, malnourished."

"Who's in your family? Write them a card now, have them bring the package to Butyrki for Object Eight. Hurry it up: I'm leaving in a half hour. Is that clear?"

"Yes, sir. Write a postcard. Hand it to you. Permission to go?"

I turned sharply, with a jerk, stamped my right foot, started off with my left. A few minutes later I was running back with the card.

When I told Panin and Solzhenitsyn of my success, we discussed the superiority of military behavior by the book. Clearly defined, standardized gestures and words, even though they expressed dependency, subordination, and obedience, still allowed you to maintain your human dignity. A soldier's demeanor differs from a slave's or flunky's. I recalled that at the front, too, a marked smartness according to regulations was practically the only and certainly the least dangerous form of resistance to the officious boorishness of certain colonels and generals. Anatolii Gavrilovich Voinov, a lieutenant in the tsarist army and a major in the Red Army, taught us new recruits: "Dissatisfaction with superiors can be expressed only at attention through the wordless movement of the big toe, and it goes without saying, in a shod condition."

During the second week of my stay, I became ill. A harsh cough racked my chest. I ached everywhere. My temperature reached 40° Celsius [104° F]. The feldsher [paramedic], a first lieutenant, a young woman with a frontline ribbon, said: "The doctor won't be here for another three days. He comes twice a week. That means we have to send you to the hospital, in Butyrki."

Cruelly frightened, I begged: "Just don't send me anywhere. I can work in bed. Translating. This is just an ordinary cold."

She hesitated, but agreed to wait a day or two. Friends brought me food from the dining room. Swallowing a lot of aspirin, I would pile my padded jacket and some other rubbish from the supply room over my blanket. My greatest fear was that they would take me away from sharashka heaven, and after the hospital, forget to bring me back.

Never—not before, and not since—was I so happy to be cured. And to prevent a recurrence, I embarked on a strenuous strengthening regimen. I exercised morning and evening in the yard. On my walks, I tried to breathe as deeply as possible. I washed down to my waist with cold water. Then I started rubbing myself with snow. And I never got another cold to the last day of my term, seven years later. (But on the outside, the very first autumn, and in Essentuki* of all places, I was felled by pneumonia.)

Sharashka grub in the first postprison days seemed luxurious. At breakfast you could sometimes even get seconds of wheat cereal. The lunch soup —and it was soup, not gruel—occasionally had pieces of real meat. And

*A health resort in the Caucasus.

the main course of buckwheat kasha was thick, with obvious traces of meat. And there was always a third course—*kisel'*, a fruit jelly sauce. But all these marvelous foods did not overly fill us up. We were constantly hungry. There wasn't enough bread—500 grams a day.

We awaited packages with impatience. But we didn't start getting them until January.

The three of us welcomed the new year of 1948 on Panin's cot, on the second tier of the bunk system, made up of ordinary iron beds.

One of our cellmates, who received packages, gave us a quarter of a can of condensed cocoa. We saved the sugar from breakfast and some bread from dinner. And we drew two pots of boiling water.

The duty supervisor that evening was very understanding. "I know it's New Year's. But we must have order. After lights out—quiet. Other zeks want to sleep. So you be careful not to make any noise. If I hear it outside, or if anyone complains, they'll have my hide, and you'll be punished. You'll start the New Year in the cooler."

But that night there were groups of celebrants in other parts of the cell. Everyone partied in the dull glare of the night-lights. Almost every bed had small attached night-lights, made by our technicians. There were many homemade radios, which upset Solzhenitsyn almost every night. He had trouble falling asleep, and the buzzing of earphones, forgotten by sleepy listeners, disturbed him, drove him crazy. He would jump down from the second tier of the bunks, find them, and unplug them. In the New Year's poem I wrote, I had the following lines:

> Quiet is the sharashka night,
> The stars shine in the dark bars,
> The screw can't overcome his
> Sleepiness. Who then is
> Cursing hoarsely, and
> Scurrying about the bunks in his underpants?
> It's angry Sanya Solzhenitsyn
> Seeking the unstilled earphones.

Panin triumphantly raised a mug of fragrant cocoa. "Gentlemen, I don't know how to give speeches, I'm not silver-tongued, like you two. But I am older than you and I began my stations of the cross before you. Therefore, allow me to proclaim a New Year's toast. Dear friends! I am certain I may call you that. We are soberly greeting the New Year, and I want to make a sober wish. It is customary to say, 'A New Year! New Happiness!' But what happiness can we have? We all dream of freedom. But that is an unrealizable dream within these walls, in this country. And so I raise a sober toast to the possible. I drink to the New Year, in which we will not go hungry . . . and will remain friends. Gentlemen . . ."

The three of us lived together another two and a half years, until the summer of 1950. We were not hungry. And we were friends.

The earliest riser was Mitya Panin. Even before reveille he hurried through his exercises and headed for the backyard, where he sawed and chopped wood by the kitchen door. "Suppressing the flesh" even in the coldest weather, he strolled without a hat, his jacket thrown over his shoulder, his shirt open at the chest sailor-style; in the spring, as soon as the snow started melting, he took off his shoes and stepped out barefoot, trying to walk on the most inconvenient paths, on gravel and coal bits. Some mornings he dragged Solzhenitsyn and me out for the "wood exercises." The supervisors encouraged such industriousness. They had to keep an eye on us, and this brought them closer to the generosity of the cooks, who were helped by prisoners thirsting for outdoor work and who fed the supervisors while they watched us.

In the mornings we usually worked and strolled in silence. Prison awakenings are not merry. After pleasant dreams of freedom and family, reality is that much worse. It was no better after nightmares or difficult sleepless nights, filled with thoughts that persisted to despair and marked by the suffocating depression of loneliness amid a multitude of strangers who were inseparably forced together—wheezing, snoring, moaning, or screaming wildly in their sleep.

During the lunch walks, which were the most crowded and noisy, it was harder to have a talk with one or two people. But in the evenings there were fewer people taking walks, especially in bad weather. Many stayed indoors. Some washed their socks and handkerchiefs in the sink, others played dominoes, which they called "killing the goat," chess, checkers, still others gossiped in the smoky corridor or simply lay about on their cots.

The three of us usually signed up for evening work, and tried to stay out on our walk as long as possible before prisoner count.

Sometimes an insurmountable desire arose to be alone. But only to friends could one say simply, "Today I want to walk alone." And then the two tried to protect the third. This was easier in winter. We dug our own path in the snow between the bushes.

Solzhenitsyn asked for solitude most often. He strode along the path, tall, thin, in a long military overcoat, the earflaps of his army hat lowered. And Panin and I patrolled by the entrance to the main square of the yard, for which the sharashka wags came up with a number of pompous names: The Square of Trampled Hopes, Gabodrome, Donkey Manège, and so on.

We had long conversations—on the fate of Russia and Europe, on religion, philosophy, history, literature.

In the very first days, Solzhenitsyn said to me: "Could you give me a chronological history of the revolutionary movement in Russia? Well, it's understandable that you can't remember everything. But I need the general chronology, the connections between events, profiles of the people. But most of all—without bullshit, without cover-ups, and as much as you can, objectively, without prejudice. Naturally, you are prejudiced. You're a Marxist-Leninist and that means you'll always be a Party man. But I understand that and can make the appropriate correction. You just talk, tell me everything you remember. But don't obfuscate, don't agitate, and don't hide anything. Tell me other versions, other points of view. And don't interfere with my making my own judgments and choices. Don't try to brainwash me."

Our peripatetic "history seminars" were often interrupted by arguments and fights. Panin was the most radical and intransigent. Convinced that the Bolsheviks were Satan's weapons, that the Revolution in Russia was the result of intrigues by evil-wishing foreigners and aliens, he believed that salvation would come only through a miracle from on high. But one had to prepare for salvation, cleansing the soul, one's thoughts and language. With that aim in mind he firmly refused to use foreign words, which he called "bird words." Instead of *revolutsiia* he said *smuta* ("disturbance") or *perevorot* ("upheaval"), instead of *kommunisty* he used *bol'sheviki*, and he called *inzhener, zizhditel'* ("builder"). He even managed to write his manuals on blacksmithing using only his "language of extreme clarity." For example, he did not use the foreign loanword *metal*, replacing it with the precise name: iron, pig iron, copper. Instead of the foreign word *stal'* ("steel") he wrote "iron with carbon," or "carbonized iron," and so on.

He allowed exceptions only for "sacred concepts," such as the words *tserkov'* ("church"), *religiia, arkhiepiskop* ("archbishop"), *d'iakon* ("deacon"). And he grew very angry when he learned that Church Slavonic arose from ancient Bulgarian. "That can't be! They're Turks! Ordinary Turks, blabbing in broken Slavic dialect. Our ancestors borrowed their language? I don't believe it! That's impossible! That's a Bolshevik lie."

In skirmishes like this, Solzhenitsyn and I were allies. But when we were left alone, he opposed my dialectical-materialist arguments with stubborn disbelief. In those days he considered himself a skeptic, a follower of Pyrrho, but he already hated Stalin—"the ringleader"—and was beginning to have doubts about Lenin. Over and over he questioned me persistently: could I prove that if Lenin had lived, then neither the dispossession of the kulaks, nor forced collectivization, nor the famine would have taken place. Back then I thought that all those horrible events were the consequences of tragic, fateful circumstances, but I felt that one of the essential prerequisites for these tragedies were certain peculiarities of Stalin's character. His genius I did not doubt. I imagined it as vectored and single-focused, speeding toward one aim every time. Which is what led him to inevitable miscalculations, fateful mistakes. But Lenin I confidently considered "radial," that is, a multifaceted, universal genius, and tried to prove that if he had lived longer, we would have built socialism at a significantly lower cost.

Solzhenitsyn countered: "Those are empty conjectures. You accuse

Mitya and me of oversimplifying with our schemes, yet you yourself have invented a totally artificial scheme. Why do you have the ringleader as pure vector with no radii? After all, he's written on the national question—'the marvelous Georgian,' Lenin called him. He declared Mayakovsky 'the best, the most talented poet' in literature. And he discovered 'a thing, more powerful than Faust,' that is, Gorky's *The Maiden and Death*. And in both music and biology he's restored order. 'The coryphaeus of all sciences.' Then why is he only a vector? No—you underestimate him. Nat gud, dear *katso*, nat gud!" He imitated Stalin's Georgian accent. "That kind of underestimation deserves more than a Paragraph 10; it smacks of treason."

For a long time I remained an incorrigible "Red imperialist." In my consciousness ripened a symbiosis, highly typical for the period, of Soviet patriotism and Russian nationalism. Perhaps the main proof of Stalin's genius for me were his annexations. After all, we got back everything we had lost of the former great Russia, and had added more. We stretched from the Elbe River to the China Seas. They were all real victories, and victors are not judged.

Solzhenitsyn dismissed these arguments, too. He told me that in some book of memoirs about 1917 he read a description of a soldiers' meeting. An elderly frontline soldier interrupted the orator who was shouting that Russia needed straits, an exit into the Mediterranean. "Fuck those seas! What are we going to do, plow them?"

He opposed this hearty peasant truth to my great-nation Stalinist raptures. He did not believe that Russia needed conquests, did not believe that Stalin was concerned with the people—Lenin and Bukharin maybe had thought about them, but Trotsky, Zinoviev, Stalin, and Kaganovich, they didn't give a damn what Russia, or Germany, or China was. For them what counted was their theory, the victory of Marxism-Leninism on a world scale. To that end all means were good, everything worked, everything was profitable. You could praise Ivan the Terrible, and hold church services, and invent Russian priorities, but the goal was still the same—world revolution.

In evaluating concrete events, historical details, in judging what was good, what was bad—we almost never disagreed. But when I proved the inevitability, the historical determination of the Revolution, the Civil War, the terror, the collectivization—he would explode.

"Whoever proved it, that historical necessity? What if Kornilov had overcome that trifler Kerensky? What if Krasnov's cossacks had broken up the congress of Soviets, shot Lenin and Trotsky? After all, the possibility existed. Does that mean another historical necessity would have occurred? Why can't the subjunctive mood be used in history? Who forbids it? Alexander II might not have been killed. And then all domestic policies would have evolved differently. And if Rasputin had been taken away sooner . . . You keep harping on objective conditions, socioeconomic prerequisites. Historians invent those explanations with hindsight. They maintain that it was just this way because it couldn't have been any other way."

He said that he used to believe in the basic tenets of Marxism, but then began having more and more doubts. Because he could not believe in the historical analyses of those whose prognoses turned out to be wrong. For even the greatest ones—Marx and Lenin—were wrong in their predictions. And Stalin was the worst; he announced a world crisis as the last crisis of capitalism, then invented a new name for it—'special kind of depression.' In 1941 he promised victory "in a half year, a year."

We argued, stamping through the snow, whispering, so others on the walk would not hear us, swearing and cursing so that the "coloration" of the conversation would not stand out from the usual zek chatter. I tried to convince him, citing examples of Marxist predictions that had come true. He countered that these were exceptions that proved the rule—like weather reports: they lie and lie, and suddenly they guess right—rain or snow, yes or no. "Ah, you think diagnoses can't be compared to prognoses? Then why do you call it a science? In physics, in chemistry, in biology a law is a law because it repeats in the future. The laws of Archimedes and Gay-Lussac apply both to diagnosis and prognosis. Now when you tell me about language, about laws in linguistics, I believe you. But in this, no. You're a prisoner of your dogmas. And I can see how much bull has been made of them."

In the coziest nook of the library, behind the shelves, we had our evening getaway. There we fried potatoes on a hotplate, dubbed "the fireplace," drank the strongest tea, and talked about everything under the sun, avoiding arguments—because various people came to the other part of the room.

The evening talks "by the fireplace" most often were peaceful reminiscences and thoughts spoken aloud about literature, painting, music. Solzhenitsyn said that in the final analysis everything could be explained. What was necessary was strong and experienced thought. He told us that his wife, Natasha, explained both Chopin and Beethoven to him, and naturally interpreted everything correctly, because she was not only a musician— she was studying at the conservatory—but was also a scientific worker, a chemist, in graduate school. "What, your wife is also a chemist? Another coincidence."

Each of us tried to convince the others that he understood music and described what he thought about, what he pictured when he listened. But we agreed in a very few cases—for instance, when there was a radio broadcast of Mussorgsky's "Dawn over the Moscow River." Then it seemed to me that like my two friends—the skeptic and the romantic—I not only heard, but saw. A quiet morning river. Fog. Grassy, clayey slopes. Birds singing in the bushes. Ancient log-cabin Moscow. Belfries, cupolas, steep plank roofs—dark gray against the sky—the first cocks. The sky turns from dark blue to green, then orange, pink, light blue . . . Human voices. The first church bells . . . Morning!

Mussorgsky's picturesque music was doubly pleasing because it was so explainable.

The sharashka library was made up of Soviet technical books and of war spoils: German, British, French, and American scientific and technical journals. Some foul-up at the ministry book-collecting department or at the post office led to our sharashka receiving several issues of American military journals: *Field Artillery Journal, Coast Artillery Journal, Antiaircraft Journal, Aviation,* and others. No one censored them, and in some we came across fascinating articles on political topics, for instance, Fuller on the prospect of a third world war. I retold them to my friends. There were also a few books on philosophy, history, and linguistics by unfamiliar names. And even some fiction.

I had a lot to translate. But soon I got a handle on it and easily over-fulfilled my quotas—twenty-four pages every four workdays. I translated German and English most frequently, French, Dutch, and Czech texts more rarely. Primarily on radiotechnology. By the end of the winter I was reading and translating without dictionaries. There was time left over for outside interests, which we called "training for improving one's qualifications," in those instances when someone in authority looked over your shoulder and saw unusual books and notes.

Panin, in the evenings, concentrated silently by his carrel, thought about new methods of shoeing or chose words for his "language of extreme clarity." Once he said that he had decided to acknowledge Hegel's dialectics, which he called "the teaching of contradictions." According to him, this came about unexpectedly for him and just as decisively as back in the camps when he suddenly accepted Mayakovsky.

"In every way, he was just like an inmate work superintendent in the work camps. Arrogant and boorish but a powerful verse creator. I realized that, listening to an actor read. Powerful and inspired verse. He pretended to be godless, to fight God. But his words came from the Holy Writ; the words, and the passions."

Solzhenitsyn was always reading Dahl's *Dictionary,* making notes in small homemade notebooks or on pages that he later sewed together. He wrote in tiny letters, abbreviating words or substituting mathematical or stenographic symbols. At the time, he was learning stenography from a home-study book. He read books on history and philosophy and *War and Peace.* The volume from an old collection of Tolstoy's works was his personal property, and he never lent it to anyone. When I finally got his permission, I saw that the text and margins were scribbled over with notations. Some seemed blasphemous to me. He marked "doesn't work," "clumsy," "Gallicism," "wordy."

He shrugged off my reproaches. "Don't try to intimidate me with authorities. That's what I think. And I wrote it for myself. Tolstoy's language is obsolete."

And he reminded me what I myself had told him about language, as a living creature, steadily developing, changing, and said that Pushkin's language was different from Derzhavin's and we couldn't, didn't have the power—no matter how much we wanted to and tried to—to stem the development, preserve the language unchanged, the language created by the great classics.

Solzhenitsyn kept hidden in a secret place a large volume in which were bound several works on the ancient East.

We were both amazed by the unusual topicality of the intensely sad and good thoughts of Lao-Tzu:

"Weapons are the arms of unhappiness and not of nobility. The noble man conquers unwillingly. He cannot be happy killing people!"

"The more prohibitions and limitations, the poorer the people. The more laws and regulations, the more thieves and outlaws."

Lao-Tzu said a half millennium before Christ: "Respond to enmity with kindness."

Confucius countered a century after Lao-Tzu with: "And then how will you respond to kindness? Pay with justice for injustice, but pay kindness for kindness . . . Do not do unto someone else what you would not want done to you."

They preceded the preachers of Christian morality and the categorical imperative of Kant by centuries. Thus were confirmed my conceptions about the unity of humankind, which arose in my Pioneer childhood, in the days of my Esperanto fantasies.

But every time that we discussed this among the three of us, an endless argument arose.

Panin, without contradicting the essentials, decisively maintained that all such statements were simply empty heresies; he had no time for some ancient Chinese. He allowed that there might have been some wise men among them, spiritual ascetics, but there was no reason for him to read or understand them. The revelations of true faith are perceived by the heart, not reason.

"When you talk of material objects, about sizes that are computable, measurable, about problems that are fundamental or scientific, then you must trust only your mind. But the comprehension of God and the consciousness of belonging to the people is accessible only to that high spiritual apprehension that is higher than all minds. 'This is a great mystery.' So there is nothing to gab about. Now when you've read the book *Dogmatic Orthodoxy*, then maybe you'll understand what that means. And don't hope to suppress me with your education. Unlike the true sciences, which study and explain actual natural things and natural forces, unlike the sciences of number and measure, all your word sciences are hurly-burly. It was said of them that 'dissent and heresies are the children of sciences.'"

..enitsyn laughed at the zealousness of our friend, but he looked on
..y thoughts on the unity of mankind with just as much suspicion, and
sometimes even with hostility.

"Even Stalin the gang leader realized that all your Cominterns, Profin-
terns, and MOPRs* are just nonsense. When things smelled of gunpowder,
when he sensed danger, he remembered Russia, and Russian military leaders, and Alexander Nevsky, who's incidentally a saint, and Suvorov and
Kutuzov. And he began appealing to the Church for help."

I tried in vain to prove that our internationalism, Soviet, Marxist, Leninist, did not deny nations, did not suppress national independence, but on
the contrary, was called upon to aid it in every way; that "inter" meant
"among" not "without"; and that our aim was *inter*national relations,
friendly, equal relations between various peoples. It seemed self-evident to
me. But I couldn't convince anyone of it.

When I told Solzhenitsyn the history of the various parties, and reached
the Socialist Revolutionaries, recalling the leaders, including Gorovits,
Gershuni, Gots, he interrupted me in astonishment, almost in disbelief:
how can that be—Jewish surnames, when the SRs were a Russian peasant
party? And he was astonished once more when I began to refute what he
considered universally known: that all the Trotskyites were Jewish and all
the Bukharinites,† on the contrary, were Russian.

Panin reproached me for the sinful rejection of my people—for not
wanting to avow myself "first and foremost a Jew." "After all, you do look
like an Old Testament prophet in bearing, appearance, and manner. What
of it, that you don't know the language! You don't know yourself, either!
But it's clearer to an outsider. God has determined your fate: you are born
a son of the chosen people. And you, you stillborn Jew-Israelite, keep
denying, proving you're right, covering up!"

Solzhenitsyn seconded him. Naturally he believed in the sincerity of my
convictions, that while being a Jew I still felt myself a Russian. However,
he could not agree with that or with my self-definition: "A Russian intellectual of Jewish descent."

"Sure, you know the Russian language, literature, and history very well.
But you know German very well, too. Not as well? All right. But German
history and German literature certainly as well. That is your calling. If you
were to live ten or fifteen years in Germany, you could absolutely consider
yourself a German. Just like Heine or Feuchtwanger. But neither Mitya
nor I ever could. Why talk about us? Take our janitor, Spiridon. He's

*Comintern—the Communist International (1919–1943); Profintern—the Red International of
Unions (1921–1937); MOPR—the International Organization to Aid Revolutionary Fighters,
a non-Party organization of the 1920s. (Translator's note.)
†Nikolai Ivanovich Bukharin (1888–1938), a Party official and economic theorist, executed
after a show trial in 1938 for opposing forcible collectivization and industrialization. The
Trotskyites were left-wing and the Bukharinites right-wing within the CPSU. (Translator's
note.)

semiliterate. He never read *Tale of Igor's Campaign,* he's never even heard
of it. All he knows about Pushkin are some dirty jokes. But even if he were
to spend his entire life in Germany or Poland—he would always remain
a Russian muzhik."

In these arguments I was particularly angered by my own impotence. How
can you argue against "if"? Or when your most convincing conclusions
are set aside in a friendly way that nevertheless brooks no discussion and
is decisive: "We believe that you think that, but you only imagine it and
you want to subordinate to reason those things that are not subordinate to
it—heart, blood, the mysterious world of genes that was created over the
millennia."

Arguing with that, I maintained that instincts, the subconscious, elemen-
tal world view, are essential for an artistic perception of the world. However, national consciousness is first of all *consciousness,* and it is created by
rationally apprehended conceptions about the world.

A living feeling of belonging to your "kin and tribe" is also inculcated
indirectly, and in the most varied environments.

To a certain extent it is inculcated with mother's milk—that is, in
infancy, with the first sounds of the native tongue, native songs. But it does
not appear in the fetus. And national consciousness is truly created and
developed in youth.

"Love for the native hearth, Love for our fathers' graves"* are inherited
not through birth but through upbringing.

In Butyrki, not long before I left for the sharashka, I had a visit from
Mother and Nadya. We stood, separated by two steel mesh fences, between
which the supervisors paced.

Five or six meetings took place simultaneously. The hubbub was deafening at times. The supervisors shouted: "Keep it down! You were told to
quiet down! No hollering!"

Mother and Nadya told me that the Military Board of the Supreme
Court on an appeal by my lawyer had reduced my sentence to six years
—that meant I had another three years and some to go. But the lawyer
assured them that in a few months he would be able to appeal to the plenum
of the Supreme Court. The fact that the board had already reduced the
sentence was a good sign.

I came to the sharashka knowing that I was sentenced to six years and
hoping to be freed earlier. I had already been acquitted once, and I remembered so clearly that January day when I walked out of the gates of Butyrki
Prison. It was less than a year ago.

When my friends and I talked about the future, I based my thoughts on
the probability that even at worst I would be freed first—by the summer

*Pushkin. (Translator's note.)

of 1951; two years later, Solzhenitsyn; and another year and a half after that, Panin.

Mitya disagreed. "Don't lull yourself with dreams, gentlemen! They won't let us go. They might if we were still in the camps. From there, maybe, we would have been let out into the big zone—into exile. But from the sharashka, never. We've been let in on secrets here. For all the blessings here—the mattresses, sheets, the fruit jelly sauce for dessert—we'll have to pay dearly. We'll be lucky if they simply add to our sentences here. They can just as easily send us to the left, as the Chekists used to joke—"to the earth department." No, gentlemen, there's no point in counting years; we're condemned for life."

However, I resisted stubbornly, believing there would be changes for the better. I believed not only because of my innate optimism, but, as it seemed to me, through sensible calculations. The success of Stalin's domestic and foreign policies had to weaken the pressure for "increased vigilance." And expanded relations with countries that were people's democracies would naturally have a beneficial effect on our public life. The government's confidence would grow in its security, in the stability of the state, and naturally the punitive policies would soften.

Solzhenitsyn had doubts, but I could see that he, too, wanted to hope. Panin was convinced that "this godless, and therefore immoral world" could never improve.

There was no point in thinking about working in the next few years in literature, history, or philosophy; they wouldn't let me near ideology. But linguistics, and in particular, paleolinguistics, which studies the most ancient sources of modern languages, seemed ideologically neutral to me and at the same time an extraordinarily interesting field. For even the ancient history of a language is manifest in its living reality—in the vocabulary and its entire structure. Delving in history, you can trace the long-standing links between various peoples and races, their mutual influence and interaction.

In Marr* I read that the language of sounds followed the language of gestures—hand, sign language. This was asserted by certain other scholars. Lévy-Bruhl's book *Primitive Mentality* turned up in the sharashka. The consciousness of primitive people related or even totemically identified completely different objects, which sometimes "belonged" together only remotely, conditionally. This had to be evinced in language.

Thus arose the idea, which I privately considered to have the simplicity of genius, to trace the most ancient sources, first of all of Russian and its related languages, by studying the etymology of words meaning "hand" or "arm," words indicating parts of the hand or arm (finger, fist, shoulder, elbow) and actions performed by hands (take, give, dig, hit, beat, throw,

*Nikolai Iakovlevich Marr (1864–1934), a linguist and Orientalist. (Translator's note.)

and so forth), and the names of various objects that could be considered a part or extension of hands (rock, stick, stake, shovel, ax, knife, sword, dagger, and so on).

Juxtaposing words from many languages of this time, I hoped to determine the oldest connections among languages. For this I needed as many foreign dictionaries and as many conversations as possible with people who spoke the languages for which I could not obtain dictionaries. My family sent books and dictionaries that they managed to get through friends.

Every spare minute I thought about "hand" roots, derivative and related words. I was as engrossed in dictionaries as in the most fascinating fiction; I compiled tables, compared, thought. Much, naturally, I thought up, invented. My enthusiasm gave birth to the desired conclusion. But my starting assumption and several etymological observations and hypotheses still seem reliable to me. And I would very much like to see them followed up in a more serious manner.

We had to work more and more intensely with every passing month. And the work was engrossing. But still I continued from time to time to dig around in dictionaries, questioning people who knew Caucasian, Turkic, Siberian languages.

On March 18, 1948, I was called in to see the security officer of the prison, Major Shevchenko—a broad, pathologically puffy fat man, with a blurred, pale-yellow face—we called him Buddha or Dalai Lama. He handed me a piece of paper, a standard printed text with typed inserts. The plenum of the Supreme Court in correction of the incorrect decision of the Military Board had sentenced me to a ten-year term of incarceration. (Until June something 1955. That meant more than seven years to go!)

So, it was the damned Ides again. Just as in March 1945 when it all began.*

For the first instants, cold emptiness. I felt my heart beating—before, I had noticed it only after heavy labor, a steep slope, or a long run.

No more hopes. Was it worth living? At least, I was in the sharashka. Here you could hang yourself so that it wouldn't be noticed for a long time. Such thoughts came to me for the first time in my life, I think.

But people live with longer sentences. Why was I any better?

Major Shevchenko was staring at me closely. In the narrow slits between the swollen, almost lashless lids were glimpses of indeterminable color. "But don't . . . don't, you know . . . despair, give up the reins, as they say. You're still young. And your health seems good. You'll live on the outside, too. You have a family, uh—wife, children. Daughters, is it? They're

*Even now, as I write these lines, even though I have been free for almost a quarter of a century, I still have a superstitious fear of the Ides of March. Numerous and sundry misfortunes befell me in various years between March 15 and 20. And no matter how I berate myself for my weakness, I cannot rid myself of tense, anxious forebodings on those days.

waiting for you. And they'll see you. And you have a mother and father. They're hoping, too. That's whom you should be thinking of. And you yourself have a good education, they say even, uh, an outstanding one. Highly qualified. And your work here is, um, interesting, beneficial for the state and science and personally for you, um, in several ways. And for these days, good conditions. You know yourself what it's like in other places. And maybe for the future . . . So you control yourself. You're a man, you um, were a soldier."

Listening, I grew wary. Aha, he was going to try to recruit me now. What else could I expect from a "godfather"?

"Don't think that I'm, um, proselytizing, saying what I'm supposed to. It really is so. Really. Man to man. Now, I'm three years older than you, but no one can believe what's become of me. All because of heart disease. I had serious shell shock; I was also at the front. But now I'm alive only because I, um, take care of myself. I suck, lick, swallow pills. And I walk the way, um, one walks behind a coffin. And yet I want to live a little longer. That's why I try not to get overexcited. If I worry even a bit, right here"—he placed his broad, fat paw on his chest—"it aches, and flutters, and, um, palpitates; it's terrible. Health is the most precious thing. You understand Ukrainian, don't you: 'Gde by zdorov'e ne zagubiv, vzhe nigde ne naidesh'.' [Wherever you may lose your health, you won't find it anywhere.] So this is my advice, um, guard your health, don't let yourself go. Understand? Well, go on, work . . ."

Even later he did not try to recruit me or my friends. And yet he undoubtedly received denunciations from stoolies and naturally gave them assignments.

He handed out our letters, opened, naturally, and he probably glanced through them.

About three weeks after that March conversation, giving me the books and magazines sent to me for my birthday, he said: "They give you good books. They want, um, to make you a little happy. More dictionaries. Now a Turkish one. They say you know many languages? And you're still interested? Well, why not—it's, um, beneficial. But you also care about poetry, and novels. And there are others here who like, um, to read. You give your comrades books, don't you?"

I grew wary again: what was he leading up to? But he didn't expect an answer.

"So, over there"—on the windowsill were piled up about three dozen books, some rather worn—"I brought these books for every one, um, of you. The director and I talked about it—we must have our own library. And since you receive many kinds of books, we're appointing you, um, librarian. We'll put a bookcase in the corridor, you can find yourself some assistants. Now Solzhenitsyn is in charge of the library in the unit. I asked him to take on this one, too. But he refused, he says, um, he's overloaded with work. Night and day he has to think. He promised to help whoever else, for instance, you, and I, um, hope that you won't refuse. We'll get more books later. The head of the prison said that he'll appropriate funds. You and Solzhenitsyn put together a list of books you'd, um, like. But only fiction. Science books you can get at the site."

Several times later on, Major Shevchenko brought new popular editions of the classics and Soviet writers. He was ill more and more frequently. He was replaced by a ruddy-cheeked dandy and boor, Lieutenant Colonel Mishin, who tried to recruit everyone who came into his office for a letter or "for a meeting."

Major Shevchenko—the only one of all the security officer godfathers I ever saw—was simply human. And truly kind to me in very difficult times.

During those days my friends strove to be gentle with me. Even the most embittered prisoners, who seemingly have grown accustomed to their own and other people's problems, disappointments, and deprivations, cannot remain indifferent when a comrade's term is added to.

Panin knew from personal experience how it felt. And Solzhenitsyn, even though he tried to seem severe, a veteran forged in the battle, and an inscrutable "native" of the GULag Archipelago, experienced in all prison ordeals, still retained the impressionability and responsiveness of youth. He and Panin took turns or worked together to distract me from bad thoughts, pestered me, teased me, started long conversations on the most peaceful topics of philosophy, history, or my linguistic research. Panin even tried to enlist me as coauthor of the "language of extreme clarity" and with unusual humility put up with sarcastic or angry retorts.

I couldn't see Nadya and my parents more than two or three times a year. However, we no longer met in the barred boxes of Butyrki, but face to face, at an ordinary desk in the investigator's rooms of Lefortovo.

These visits and letters were holidays. Not only my family wrote to me. All those years I received marvelous letters in verse and prose from Inna Levidova. I got kind regards from many friends. Every birthday Berta Korfini sent a cake.

The memory of friends helped me live.

Music and poetry also helped.

A large receiver stood on Solzhenitsyn's desk. In the evenings we listened to concerts of instrumental music. Never before had I reacted to Mozart, Beethoven, Glinka, Tchaikovsky, Mussorgsky in the way I did during those sharashka evenings. We pulled on the earphones—there were no other eager listeners about.

Panin respected our weakness for "abstract" music; he did not disturb us and chased away others who might. But some thought that we were "just showing off," pretending that we preferred the plunking and plinking to *chastushka** ditties, choruses, and operettas. And they merely scoffed when we put on the earphones. "Look! The intellectuals found themselves another symphony."

Of course, there were also experienced melomaniacs, who significantly berated what I liked and praised things that I hadn't even noticed.

And even more than music, we needed poetry. In the quiet evenings behind the shelves, we read Pushkin, Tiutchev, Blok, Gumilev, Yesenin, Mayakovsky, Pasternak, Simonov. We often argued. For Solzhenitsyn at that time Yesenin was the most important poet. Once, when I started reading translations by Bagritsky, he even grew angry.

"What do I need those Brignal Banks for? Moon-June . . . boon-boon. That's all foreign boon-boon. I need Russian poems, about Russia."

Solzhenitsyn was writing a long autobiographical novella in verse about how he and a friend went by boat along the Volga River from Yaroslavl to Astrakhan. In those days, I liked his poetry, which was occasional and descriptive like Nekrasov's.† I particularly liked two places in the poem. The author and his friend encountered a grim barge, heavily populated with bedraggled, emaciated, shorn men. The youths, grown up without fathers, and the convicts, torn from their children, looked at one another. And then, at night, the author and his friend are awakened in their tent on shore by shouts, curses, dogs barking, blinding beams from flashlights. A horde of pursuers, on the trail of runaways, bursts into their tent . . .

For my birthday, he wrote me a verse epistle, which then also seemed good to me, even though rather sentimental. It described how I would meet my daughters, how I would tell them about life

> On the isle of men
> Where they don't know women
> And don't like wine . . .

I wrote poetry, too. I began in the first hours after my arrest. But I never, neither then nor later, ever imagined myself to be a poet, as sometimes happens when you're fifteen or sixteen:

> I have now returned
> To verse once more
> Only because the meter
> Makes memorizing neater.

Thoughts of how to preserve my memory and with it myself plagued me more and more persistently when I was left alone without books or

---

*Rhymed folk verses, often political or topical. (Translator's note.)
†Nikolai Alekseevich Nekrasov (1821–1878), a Russian poet, exponent of the realist and "civic" tendencies. (Translator's note.)

back in prison when new calamities befell me. Then the poems sprang up in profusion: exercise for the memory, exercise for the soul.

> Remember! Remember!
> Everything will pass, streak by,
> This day, this month of May,
> All this will not reappear.
> The fresh green of the grass
> The dapple of the orange flowers,
> The jokes of the boy guards
> The taste of the makhorka butts.
> Remember! Remember!
> Prison. Lilacs. And this May.
>
> (Stettin, 1945)

And I did try to remember. And in order to do that I scribbled many poems, funny and serious, short and very very long. During the first sharashka winter two appeared that my friends considered better than the rest.

> Whoever has heard in prison the turn of the key—
> A click,
> A click,
> And once more—a click . . .
>
> In his memory long will sound
> That metallic scream
> That bitter sadness . . .
> In delirious nights the one-eyed judas-hole
> Will goggle at him.
>
> All will pass. But then, many years later,
> He will suddenly moan in his sleep.
> He will see black bars on the window.
> The white dawn is cut into fourths.
> The door stamps hollowly and the lock jingles.
> Click!
> Click!
> And once more—a click!

The second poem was born of the nights in the sharashka itself. Sometimes it seemed to us that we were somewhere outside of town. From the windows we saw the dense trees of the Botanical Gardens and the then few buildings of the sovkhoz—greenhouses, gardens. Moscow was barely discernible above the horizon. At night the sky in that direction was pinkish purple—the glow of Moscow's lights. Street noises barely reached us. But at night we could hear the trains. Somewhere not far from us passed the tracks of the Riga and Yaroslavl railroads.

> At night the horns sound sadly.
> At night the sad horns sound.
> Inaudible in the pounding of the wheels,
> In them are sobs of station farewells,
> The sadness of inevitable parting.
> At night the distant horns sound
> Calling to freedom, to freedom, to freedom.

2

TWICE
A TRAITOR

As soon as "Get ready for inspection!" was heard behind the door, he jumped up first. But he stood at the very end of the last row. Lanky, rather stooped. A broad face almost without wrinkles; small light-blue eyes. Long hands, broad, dark, rough palms. He worked as a janitor. And in the evenings his knotty fingers with stone-hard nails deftly handled a small needle. He darned socks, hemmed, patched things for himself and some of his cellmates. He didn't play chess, or checkers, or dominoes, he couldn't read—his vision was bad and he didn't have glasses.

He never started a conversation with anyone, but replied readily; he told his story in detail and slowly, as though choosing words to match.

"I'm from the country—Gumbinnen. Have you heard of it? Exactly, in Prussia. There's a village nearby, where I had a place since one thousand nine hundred and twelve. But I was born in Russia. We're Russian. I was born in one thousand eight hundred and ninety. Saratov Province, Balashavsky District. Born a peasant. But I'm an orphan. I don't remember my mother at all. When she died, I wasn't aware of anything yet. Father was a carpenter. He worked in town and died there. I lived with my grandfather. He had a large place, undivided. Uncles, daughters-in-law; all had children. One dies, two more are born. And there were always more mouths than hands. Well, I was without a father or mother; everyone bossed me around. And everyone let me have it—some a kick, others a punch, and sometimes a stick on the spine. Only my grandmother had pity for the orphan. And then she died, too. I still didn't know how to read. I learned a bit in the barracks. And put on my first pair of boots when I was drafted. I wore *lapti* [woven birchbark shoes] before. Until I learned how to weave my own, I wore hand-me-downs.

"At first, after the village, the barracks seemed very good: as much bread and kasha as you want, always a side of meat, uniforms, boots, clean bedding. But they drilled us without stop, of course. And it was so boring! As a peasant I had harder work, but it wasn't as boring as soldiering. One day you till, plow; another you harrow, sow. Sometimes you take the cows out to pasture; another day you mow hay. And the air is so light. And sometimes, for an hour or two, sometimes a whole day, you're all alone, by yourself—you can pray to God if you want, or play a song—and you breathe free. But as a soldier you're always like a sheep in a herd. All you do is hear: 'At ease . . . Line up! . . . Chin up, suck in your gut!'

"The second year they put me in the border patrol. There's no peace there at all. Either you have to chase those . . . smugglers, or there's an alert —'Arms! . . . Run! . . . Lie down! Crawl like a snake, hop like a frog!' Our sergeant major was an animal! The company commander was a lieutenant, and he was usually drunk or fooling around with the Polish girls. So the sergeant was tsar and God; our squad noncom was terrified of him. 'Yes, sir! Right away, sir!' That one would holler at you, but this one smacked you on the cheekbone. And the least thing—full gear with your rifle. Sometimes he'd put sand in your backpack, to make it heavier, and then stand you like a post in the cold, the rain, the hottest heat. One soldier practically froze to death one winter. They barely revived him, and they had to cut off his leg. He became a cripple. I can't count the number of times I was punished like that. You stand on a hill—so that they, the officers, can see you if you dare move a muscle—and on the other side is Prussia. A clean country. All the houses have tile roofs. The peasants wear boots even in the fields. You can see the horses are well fed even from a distance. And they plow with two-horse plows. Iron ones. They gleam in the sun. They don't sow from a bast basket, but with horse-drawn sowers. And the cows are sleek, matching, skewbald, black and white. And the shepherd, like the master, wears a hat and polished boots. So you look and look—and you're standing there like a statue: your head aches, your eyes burn, and so much sweat drips into your boots, you could wring out your foot bindings.

"In our squad, the ones with parents or relatives who felt sorry for them, they got packages from home, sometimes a three-ruble bill—and the city ones even more—so they'd go to the noncom: 'Here's a little present, please don't refuse.' And their life was easier. No one even wrote me a letter. Those of us—homeless orphans—were worked harder. Duty details out of turn, and in full gear. And if you grumble, 'Why are you punishing me for nothing?' it gets worse. And they threaten you, too—they'll put you into the convict squads. One of our soldiers wasn't Russian. A Tatar from the Caucasus. They teased him, called him Makhmetka. He was quiet, willing—a kind soul, ready to accommodate everyone. And the sergeant tormented him every day. Drilled him for nothing—running, crawling, crouching. And kept training him how to salute, how to address everyone —'Your Excellency,' 'Your Supreme Excellency,' and even 'Your Imperial Highness.' The poor fellow had trouble speaking as it was, but with fright, he just went dumb. He stood there crying. And the sergeant punches him in the teeth, and on the jaw, and in the nose. 'I'll clear your throat!' And the noncom did the same, and there were soldiers who just went hee-hee and ha-ha. So one night when Makhmetka was on duty, he took off his boots, put the rifle in his mouth, his bare foot on the trigger, and shot himself to death. After that I decided that I wasn't going to stay with those tyrants either. That day I stood for two hours in full gear in the glaring sun. I didn't satisfy the sergeant—I didn't polish my boots right. And that night, when I went on duty right at the border, by the brook, I threw my rifle in the bushes—the devil take it—and farewell Russia!

"And then in Germany, in Prussia, they held me for three days in the guardhouse. An officer in glasses came. He was so respectful, and he spoke our language well. And he treated me like a master, politely, and asked me in a proper fashion who I was, where I was from, how I had served, why I ran away. And then they took me to Gumbinnen, and sent me to work on a farmstead—a count's estate. I spent three summers and three winters there. I began to understand German. There were other farmhands there —*Landarbeiter* in their tongue—some German, some Polish. And the Poles' talk sounds like Russian. I learned German with them. The whole estate was run by the Pan Inspector. Along in years, stern, but fair. He understood Polish well and a little Russian. He put me with the horses first. The horses were good, hefty and handsome. And I've always loved animals. And I took care of them like my own. I fed and watered them when it was time, the right way, and combed out their manes and tails hair by hair, and cut their hooves. The Pan Inspector would come, take out a white hankie from his pocket, rub the withers of one and the groin of another, and say, '*Gut.*' And offer me a cigarette: '*Bitte, rauchen*'; that means, 'Please, have a smoke.'

"When the war started—the first one, the tsar's—the gendarmes came to the estate, looking for me; they were afraid because I had been the Russian tsar's soldier before. But the Pan Inspector didn't turn me over to the gendarmes. He sent me with the horses far away from the farm. There were other stableboys—Poles, but also citizens of the Russian state. So we took the herd . . . We could hear the cannon behind us. And the Poles kept scaring me: 'When the cossacks will catch us, they'll chop us up with their sabers or hang us.' But then the war turned back, and we returned by winter. And that fall I married. She was a widow with small children, a son and a daughter. Her husband had died young. And he had no relatives and she had none. Complete orphans, like me. Her place wasn't all that big —seven *morgen* of comfortable land. And a cow, and pigs, and chickens, and ducks . . . How could she handle it alone? So she went to the estate —to work in the fields, in the yard. They paid a pittance. But the Pan Inspector gave her help, sent people to plow, and sow, and harvest. He sent me—in the spring with a plow, in the summer with a scythe. And I helped out in the yard, too. I liked her. She was a good *frau* both in looks and habits—she was clean and industrious, quiet and merry. And she liked me. I was young, strong, good for any kind of work, and also quiet and merry . . . Her name is Maria, like my late mother.

"Maria and I got married in one thousand nine hundred and fifteen. A pastor married us. A good old man. He asked me, 'Do you believe in Christus?' Christus—that's their name for Christ. 'Of course I believe and I know how to pray: Our Father.' So he said: '*Gut.*' There is only one God.

The Germans call him *Liebegott* or *Herrgott*, the Poles say *Pan Bóg*, and that's all the same as our *Gospodibozhe*. The words are different, but God's the same.

"Maria and I lived well. She gave birth to three more—two daughters and a son. But I loved the first two like my own. The eldest daughter— she was also Maria—she got married back in one thousand nine hundred and thirty-one. Her husband worked on the *Eisenbahn*, the railroad; they later moved to Berlin. The eldest son, Christian, was drafted before the war, made it to noncommissioned officer; he was killed in France. We all cried over him. He left a widow, two children. They lived in town, in Gumbinnen; her father had a *Gasthaus*, an inn. Our younger daughters— Anna and Louisa—I called her Liza, in Russian—also married peasant sons from our parts. Anna's husband, Fritz, was a private first class; he disappeared on the *Ostfront*—in Russia, that is. Maybe he shot at my nephews there? Or one of them killed him? And Liza's young man, Kurt—they got married during the war, when he came home on leave, a noncom—he fought in a tank, in Africa, right in the desert, and then in Italy; there was no more news from him. And our littlest one, Petka—in German they say Peter—they took him into the army directly from school—he was born in one thousand nine hundred and twenty-three—and also to Africa. But, thank God, he was captured. He wrote from Canada, that he was healthy, not abused, and that the work wasn't hard, in the forests . . . That's how it is—I had relatives all over the world. And I returned to my homeland. Right here, to prison.

"When this war started—in Russia, that is—they took the last men from our village. And things got stricter. Give money, and grain, and meat, and eggs . . . Well, I always turned things in on time. There were those authorities, who asked: '*Herr Simonoff, Russe, Bolshevik?*' I would just spread my hands. *Russe*, of course, *Russe*, but no Bolshevik. And that's true —what did I know? My family, my field, my house, and the whole farmstead. Our place wasn't in the village itself, but about a verst and a half outside, by the woods. We went into the village only on Sunday—to the *Kirche*, and then to the inn, to have some beer, and I'd have a small shot or two of *Korn*—vodka, that is. The children would go to the movies or the dance, and Maria and I went home, to feed the cows, horses, pigs, and fowl. We lived quietly. We didn't bother anyone, and no one really pressured us either. I paid, turned in everything that was demanded, and lived quietly.

"But my soul ached when I saw our prisoners of war. They herded over fifty of them to the town and to the village to the big farmers—the richer landowners. All emaciated, skin and bones, ragged, filthy. You couldn't tell who was young and who was old. God, I thought, these are our soldiers?! The gendarme watchman laughed: 'Look at your Russian army, Simon.'

"Tears boiled in my eyes and I couldn't find the words. The chief of the village and the whole county was called *Bauernführer*; an elderly man with

a mustache, he wore a uniform with an armband, red with their cross—
black and bent—officer's boots and rode on a motor bicycle. He gave strict
orders that no one come close to the prisoners—they were contagious. But
the watchmen, the ones that were older and had sense, felt sorry for them.
And many times, as though passing accidentally, would shove them some
sausage. After they got a little food into them, they calmed down. They
were allowed to walk around free. And I talked to them, asked them how
people lived in Russia, what kolkhozes were.

"Well, one says, everything is fine at home and will be even better; all
people are equal, there are no landowners, and some peasants have become
big bosses, all power is in the hands of the workers and peasants, Stalin is
the world's wisest military leader, and the Russian army is the strongest,
it will conquer the Germans soon and hang Hitler.

"Another says, don't you believe him. Everything's a mess in Russia, all
the good farmers have been exiled to Siberia at hard labor; it's worse
working for a kolkhoz than for a landowner, the famine was so bad that
entire villages died out, Stalin is the Antichrist and a bloodsucker, the
Germans have reached the Volga and the Caucasus, they'll take Moscow
soon.

"A third said something else—that the one and the other lied, and to tell
the truth, there's good and bad in Russia. There really was a famine, and
the Germans really were as far as the Volga, but more people are educated
than under the tsar, and there are many new factories and whole new
towns, and the Russian army is stronger than the German.

"Two prisoners, one a Siberian, the other a Ukrainian, tried to convince
me: 'You, pops, personally have nothing to be afraid of. Since you're both
a Russian and a laboring peasant, you worked yourself and kept no hired
hands, our government will respect you.'

"I believed and didn't believe. And as things were changing for the
Russians at the front, all the prisoners were taken away from our area. Only
civilian Poles were left. They said: 'When the Soviets come, they'll destroy
everything, everything will burn, they'll kill the men and rape the women.'
And the *Bauernführer* ordered all the men turned into soldiers—that was
called *Volksturm*. But here I decided—I'd rather hang than take up arms,
fight against my native people. And if they—my own people—kill me, at
least I'll die with a clear conscience.

"Maria and my daughters were very much afraid. 'Let's go, let's go. In
Berlin at my sister's, we'll be crowded and hungry, but we'll be alive. We'll
die here.' I got them packed when the sound of cannon was near. I loaded
the *Wagen*, a large cart, and harnessed the mare. We had one old horse left.
Before the war I had a pair of fine horses, but I had to give the fine stallion
to the Wehrmacht. They went in a wagon train from our village. But I and
a few other men were talked by the Pan Inspector into helping him lead
the count's horses and cattle away and take away some other property. But
he promised us big *Wagens*, so that we could load our pigs and fowl. And

he promised us feed and said that we could drive our cows with the count's herd. But that Pan Inspector was a weakling of a man: he was lost and kept waiting for somebody's orders. We ran here and there. And then the Soviets rolled in on their tanks.

"Well, what can you say about them? Soldiers like any others. They had been fighting a long time; some were tired, some were embittered. There were of course some wild ones—they chased women and girls, raped them. And they looted whatever came their way; and they pillaged and set fires. But there were good fellows, too, with good souls. I was friends with those. I explained everything—the way it was, how I had lived; I showed them my place, what was left of it. I gave them potatoes, bacon, butter, home-canned foods, and they gave me tobacco, vodka. And the officers were good; they called me in to translate their conversations with the farmers who were left. And one young captain kept joking: 'You, father, we'll appoint you chairman of a kolkhoz, since you're a good worker and a Russian man.'

"And then one morning some lieutenant came with a soldier, 'Come on,' he says. 'Let's talk for an hour.' I went as I was. We got in the car, drove to another village, and they immediately stuck me in a cellar, in the cooler. I sat there for two days; they didn't give me a piece of bread, and it was all I could manage to get them to let me out into the yard, to piss. On the third morning they took me, filthy, chilled, my teeth chattering, into the house, into a clean room. At the table sat a major, respectable, gilt epaulets. He began pleasantly enough: 'We,' he says, 'are counterespionage—SMERSH, that is, "death to spies." We know everything through and through, we know all. So confess exactly what tasks the Germans have given you.' I couldn't understand what he wanted, which tasks he meant. I told him everything—how I lived, how my wife and children were afraid of the Soviets and left, and how I also wanted to, but was too late. Then he started shouting, mother-cursing, and threatening: 'Confess, and we'll pardon you; don't confess, we'll skin you alive, break all your bones, and hang you as a spy.' I told him the whole truth again, and he started beating me . . . with a stick, on my shoulders, and my head. Harder, worse, than that sergeant that I ran away from. Except this one I wouldn't be able to run away from. He beat me himself, and then a lieutenant helped him, with his fists and the stick. I just cried: 'Why are you punishing an innocent man?' And they swore at me: 'You, motherfucker,' they said, 'are a traitor to your country, you were selling Russia to the Germans.' I argued, swore to God, gave them a holy vow that I wasn't a traitor. I didn't sell anything to anyone, but lived quietly, like a peasant, a Christian.

"Well, they got tired of beating me and stopped. They said: 'We're sick of you! Here are the statements—sign.' But I couldn't sign. I remember only block letters, and I can't read without my glasses. I was arrested in the yard, and I didn't take a piece of bread, to say nothing of my glasses. I couldn't see anything on those papers, so I didn't sign. I'm awfully quiet, but I understand things: they wrote whatever they wanted, and I was supposed to confess. 'No,' I said. 'Kill me and execute me, I'll die, but I won't give in to lies.' Well, they hit me once or twice more, cursed horribly, and sent those papers to the court that's called a tribunal. Over there, no one beat or cursed me. They just asked questions. Three officers sat at a table. The middle one, the chief judge, a lieutenant colonel: silver epaulets, serious, in glasses. He asked politely, 'Do you confess that you are guilty?' 'No way, Mister Colonel! I am innocent.' He said: 'Do you confess that you gave a soldier's oath to serve the fatherland?' 'Yes, sir, I swore.' 'And do you admit that you threw away your soldier's arms and ran away across the border to Germany?' 'Yes, sir,' I said, 'that did happen, but I wasn't running away from my homeland, I was running from a beastly sergeant major, from hard-labor suffering.' He seemed to laugh. 'That doesn't mean anything. A soldier is a soldier forever and an oath is an oath forever. And you ran away to Germany, which is a vicious enemy of the homeland. Since the year that you ran off, Russia has already had two wars with Germany. And that means that you are doubly guilty, as a traitor to the homeland on the state border. In wartime that is punishable by the highest measure—shooting or hanging. But since the war has ended in our victory, and since you are of advanced years, and since Soviet courts are'—here he said such a funny word that I had never heard, something like humus, or human courts—'we are sentencing you to ten years of correction in labor camps.' All my belongings were—how do you call it —confixated, and I was given another five years of disfranchisement.

"Well, so now, two years have passed. I have eight left. I'm fifty-seven now. And Maria—if she's still alive, if the war didn't finish her off—is two years older than me. So when will we ever see each other again? And where? Unless it's in the Kingdom of Heaven."

3

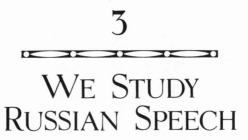

WE STUDY
RUSSIAN SPEECH

Of all the words of the mighty and primogenitary
Russian language, full-voiced, meek, and awesome
. . . a language alive, created and under creation, I love
most of all the word *freedom*.

—KONSTANTIN BALMONT

In the winter of 1948–1949 the sharashka was turned over to a new boss—
the MGB. The new director was Anton Mikhailovich V.—the very same
colonel and engineer who had questioned me in Butyrki. New groups of
imprisoned specialists kept arriving. They were mostly signal men, radio
engineers and technicians, but there were engineers in other specialities,
as well as physicists and chemists.

Solzhenitsyn was handing over the library to three young, and as it
seemed to us, extraordinarily attractive women. He asked the new authorities to include me in the work group, too. We had to inventory not only
the old books, but the several thousand new books and magazines.

Working next to women—hearing their voices, seeing their smiles, in-
haling the scent of cheap cologne and sweat, accidentally brushing up
against them in the close quarters, and joking—was both joyful and upsetting.

We tried not to hurry. We competed in conscientiousness and pedantry.

The engineer Aushev, head of the section on technical documentation,
was in charge of receiving the library. At first glance he seemed unap-
proachably austere and appeared to be looking at us disdainfully through
his thick, horn-rimmed glasses. He was taciturn, maintained an unchang-
ing strict mien and a dry, businesslike tone. But gradually we got to talking,
and learned that he had been in under Article 58–9 (sabotage), had worked
in a sharashka, and had stayed on as a free, hired scientific consultant. It
turned out that Anton Mikhailovich was also a former zek, sentenced in
1930 in the Promparty Affair* and paroled early for his inventions and
proposals for improving efficiency.

---

*Engineers throughout the country were accused of creating their own party, the Promparty
(*Promyshlennaia partiia*, or Industrial Party), having ties with the British, and planning to take
over the state, installing Ramzin as premier. After the show trials of 1930, when most of the
accused "confessed," the engineers were not executed but sent to work in sharashkas. (Translator's note.)

That meant we could hope, too!

Anton Mikhailovich called a few of the inmates into his office. "Ah, Lev Zinovievich, *Guten Tag! Bonjour!* I'm so glad to see you in good health."

Unusual were both the jovial greetings and the fact that he was using my real patronymic and not the Jewish one on my birth certificate—Zalmanovich—as I was always called by jailers and investigators.

"So, gentlemen, I've asked you here to give you some extremely pleasant news. From now on you are workers of a scientific-research institute. A particularly important and particularly secret one.

"You and I have to develop new systems of secret telephony. We must invent and prepare a telephone so that over several thousand kilometers a connection can be maintained that is absolutely dependable and absolutely impervious to wiretapping or interception. I stress—*absolutely*. Currently, several types of secret telephones exist. But no system has absolute guarantees. Several of you probably have dealt with the HF telephones. They were used at the front on a large scale. An HF connection prevents only direct tapping of the line. The lines carry a high-frequency current, modulated by a sound signal from the membranes. The eavesdropper gets nothing but a steady squeak. But all you need is to find a filter that strains the high frequency (and with modern technology that is a very simple task) and the conversation becomes clearly audible. In recent years more complex systems have been in use—mosaic encoding, or time-frequency segment scrambling. During the war years it was used by our allies, by our enemies, and by us. The sound signals are separated by frequency filters into three or four bands and with a magnetic recording disk are split in time, for short fractions—a hundred to a hundred and fifty milliseconds. The coder mixes the frequency-time segments. And the line carries this mishmash of squeaks and noises. At the receiver, the transmission is decoded and the original speech is reconstituted. These systems are more or less stable because the enemy cannot eavesdrop on a conversation until he creates a similar encoder-decoder. For now! But eventually, he will. So our most important goal here is to achieve the *absolute*. I think it's Balzac who has a novella called *The Quest of the Absolute*. So that's what you and I will be doing. The work will be intense, difficult, and highly responsible, but also extremely interesting. For those who can truly become engrossed in science, in a technical problem, for those who don't think from here to here, within the framework of the workday and the pay scale—in short, for the real scientist, the real intellectual—all these tasks are not so much difficult as attractive. They hold the source of the greatest pleasures of the mind. And last but not least, when we successfully resolve our problems, this will bring you quite real blessings. Early release. High awards. It will be enough for me to say that the work of our institute will be directly supervised by Comrade Beria, who will report personally to Comrade Stalin."

.   .   .

When we were finishing up the transfer of the library, a new prisoner arrived, pale pink, gray-haired, in a baggy jacket—he had apparently lost a lot of weight—Aleksandr Mikhailovich P., an economics engineer, sentenced to ten years under Paragraph 10. He had already served a third of his sentence. He said that Anton Mikhailovich had placed him in charge of a special research group that included Solzhenitsyn and me, and later more workers would be added, as many as we wanted. "Are you a philologist? They say you know many languages? Then you're a linguist? And you—you're a mathematician? Both are just what we need. The three of us constitute the guiding nucleus of the statistical research of the Russian language.

"What do you need to develop new apparatus? You need to know the material that it will be working on. If we were dealing here with photographic apparatus, we would start studying film, paper, lenses, the physics of light, optics, and so on and so forth. But we are developing a telephone here, and we will study language, speech. You've heard of the science of phonetics? What, you even taught German phonetics? We need Russian phonetics, but I think that there must be common scientific principles. Thus, the first thing we must do is study the materials of our telephone system—the Russian language. We will study it phonetically and mathematically, that is, statistically. How many and what kind of letters. Don't laugh—I mean, how often the letters occur, how the various letters are transmitted along the telephone lines. We must carry on scientific work, and what's central to scientific work? To discredit your predecessors. Yes, yes, exactly. Learn everything that came before and prove that it was all in error, insufficient, wrong, misguided, unfounded. Today we prepare a plan of work and report this evening to Anton Mikhailovich. What do you mean, 'impossible'? You can't imagine what plan? Well, say that you don't know a thing and can't imagine a thing. I know even less. But I do know that we need a plan. Any plan. It doesn't matter whether it's wise or foolish, realistic or unrealistic. Plans are never fulfilled. But they can always be overfulfilled. Now we need a piece of paper with the heading 'Plan.' All right, if you're so high-principled, then write 'Projected Plan.' And a correspondingly handsome subtitle. And then several points expertly formulated: 'Study' . . . 'Research' . . . 'Examine' . . . 'Check' . . . 'Outline' . . . 'Run' . . . 'Develop' and so on and so forth. Anton Mikhailovich will scribble all over it, change it, and we'll do something completely different."

We were called into a conference with Anton Mikhailovich and his deputy in scientific matters—engineer major Abram Mendelevich T., a thin-faced, curly-haired, swarthy four-eyes with the gold Stalin laureate medal. It was decided that we would run a statistical analysis of the syllables of the Russian language. Our goal: to determine, even approximately, the total number of basic speech-forming syllables. Which syllables are encountered most frequently, the approximate word order of their frequency, and how much they depend on the content (theme) of the conversation.

Our brigade leader, who was always reminding us to discredit our predecessors, was very pleased to learn that such research had never been undertaken in Russia on a large enough scale.

The new librarian, a pretty MGB lieutenant, obtained magazines and newspapers from Moscow libraries. She immediately set up a subscription service with the lending library and the libraries of the Academy of Sciences, the Central Technical Library, the foreign library, and others.

Solzhenitsyn developed the mathematical conditions for the study. He ordered textbooks and new works on statistics and the theory of probability. And I surrounded myself with books, magazines, and brochures on general linguistics, phonetics, and the history of Russian.

We worked on the plans for the upcoming study during working hours and on our walks. Solzhenitsyn explained the theory of probability to me and drummed the principles of mathematical statistics into me, while I gave him lessons in linguistics, theoretical and practical phonetics.

The workplace of the phonetics brigade remained "the old semicircular room." (That was our name for the library room.) First we chose our texts. After brief arguments, we agreed to conduct research in four directions. First, the language of modern literature—for this we took excerpts from novels and stories. Second, spoken language. For this, the research subjects we chose were new plays, as well as dialogues from prose works. Third, the language of journalism and oratory—newspapers articles, speeches, and reports—and fourth, the language of technical literature.

In the course of our work, these four streams were reduced to two: conversational speech and literary (book and newspaper) language. It was harder to agree on how exactly in the course of the study to distinguish a sound component of speech. The two of us convinced the brigade leader that, for instance, we should see not three syllables in the word *zdravstvuite* ("hello") but only two—that is, the way it is actually pronounced: *zdra-ste* or *dra-ste*—and in at least half the cases, even as a single syllable, *drast'*. And also that we had to substitute letters that conveyed the real pronunciation, for instance, not *drugogo* ("another"), but *drugova*, not *gorod* ("city"), but *gorat*, and so on.

Solzhenitsyn, on the basis of the theory of probability, determined the smallest number of texts that were necessary for analysis—in each of the four "streams," no fewer than 20,000 syllables, that is, a total of 80,000; just to make sure, we decided on 100,000.

The brigade leader tried to take part in our preparatory work, and we tried to hear out with as much patience as possible his expansive and usually pointless instructions. But he turned out to be helpful as an energetic administrator, organizer, and technical executor. He compiled lists of necessary books, neatly, in duplicate—one for the librarian, one for us—went to the authorities to ask for and select "cadres," cut up index cards out of heavy paper, counted, and supervised the work of the counters.

On some days there were up to ten people counting. Both zeks and free employees. Solzhenitsyn and I prepared the texts the night before, that is, divided them in pencil into syllables and substituted letters. We checked each other, since we had agreed to mark sounds with special signs.

The counters began working first thing in the morning. In front of each lay a pile of paper strips, prepared by the brigade leader, and stood three or four tablets with large letters—the phonetic signs of our simplified system of phonetic transcription.

Every syllable got its own separate strip of paper. Our brigade leader had worked as a quota setter in the camps and taught us counting by "envelopes"—four dots and six strokes make ten.

The reader first slowly pronounced the entire word, then separately by syllables. The counter, hearing "his" syllable, had to say "mine" or "mine-new," then start a new card.

In this way in three weeks we worked on over 100,000 syllables and of them counted a little more than 3,500 phonetically different ones. And yet fewer than 100 most frequently occurring syllables constituted almost 85 percent of the entire mass of studied texts.

We were convinced that the syllabic composition of our speech was generally rather consistent, independent of genre and topic. Differences were expressed primarily in relatively rare sound combinations. The most frequent in the general count and in the separate streams were the same ones. The first places, as a rule, were held by И,НА,НЪ, and ВЪ.

When the statistical evaluation was coming to an end, our team was made part of a newly created acoustics laboratory, which was headed by Abram Mendelevich T.—also the institute's deputy for scientific matters.

Anton Mikhailovich heard our preliminary report with obvious satisfaction. "Ver-ry interesting! Ver-ry. Even if you've made mistakes in the frequencies. In that order of magnitude we can overlook details. They have no significance, or play no role, as the quasi literate say. What's important for us is the general data. The bottom line. The gross indicators. After all, we hear not the letter, but the syllable. We have thirty to thirty-two letters. All right, all right, they're not letters but sounds. You shouldn't correct your superiors. You were a major, weren't you, I believe? Ergo, you must know that a superior is not late, but held up, not asleep but resting, not wrong, but incorrectly briefed. That's an iron law!

"Your brigade has made me happy. And the happiness of superiors is a great reward in itself! But I will also explain the reason for the happiness. The unit of measuring intelligibility in a communications line has long been the syllable. Articulation tables for testing telephone systems are made up of syllables. How many combinations of two or three letters—excuse me, sounds—are possible if their total number isn't even thirty, but, say, twenty?! And yet there are also monosyllabic words formed from more than two or three or more discrete units, for instance, 'sport,' 'script,' 'act,' 'branch,' and so on. You, Aleksandr Isaevich, probably can compute that without great difficulty. Precisely—an astronomical number. I guess that not all combinations are possible. However, what you have discovered—three thousand six hundred something . . . plus perhaps even another hundred or two infrequent syllables—that's a finite number, friends, completely visible. And therefore, for us telephone people, highly intriguing. Pleasantly intriguing. And so you will be presenting a paper at the first scientific conference of the institute. Please prepare brief, but maximally informative, talks."

The sharashka spread out across the entire building. The barriers were removed, and a large number of new rooms were opened. In the largest of them, where later the design office was situated and where all the meetings of the "free employees" took place, was the site of the first scientific conference.

Mixed in with the officers, scintillating silver shoulder boards, and civilian free employees were two dozen or so men from the "special contingent" in worn suit jackets, jackets, and tunics. (The prison garb had not been introduced yet. By summer we were all dressed in blue denim coveralls.)

Three read papers. First I spoke about the sound makeup of Russian speech, the theory of phonemes. I emphasized most of all the differences between written and spoken language, between the conditions of intelligibility of a text "to the eye" and of speech "to the ear." Then Solzhenitsyn spoke about the mathematical principles of our research on syllables, and in conclusion the brigade leader reported the statistical summary, explained that we had discovered the "syllable nucleus" of Russian speech, and really pushed the direct benefits of this discovery for telephone specialists. Confidently "discrediting" the articulation tables used before as not corresponding to science and the living language, he maintained that there was an urgent need to begin compiling new and truly scientific tables.

The debate began. First to speak was a prisoner, a professor of mathematics, Vladimir Andreevich T., a Leningrader, and an educated, ironic talker who was used to always being the "life of the party" and setting the tone. He stared at the ceiling, raising his graying spadelike beard, and held that all this talk of phonemes, phonetics, and other such linguistic claptrap was purely academic, perhaps even an entertaining fantasy, but quite removed from real life and even more so from scientific and technological practice.

Anton Mikhailovich, closing the conference, said that the statistical survey was original, in certain aspects moot, but certainly useful work from a practical point of view. The important thing now was not to rest on that achievement, not to get caught up in "pure science." Our respected theoretical linguists and mathematicians had to subordinate their efforts to the demands of our practice. And work in daily contact with engineers and technologists. Directly in the laboratory.

Vladimir Andreevich told us in the cell: "I hope you're not angry with me for attempting a scientific argument? I got carried away for a moment; I imagined that I had an intelligent audience. I hope that at least you understood me?"

He had been arrested and convicted in Leningrad during the blockade. According to him, he had not hidden his disdainful hostility even before then for "that paradoxical deformation of the Russian state that arose after the well-known events of 1917." He admitted that in the last few years, especially during the war, several tendencies became manifest that could be termed resetting the dislocations and healing the breaks.

"And, as it always is here, with rather radical, bloody means. But I'm a skeptic. Broken dishes can be glued, but a national culture shattered to bits is a bit harder."

Vladimir Andreevich did not like to take walks; he preferred to smoke in the corridor, where long tables stood between the rooms for the conflicts of the domino and chess players. He called his usual conversation partners the "chitchat club." Sometimes I dared to disagree with him. For instance, when he announced that the life of the Russian theater ended back in the 1920s.

"Meyerhold was a faker, a hooligan, a destroyer, an eternal *enfant terrible.* But nevertheless he had some relation to the theater. And so they bumped him off. And what replaced him? Ensembles of song and dance. Those, what do you call them, troupes of various ethnic nationalities. Carnivals. Fairground trifles, not theater! Back in Petersburg, Iur'ev was the last monarch of the Russian stage. There are no actors like that left in Moscow. Ah, the Art. Theater! The Moscow Art was at one time a curious and even significant phenomenon. But in the last two decades it has become a gray, ordinary, run-of-the-mill troupe. Alekseev, or Stanislavsky as he called himself, was of course a talented actor. Though a bit monotonous, with typical Moscow merchant-class bathetics and melodramatics. I always preferred the Petersburg stage. Even the Moscow Imperial Maly Theater reeked of the Philistine spirit a bit. But the infamous 'Stanislavsky method' is something that is closer to the rules of street traffic, to medicine or psychiatry than to art.

"Not at all, my dear fellow! You're in error. I'm no classicist or retrograde. That's the way you were taught—who isn't with us is naturally a reactionary. Quite on the contrary, I very much loved, for instance, Nikolai Nikolaevich Evreinov's Crooked Mirror,* of which you haven't a clue. Ah, you have heard of it! Well, it's very pleasant to discover such rare informativeness in a scion of your, um, generation and your intellectual milieu. In that case you must of course understand that I am in no way

*The Crooked Mirror, founded in 1908 in Petersburg, was representative of the small-theater phenomenon, presenting parody and satire. Evreinov (1879–1953) died in Paris. (Translator's note.)

an old-fashioned thinker, not what you Germans call an *alte Perücke.* I've been to the Stray Dog Café,* and I always value highly such modernists —or, in your terminology, bourgeois decadents—as Nikolai Stepanovich Gumilev. What, you appreciate him, too?! And you're not put off by the circumstance that he was executed, or, as you people put it, 'slapped' by the Cheka for his participation in a monarchist union? Ah yes, of course, 'Captains,' 'Africa,' 'The Niger.' But of course, in our day all the Gymnasium students were crazy about some of his poems. Perhaps you've heard of Osip Mandelstam as well?"

I told him that Vladimir Lugovsky had delightedly read "Age of the Wolfhounds" in 1940 at the name-day party for a female graduate student at the Institute of Philosophy, Literature, and History, and many, including myself, had liked it very much.

"You're not mistaken, are you? A proletarian poet enjoying the poetry of a 'contra'? And no one denounced him? And none of you was taken away? I don't dare doubt you, since you insist. But I am amazed, amazed! Russian life is truly inscrutable.

"Yes, well, I held the Moscow Art Theater in very high esteem. Alekseev himself and naturally Shverubovich-Kachalov. An excellent voice, a truly velvet baritone. Good manners. Say what you will, but the nobility's *Kinderstube* is not the same as the children's room in a house over the corn chandler's. Also often good was Olga Leonardovna Knipper, the wife, no, rather, the widow of Chekhov. And Nemirovich-Danchenko was not a bad entrepreneur—yes, yes, I do mean entrepreneur, certainly not a director. I remember perfectly well what the Art Theater used to be like. And its modern counterpart doesn't even compare to it. I saw—this was before the war—*Three Sisters* and *The Bluebird* and *Anna Karenina.* Well, *Sisters* and *Birdie* were museum pieces. Lifeless shells. And as for *Karenina* . . . I'm not too wild about the novel. But on the stage . . . Madame Tarasova is a self-important Soviet housewife, and not the wife of a privy councillor. Khmelev is better. A serious actor. But he's playing not an aristocrat, not a tsar's courtier, but your well-placed bank director. Prudkin is a typical ensign or Junker under Kerensky. After the February Revolution they began letting Jews have officers' ranks in the Junker schools. Youths from the intelligentsia families rushed there. Among them were front liners— 'volunteer appointees'—and soldiers recently wounded. Now you probably don't know that the Junkers who 'defended' the Winter Palace in October were at least half Jewish. Back then anti-Semites maintained that that was precisely why the palace fell. That's all nonsense, just legends like the 'storming of the Winter Palace.' There was no storming, you know. The Provisional Government was rotting at the root, decayed and lost. Having put down the Kornilov Rebellion, it deprived itself of an army.

*The Stray Dog, an informal literary cabaret founded by Boris Pronin, was a battleground for the Acmeist and Futurist poets and a favorite intellectual hangout. (Translator's note.)

The military units in Petrograd either sympathized with the Bolsheviks or simply didn't want to fight with the Red sailors, or with squads of workers, or, least of all, with their brothers—soldiers like themselves. And so they cracked their sunflower seeds, tickled kitchen maids, and the more daring even got hold of vodka. The palace garrison included the Junkers and a woman's battalion. No one was actually in command of the Junkers. They still believed Kerensky, but he had fled. And the woman's battalion was a real joke. Madame Bochkareva in charge of several hundred fine seamstresses, hysterical young ladies, and repentant prostitutes. The Winter Palace didn't need to be stormed. All the doors were wide open—come in if you want. There were no casualties. Just a few Junkers who shot themselves out of shame and despair.

"In those days I walked around calmly throughout Petrograd. I never noticed any battles anywhere. The trolley ran as usual. The restaurants and cafés were overflowing. The theaters gave regular performances. All the newspapers were being published. In a few places there were shoot-outs. Not battles, but short exchanges of fire. Here and there larger crowds than usual huddled around the poster posts or newspaper stands. But that year there were constant meetings being held somewhere. Then it turned out there had been a revolution. The ministers no longer existed and the soviets and people's commissars were running everything. The soviets had existed earlier; it's amusing to say, in some cases they handled things with much more authority and decisiveness then than they did later, when the entire state was called 'soviet.' The soviets had existed before and so did the commissars. They were called commissars of the Provisional Government. So the changes did not seem serious. Just a palace coup. One provisional government replaced by another. And it was only in the winter, when they broke up the Constituent Assembly, did I begin to sense that something catastrophic, even apocalyptic, was happening. And more so in the spring, when we capitulated to the Germans, when they started shutting down the newspapers. It was then that we were supposed to have taken 'a leap into the kingdom of freedom.' That's what you call it, I believe."

Vladimir Andreevich hated to be contradicted, but he tolerated my presence in the chitchat club because I could appreciate better than the others his literary-theatrical erudition, and several times I had been sincerely impressed by his extraordinary memory and education. We argued rarely and then for completely unexpected reasons, when I was caught unawares by one of his paradoxical or anecdotal pronouncements. That's what happened when he stubbornly maintained that Shakespeare had never existed, and that all his plays and sonnets had been written by Francis Bacon. This was indisputable, he said, since even before the war a certain English mathematician friend of his had deciphered for the first time the mathematically coded autoepitaph of Bacon and so forth. But what angered Vladimir Andreevich was not my contradicting him per se, but only that

I reminded him that Lunacharsky* had said and written pretty much the same thing, when in his "anti-Shakespearean" musings he had leaned sometimes toward the Earl of Derby, sometimes toward Bacon. To compare him with that "snob commissar," "that Bolshevizer in a starched shirtfront"!

"For that I can only discontinue our useless logomachy."

On the days of the October and May holidays, some prisoners were "isolated." The criteria for selection were purely formal: those sentenced for "terror" and for escape from incarceration, and those who had been tried more than once, "recidivists," were culled. And also those who were considered too sociable and authoritative in the prisoners' milieu. Panin and I and Vladimir Andreevich inevitably fell into the group of isolated prisoners. I had three sentences—it was the same case, but it was the number of documents that matter; Panin had been sentenced twice—the second time in the camps. And apparently the authorities didn't like the fact that I had many friends and a reputation as a "lawyer"—I often helped the prisoners write petitions, complaints, and so on. And Vladimir Andreevich was both sociable and active and indisputably very authoritative.

The first time we were isolated rather shamefacedly. They invented an "urgent, highly secret task"—to decode a telegram intercepted in West Berlin. Vladimir Andreevich had to ponder the text as a mathematician, and I as a linguist, while Panin and a few other engineers and technicians had to develop the design of an encoder that could be used for the decoding. Among the engineers was a short Leningrader with the "traditional Leningrad" paragraph—58-8 (terrorism)—and even one nonpolitical prisoner, an often-jailed petty thief.

We were placed in a cellar room and given a special supervisor. For three or four days (November 6–8) we were fed separately, taken out on walks separately. It goes without saying that we didn't decode anything.

On following occasions we were simply taken away to Butyrki for the holidays without any pretext. The first time I tried to protest—I wanted to declare a hunger strike. Vladimir Andreevich talked me out of it.

"Drop it! All protests are empty bustle. Personally I feel at my best in prison. Here I am limitlessly free. Yes, yes, and you of all people should understand. What is freedom? Apprehended necessity! Isn't that so? You maintain that everything that happens with you people is historical necessity. The Revolution, Civil War, collectivization, liquidation, industrialization . . . And more war, and the blockade, and famine, and more liquidation —et cetera, et cetera—all that, according to you, is historical necessity. Then

*Anatoli Vasilievich Lunacharsky (1875–1933), People's Commissar of Education, 1917–1929. (Translator's note.)

why are you so angered by your personal portion of historical necessity? I hold other ideas. For me freedom is first of all freedom of thought and spirit, the freedom of personal choice. But I consider it incongruous to protest here. I'm even pleased. In the sharashka I'm forced to think about the management's problems with codes, decoders, abstract and concrete problems of cryptography, cryptology, and so on and so forth. There my choice is constrained by circumstances. After all, I must act and think just that way and no other in order not to be shipped to a lumber camp, to the mines. But here, in the cell, I do nothing and can think unhindered about whatever I want. In action and deed my choice is highly limited by walls, the iron door, the prison regulations. But within these *external* limits I am absolutely free inside! If I want to lie down, I lie down, if I want to sit, I sit, if I want to, then I talk to you, if I want to, I'll play chess. Yes, I'm more and more convinced that I was born for prison. Today the thinking Russian can only be free in prison."

Vladimir Andreevich's polemic at the first "scientific conference" astounded us unpleasantly—you don't argue like that with a fellow convict in front of the bosses. Later he spoke out even more harshly against the projected coder developed by Panin and several times denounced cruelly the serious cryptographic work of other prisoners. Everyone who worked in the special "mathematics groups" said that Vladimir Andreevich of course was an outstanding scholar—wise, talented, erudite—but also an indefatigable squabbler, peevish, envious, and intolerant of the success of others.

Of us three, he treated Solzhenitsyn best—because Solzhenitsyn listened to him attentively, seriously, did not become embroiled in arguments, and even though a professional mathematician, did not become his competition, refused to work in the mathematics group, and became involved in the acoustics-linguistics one. Panin angered the jealous professor occasionally, either by his incursions into the other's private domain of cryptography or by his too decisive and insufficiently "parliamentary" polemics in defense of his "language of extreme clarity."

He treated me with polite, restrained dislike. Later I learned that he considered me a stoolie and a particularly dangerous one at that—an intelligent one, who didn't ingratiate himself but argued, "thereby provoking him."

However, it was thanks to Vladimir Andreevich, thanks to his mean captiousness and painful attacks, sometimes nonsensical but more often to the point, that I studied more persistently—I read, researched, surveyed. For I myself knew that my linguistic knowledge was superficial, approximate, and my ideas of cryptography, physics, and acoustics were completely negligible. And first, in order to respond to his cavils and reproaches and then becoming more and more engrossed, I outlined books and articles, boned up, compared what I read with what I observed personally.

In order to progress in self-education, there is nothing better than strict, hostile teachers.

In those years of voluntary and imposed study, my mentors were the masterly Chekist-intellectual Anton Mikhailovich and the implacable, mocking "ideological antipode," Vladimir Andreevich.

"Thanks to the ones who got in our way," the poet David Samoilov said.

I thank them all the more sincerely because they not only interfered, but in many cases they helped me with my lessons.

4

CONFESSION

Engineer R. was tall and thin, wore an old, neatly mended jacket and a well-altered short, black padded overcoat; his boots were always polished. His dress and demeanor bore that unintentional calm yet confident expediency, that manly chic that distinguish true frontline soldiers and true hard workers from bustling dandies, striving for a cheap tinsel effect, from slovenly slobs and absentminded eccentrics who forget to shave, wash, change their collars, sew on buttons, and launder their foot bindings.

Taciturn and alienated, he rarely smiled, and his light eyes, set deeply beneath his high, pale brow, had a sad or exhausted look. When I spoke to him, he replied politely, amiably, but briefly, not volubly, and hurried to move away. "I have work to do . . . Excuse me, some urgent business . . . Forgive me, I have a bad headache. I'm tired . . . Sorry, I have to read this book quickly . . ."

He went on walks with shovel and broom and cleared the snow at length, assiduously, or paced in concentrated thought along a narrow path. We all gradually learned that he was a mechanical engineer, a machine builder, a Muscovite who had worked for a long time in Siberia, had been in for ten years already, since 1938, had five to go, sentenced to fifteen years under Article 58,* Paragraphs 7 and 9 (that is, wrecking and diversion)— the usual "professional" (engineering) paragraphs. Questions on the subject

*Political prisoners were called fifty-eighters because they had been sentenced under Article 58 of the Criminal Code of the USSR, which deals with "crimes against the state." The fourteen paragraphs, or sections, of Article 58 are

 1. Actions weakening state power; treason
 2. Armed rebellion
 3. Assisting a foreign state at war with the USSR
 4. Aid to the international bourgeoisie
 5. Inciting a foreign state to declare war against the USSR
 6. Espionage
 7. Subversions of industry and transport, known as "wrecking"
 8. Terrorism
 9. "Diversion," or sabotage
10. Propaganda or agitation containing an appeal for the overthrow or subversion of Soviet power and preparation or possession of literary materials of similar content —the most popularly applied and widely interpreted paragraph
11. Added if other actions were undertaken by an organization
12. Failure to make a denunciation
13. Service in the tsarist secret police
14. Sabotage or economic counterrevolution

(Translator's note.)

elicited reluctant, miserly responses: "Forgive me, I don't like recalling."

In the summer of 1948 I received the first permission, after many months, for a meeting with my family. The prison storeroom had special dress-up clothing for meetings, colored shirts and ties. This window dressing was offensive, and I decided to stay in my army tunic, still dignified-looking. The prison director permitted it, but ordered me "to wear proper boots"; mine were finishing off their long, labor-filled frontline and camp life. However, the storeroom did not have a single pair in my size. I grew afraid. The duty officer might cancel my long-awaited meeting.

R. silently handed me his excellent box-calf boots. They were just the right size.

My escort watched me walk, squeaking almost like a general, with poorly disguised envy. At our meeting my mother saw the matte shine of the luxurious boots as evidence of the growing well-being of our native prisons. And the other prisoners—that day we were all sitting at a long table in the guards' clubroom of the Taganka Prison—were all in brand-new suits and radiantly motley ties.

Mama and Nadya gave me a full bag of all kinds of grub. And Solzhenitsyn also got a tasty package. We had a banquet behind the library shelves, and I dragged over the resisting R.; he politely ate some trifle and quickly hurried off, citing some urgent work.

Two days later rather easygoing screws were on duty. By evening they were so engrossed in their personal gathering of construction materials that, no longer embarrassed by the prisoners, they pulled an unofficial truck right up to the fence and even called over a few zeks to haul the stolen logs, boards, bags, and pails of alabaster and paint, rolls of wire, and so on. However, they followed the rules—the van, which did not have a pass, was not brought into the courtyard of the sharashka, and the helper zeks were not permitted beyond the forbidden zone, a strip a meter and a half wide along the fence. From there they worked themselves, groaning and swearing, tossing their trophies over the wall and trying not to damage the barbed wire stretched across it.

But at least we could all wander around until after midnight, and in the labs and in the library we felt completely insouciant.

That evening I found myself alone on our path. I walked, trying not to see the barbed wire and the towers in the corners of the fence, but only the snow, the shrubs, the trees, and the stars.

R. came up to me. We walked side by side. I tried to tell him something. Suddenly he began talking, looking away, in a hollow, compressed tone. "Here's the thing . . . I want to explain to you and your friends. I hope you'll understand me correctly. You three are decent people and experienced enough zeks. So, don't get close to me. None of you. Talk to me as little as possible, better yet, not at all—don't have anything to do with me. I like the three of you. I know about people. But I must avoid you and ask your cooperation. I ask you to keep away from me."

He spoke clearly, calmly. We walked next to each other, shoulder to shoulder; he looked at his feet or to the side, occasionally looking me in the eye.

"Don't get close to me. I ask that urgently. You see, I'm on the hook. Understand? On the godfather's hook. I agreed— Don't interrupt. I don't want to justify myself, only explain. I don't need pity. But I must explain. In '38 I ended up in Kolyma: gold-mine labor. They shot people there. Hundreds, thousands without trial. The local 'troika'* decided. Sometimes the security officer's orders were enough. Every night they called people out by lists. Led them to the hills. Night after night. The ones left behind didn't fall asleep for a long time—no one knew how much longer he had left to live. That went on for about two weeks. Then it was over. They said that the 'troika' and the chief were shot themselves. Some of our prisoners went mad. Others grew empty. Understand? Emptied: souls and brains—empty. No hope, no faith. Nothing! What was left was the bread share. Work. Lunch. Stove. Sleep. Bread again. And that was it. Nothing else. Not even depression. They didn't want to remember—not their families, not freedom. Life from bread share to bread share. And there were those who turned into animals. Like the hardened criminals. You know: 'You drop dead today, I'll go tomorrow.' They might kill you for a piece of bread, a pinch of tobacco. Very few—very—stayed simply human. And then the war and more executions. They shot shirkers right at the mines. Most often they were simply sick. The doctor hadn't given them a medical excuse. He had his limit and if he went over it, he would be shot himself. I saw it happen several times—a goner, barely shuffling, with heart trouble or kidney colic or rheumatism—and right at the entrance to the mine in front of everybody the chief convoy guard shoots him with his revolver or orders another guard to do it. They also shot people for not fulfilling the quota—for sabotage. And for new camp cases. Defeatist agitation. Extolling the enemy . . .

"The stoolies worked hard. They said that I supposedly said that the Germans had good planes. And they began building a case on the fact that the instruments were wearing out too fast in the shops. Sabotage! I was the chief mechanic. They put me in the cooler. The security officer led the investigation. Certain death sentence. So he started buying. The choice was simple—death or sign. I promised to help. I promised. What happened after that, I don't want to remember. I can't. I tried not to ruin people. I tried to help good people. I was lucky—they transferred me to another camp, also in production. The godfather there didn't realize it right away. And he wasn't as demanding. Then I was sick for a long time. Dystrophy, nervous exhaustion. They transferred me again. The godfather found me again. 'Come on, give us signals, you're not catching any mice.' But it got

*Secret courts of the GPU, which sentenced *in absentia*, primarily for political defendants. The courts had three judges. (Translator's note.)

easier toward the end of the war. They didn't push me as hard, they didn't threaten as hard. And I kept pushing the production part. I worked till I dropped. Invented. Improved. I liked work. And to get away from them, I tried twice as hard, three times as hard. I became a harsh overseer, a dog pack leader. The hard workers feared and hated me. But I did it on purpose. That's what I wanted. Let more of them hate me. I could say: 'No one trusts me, I worry about production, I don't give anyone a break.'

"No one's called on me here yet. But they can at any moment. I have wonderful work here—one on one with the carrel—invent, calculate, draft. And I can talk only about work, so that everyone hears. But you and your friends are working on a completely different project. That means we can't have anything in common. That's all there is to it! No, please, don't say anything. I'm urging you not to. It's not necessary. You can understand how much I trust you if I've told you this. Tell your friends, only them and only once. I beg you: never bring this up again. Don't promise. I believe you without it. That's all. Good night."

Shaking hands was not a common practice then. He turned; he left unhurriedly, with a broad, steady gait.

During the morning walk I told everything to my friends. Solzhenitsyn asked me to repeat certain things. "Well, it's all clear. Let's keep it in mind. We'll obey his wish—we won't chat with him."

Panin heard me out in silence, scowling. Then he said: "Gentlemen, this isn't simple at all, but very complicated. It requires solitary thought."

On the evening walk he strode between us, hands clasped behind his back, hunched up, pressing his forked dark-chestnut beard into his bare chest, red with the cold, his dark iconlike eyes flashing occasionally, and spoke, choosing his words carefully. "I always thought that a stoolie, a plant, was the lowest, vilest creature. So vile that decent people, if they can't squash it, must walk around it, because it is stinking, poisonous, a viper. But this case is something not quite usual. Or completely unusual. Confession is very dangerous for him. And brings no profit. Therefore, there is a certain nobility there. Yes, yes, gentlemen, I dare to use that word. I think that in this case we must judge not only as zeks. I am first and foremost a Christian. But you are also Christians, fundamental Christians, so to speak. Even though you, Sanya, insist that you are only a rational computer and doubt everything. And you, Lev, stubbornly maintain you are a fervent Bolshevik-atheist. But both of you, nevertheless, in your nature, your spiritual makeup—forgive my inarticulateness—in your mores, in your relation to life, you are fundamental Christians, and therefore my friends. And that means, we are obliged to fulfill that wretch's request exactly . . . Yes, precisely, that wretch. Do not approach him anymore. We won't discuss him among ourselves—and certainly not with anyone else. But we'll treat him without hatred or disdain and as much as possible, help him. That is, help him from falling into temptation."

And that is what we decided.

5

WHY
SEE SOUNDS?

Reminiscence is capricious,
Like dreams it seems to be
   full of truth,
But it is just as wild and dark
And, probably, just as false . . .

—VLADISLAV KHODASEVICH

Anton Mikhailovich brought a stack of British and American journals. "Look here, I've marked what needs translating. And not word for word, just the gist. Give the general discussion in outline, but sensibly. Will you manage?"

"I'll try."

"Are you familiar with acoustics? In particular, with electroacoustics?"

"I vaguely remember my school lessons. It's been twenty years."

"Can you walk a tightrope?"

"No."

"Well, what if you were told: 'Here's the tightrope, walk.' The choice is walk on the tightrope or die. *Tertium non datur.* What would you do?"

"Walk."

"Now there, you see. And learning acoustics is a lot easier for an intelligent person than tightrope walking. Here's a book for you, *Speech and Hearing,* written by an American, the wise Fletcher. Some of it is out of date, but in general, it's a classic, the foundation of the foundations. This is my own copy. Guard it with your life. And learn it like 'Our Father.' Though, I don't suppose you know it."

" 'Our Father, Who art in Heaven, Hallowed be Thy name, Thy Kingdom—' "

"All right, all right! I believe you. But you're Jewish, aren't you? Aha, your nanny taught you. Mine, too. But in acoustics, prayers won't help. Start translating the journals with Licklider's articles on interrupted speech. And then . . . No, actually, do it in reverse. First, translate everything you can find here on 'visible speech.' Understand that? Not completely? That's all right. There are more things in heaven and on earth, Horatio, than are dreamt of in your philosophy. And this American thing seems to be one of them. They've come up with an apparatus that analyzes the spectrum of sound oscillations. Here, do you see the photographs of the spectrograms—here, here, these wavy shadows. You could say they're rather elegant. Yes, it does look like abstract art. How do you feel about Malevich and Kandinsky? Do you remember *Black Square?* It's nonsense of course, whimsy. But there is something to it, after all. I recently read that the Americans have invented a way of combining music and color. Just imagine: sound channels direct the light sources. They've 'agreed and coordinated' the spectrums of color and sound vibrations. And not arbitrarily at all. After all, red and blue are differentiated by the character of emitted color waves. Therefore, the low sound frequencies must control various shades of red, and the high ones, on the contrary, control blue and light-blue lights. The piano and orchestra are hooked up to this system that controls multicolored light signals and allows variation in shades. I can't imagine how they manage agreement of velocity, how they coordinate the resolving abilities of the sources of light and sound. And that in itself is an extremely interesting problem—to compare vision and hearing, eye and ear. Which distinguishes perceived signals faster and more accurately? Television is being developed now. And now the problem is no longer simply abstract, but concrete and applied, engineering and technological . . . However, I've gone off on a tangent. What were we talking about, then? *Revenons à nos moutons.* So, spectrograms of visible speech. The Americans call those pictures 'patterns'—like a design. Check several dictionaries. Do you remember that I had talked to you about secret telephony? Well, I suspect, I'm almost convinced that visible speech can be a significant aid in decoding mosaic systems. Until now ordinary oscillograms were used for that. But they make the work complicated and tedious, everything has to be approximated visually, with a slide ruler, calculating peaks. Accuracy is suspect—it's not easy to separate interference from useful signals. But with this you look and everything is clear.

"The Americans write that they use their 'patterns' for studying foreign languages, to master correct pronunciation, and also for teaching deaf-mutes. A hot-off-the-presses legend. For some reason they didn't publish these materials until 1947, although they had developed it all back in '42 and '43. And the analysis circuit isn't described fully anywhere. Just a look and a glimpse. It's quite possible that it's disinformation. In every serious laboratory there they have special workers who edit materials prepared for publication. They edit them in a way to keep secrets from being revealed and to disinform as much as possible, to disorient even other specialists. Dust-in-the-eye-throwers . . . Well, you and I must outsmart them.

"Does that interest you? Don't tell me that you understand; I won't believe it. But I can see by the look in your eyes that you're interested. Eloquent glances, as the writer would say. A bad one, naturally. Well, go to it. *Hic Rhodos, hic salto.* When you've mastered this theoretical part, we'll show you a few practical wonders."

One of the wonders turned out to be a ten-band spectrum analyzer.

Sound signals traveled directly from the microphone to the inlets of ten filters, and their outlets controlled "pens" that wrote on a moving roll of pink paper, saturated with an iodine solution. Every touch of the pen left a mark, a brown dot or line. This created clearly visible spectrums of sound oscillations. Ten "pens" corresponded to the ten channels of frequencies from 60 to 3,000 Hertz. The degree of darkness of the "line" was an indicator of the energy of the given band.

With the help of the American journals and direct observation I quickly learned to read these spectrograms, for which I invented the name "sound pictures."* The term caught on in the sharashka and was mentioned in Solzhenitsyn's novel, but never did become part of general usage.

The prisoner engineers Sergei and Arkadii developed and built a new spectrum analyzer. A magnetic tape was stretched onto a metallic disk. The sound picture was drawn on the same pink paper in a few minutes with a single thin pen, but very close together, and it looked almost like the American patterns. The wavy shadows of various shades clearly described the movement and distribution of sound energy along the frequency, in the range of 0 to 3,000 Hertz (the number of oscillations per second).

The transitions from one sound to another were becoming visible.

Apparatus AS-2, that is, analyzer of spectrum, or in our own decoding version, Arkadii-Sergei, allowed us to examine details in speech structure that all previous analyzers could not reveal. Soon after, Sergei and Arkadii created yet another one (AS-3), which gave even larger and clearer sound pictures. Gradually, I learned to read them (if it was a recording of ordinary speech and not patter or tongue twisters).

It was difficult (and sometimes simply impossible) to read words broken up by the mosaic encoder; however, once I grew accustomed to reading sound pictures of ordinary speech, I could eventually determine from depictions of unusual speech the character, method, and approximately even the code of the cipher, since the bands of the used filters—three or four—and the time fractions of 100–120 milliseconds, into which the coded signals were divided, were clearly distinguishable.

Anton Mikhailovich and Abram Mendelevich were pleased. They bragged about my ability to the bosses from the MGB and to government commissions that occasionally visited the sharashka and that were also shown the main attractions:

"And here is the only man in the Soviet Union and in Europe who can read visible speech. Only in America are there such readers—one or two men. But they naturally can only read English. And apparently he is the only one to have mastered Russian for now."†

*"Sound pictures" is the term that is translated as "voice prints" in Solzhenitsyn's *The First Circle*. (Translator's note.)
†In the days when I had the galleys of the Russian edition of this manuscript, a young friend of ours—a college freshman—was doing a paper on the physical structure of speech, and she easily read a sound picture, which she called a spectrogram.

When Foma Fomich Zhelezov dropped by the laboratory, he conde-scendingly offered his hand to several zeks, demonstrating how high up he was—he could allow himself even that.

Once we were visited by a deputy minister, a tall, distinguished, hand-some man, in a suit the likes of which I had seen only in foreign films. He was accompanied by Anton Mikhailovich, even more amiable and talkative than usual. They were followed by a retinue of officers in uniform and in civilian clothes, among whom I recognized some ten minutes later Foma Fomich—he seemed hunched over, shorter, thinner, losing himself amid the silent or quietly whispering members of the group.

That evening and a few times after that I was shown off like a "trained bear." I asked that Solzhenitsyn be the speaker—he had a good voice and clear enunciation. Only the old analyzer was used for the demonstrations. It gave sound pictures much faster, and they could be of any length. The new apparatus gave a finer analysis, more detailed, but only brief excerpts of two or three words at a take.

The boss, for whose benefit the demonstration was being given, wrote several words on a piece of paper. The text was taken to the speaker in the acoustics booth, built in the corner of our laboratory. The tape with the recorded spectrum was spread out on the table—I waited a few moments while the "drawing" became more distinct and until the speaker could come out of the booth and take a spot where I could see his hand. Like cardsharps, we had our own simple hand code. I would say aloud the sound I supposed it to be, marking it in pencil on the paper, without raising my eyes, engrossed in "contemplation." He stood opposite. If I guessed accu-rately, his hand did not move; if I was completely wrong, he lifted all his fingers; if I had the wrong sound but was close, only a few fingers went up. However, the puzzle really was not too difficult in those cases when the text was clearly enunciated by a familiar voice.

The sound pictures showed in clearly drawn, dark wavy stripes the stronger parts of the spectrum—the formants of the sounds of speech. I called them the formative frequencies. The main formant in voiced sounds is, as a rule, the second from the bottom, and in unvoiced ones, most frequently the first or even the only—which constantly changed, moving, undulating, and breaking in sound combinations that blended into syllables and words. The Americans called it the hub, and I tried to legalize the terms "deep stream" and "deep-stream formative."

In every sound picture I could observe the hubs of discrete sounds being altered under the influence of preceding and following sounds. For in-stance, in the word "bass" the hub "a" moved sharply upward from the lower "b" to the higher "s"; in the word "chap," on the contrary, it moved sharply downward. In "chat" the hub curved upward with crescent points, and in "bab," pointed down, and so on.

We did the following experiment a few times: we recorded on tape a syllable or a series of syllables, spoken clearly and slowly, as meaningless as possible (in order to rule out the usual guesses), and then very carefully and precisely comparing the length of tape with the sound pictures and oscillograms, we "cut off" the last sound. We transmitted this tape over the channel of an ordinary telephone. And the majority of people in the articulation group, as a rule, *heard* the spliced-out sounds or sounds that were phonetically close to them (for instance, instead of the "sh" they heard "s" or "zh").

By the fall of 1949, the joint efforts of several laboratories developed an *absolutely* secret telephone. The sounds of speech, passing from the microphone into the encoder, were no longer broken up in time and frequency into a mosaic, but, "debanded" by dozens of filters, they were transformed into the simplest signals. In each band, impulses that were absolutely identical in amplitude ("clipped") were transmitted in beams of varying thickness. They were mixed up in the encoder according to a certain code. Bugging the line gave only a constant, uneven squeak, whistle, and hiss. Sound pictures didn't give even an idea of the nature of the sounds. And they looked almost like mechanical noises. But the decoder at the receiving end, tuned by a key that could be changed daily, directed these signals into the corresponding filters, and speech was restored.

When this principle of coding was first explained to me, I said that in the mosaic system, speech is subjected to mechanical fractionation, after which the unchanged particles are rejoined, while here there takes place a kind of "chemical decomposition" of speech into atoms, which are then synthesized anew.

Anton Mikhailovich noted: "I don't feel that that is a sufficiently strict scientific-technological definition. It's more a metaphor, an image. But to a certain extent it reflects reality. So, my dear philologists, now we are expected to do the following: determine precisely all the conditions of maximal intelligibility in this synthesis. We must know which parameters must be transmitted *sine qua non* and on which we can cut corners. Which frequency bands can we cut? Which various amplitudes can we overlook? But the most important thing is coding."

Together with the prisoner engineer B., I translated Wiener's *Cybernetics*. He translated those pages where I simply couldn't follow the mathematical meaning and edited everything that I translated.

Our press had declared cybernetics a reactionary pseudoscience. Anton Mikhailovich wasn't worried by that. "Well, they may be right. If it's reactionary, then it's reactionary. But it must be used technologically. We never doubted the reactionary character of the German fascists, and nevertheless we shot at them with their own cannon. How is it pronounced: 'sy-bernetics' or 'ky-bernetics'? A smart cookie, that American. Though I believe he's an Austrian Jew—the Yankees appropriated him the way they did Einstein and Bohr. And got a goodly profit. The atom bomb was created primarily by immigrant scientists. But you and I, we must surpass the wise men from overseas, outsmart them.

"Thus, your first goal is intelligibility, intelligibility, and intelligibility again. You, Aleksandr Isaevich, must determine not simply the bare percentages—how many syllables passed through a channel—but determine which letters, ah yes—sounds—are more easily made out, which less so. And you, Lev Zinovievich, please analyze the physical causes of this impenetrability. How do you plan to do this? I see . . . Tape a speaker reading to the articulation brigade and then study the sound pictures. I don't see why you don't just call them spectrograms. Honest to God, it's more exact, though not as beautiful. Of course, you can call them anything, just give us accurate data. But there's a second goal as well. You listen yourself and so you know—this one and that one and the other one—all our models sound very bad at the receiving end. And even worse, the speakers are unrecognizable. Intelligibility fluctuates—sometimes better, sometimes worse—but recognizability, or rather unrecognizability, is constant. Just imagine: Comrade Stalin calls Marshal Konev or Vyshinsky or, um, Rákosi, and he doesn't recognize the voice. So that's your job, dearest reader of sound pictures. Please find out as precisely as possible how one voice differs from another. I need to hear the shortest 'hello' or 'yes' to know whether it's Captain Voloshenko or Major Trakhtman. I recognize them in the space of a second. And yet in an ordinary phone we hear a very limited band, and with a frequency response that deforms the spectrum significantly. Now, I listened to your musing on formants and so on. And then I looked at the frequency responses of telephones. And it turns out that all telephone engineers, who had never heard of visible speech and had cooked all that up by ear, they acted as though they had studied the same data as you. Here, look—the lower and upper frequencies are rolled off, and the middle ones are amplified; this belly sticks out, the very same bands where according to your observations the main formants pass. So, judge for yourself. The telephone engineers—humble empirical technologists, knowing no theories, following practical experience—have achieved highly worthwhile intelligibility in accordance with the same laws you discovered theoretically, sweating over the latest technological achievements. On the one hand, it turns out that the telephone engineers acted like that Molière character who didn't know that he had been speaking prose all his life. On the other hand, this coincidence is evidence that your observations and thoughts are trustworthy. After all, I personally am convinced that until quite recently you didn't even know what a frequency response of a telephone was. This fact is also interesting in itself, because it confirms a certain regularity that is rejected by many. I formulate it this way: healthy ignorance is one of the movers of technical progress. *Healthy*, that is, recognizing itself as ignorance, lacking smugness and hitched up with intellectual curiosity. Henry Ford understood this law very well. He didn't hire graduate engineers or even experienced practical specialists. He used to say: Their brains are frozen now, all their thoughts move in one direction, they're used to a rut, and they can't and don't want to move out of it. I need inexperienced but curious fellows, who will learn everything anew. Men like that are more courageous and resourceful; they are capable of finding completely new paths. What a clever old man! And I, too, bless your healthy ignorance and send you off in search of new paths."

I didn't need convincing. My first immersion in applied linguistics—the statistical study of Russian syllables—was completed. We compiled new syllabic articulation tables and began compiling "word" and "phrase" tables, formed brigades of young—under thirty—free employees, both male and female. In testing each new model and every separate unit of the telephone system, the articulation brigade wrote down syllables that the speaker pronounced in the acoustics booth—so that there would be no external interference. The percentage of correctly received syllables was counted by an objective indicator of intelligibility in the given channel.

We selected speakers from among prisoners and free employees who could read the tables clearly, evenly, and at the same time naturally—without shouting or stressing individual sounds—for long periods, that is, for hundreds and thousands of meaningless syllables.

The engineer Sergei Kuprianov appeared in the sharashka during the second winter.

"I come from pure Petrograd stock. I grew up on the Neva on Vasilevsky Island. A hereditary engineer, an electromechanic. But other kinds of mechanical work don't exactly slip through my fingers, either."

He worked in blockaded Leningrad, swollen with hunger, barely alive, not leaving the shop for weeks at a time; he was brought out, completely malnourished.

Even before the end of the war he returned to Leningrad and his plant. His cousin, also a plant engineer, and a man who loved the easy life, took platinum parts from war-spoils machinery and sold them to sailors from freighters for money or contraband. He was caught red-handed and turned over to the MGB. And the investigator told him that he was certain to get the death penalty with no hope of commutation. But he offered the only possible way out—"to help expose a serious counterrevolutionary plot." That ill-fated thief, without much thought, "confessed" that his relative and best friend Sergei was planning to kill all the Leningrad leaders (Kuznetsov, Popkov, and others, who were later shot in 1951 in the notorious "Leningrad Affair")* and Comrade Stalin as well, after which he intended

*The purge of the Leningrad organization of the CPSU. The charges were never revealed but Khrushchev in his "secret speech" charged Beria and Abakumov with making up cases against Zhdanov's followers after Zhdanov's death in 1948. (Translator's note.)

to reinstate free trade, disband the kolkhozes, and turn over the medium-sized enterprises to private ownership.

Sergei had a poor reputation: he did not join the Party and was considered a "whiner and squabbler"; that is, he exposed shenanigans at the plant verbally and in writing a few times. In one case he was even called to Moscow by the Ministry of State Control.

After his arrest he fought for a while. They pressured him in a freezing cooler, put bracelets on him, beat him viciously. He "confessed" to telling anti-Soviet jokes, that he liked Lenin and Kirov more than Stalin, and that during the blockade the loss of all food supplies in Leningrad was the fault primarily of the government—Zhdanov and perhaps even Stalin.

The investigator laughed at some of the jokes: "They really come up with them, the bitches!" But he continued demanding a confession about writing "tracts" and creating an underground organization.

Face to face, Sergei's cousin looked well fed, but a bit sad, smoked Kazbek cigarettes, and asked Sergei not to ruin himself, their families, and to make a clean breast of it: "The motherland will forgive us."

Finally the investigator showed Sergei a completely filled out order for the arrest of his wife and older daughter.

"If you confess, this very second, I'll tear it up in front of you. But if you keep this up, you bastard, they'll be brought here tonight. They'll be tried as your co-conspirators. That's when they'll thank you, fuck your mother! When we start peeling them and tell them that you're the one who turned them in!"

Sergei agreed to sign everything. The orders were deliberately, dramatically torn into shreds. The investigator gave him a cigarette and started speaking very amiably.

"You should have done that a long time ago. You just torture yourself and us, drive us crazy. Do you think I like bruising my fists on your bones? And this way there's benefit for you and us and the state. The enemy is rendered harmless. You and your cousin are the real enemy. That's a fact. But now, for a frank confession things will be easier for you, too. The organs will take it into consideration."

Sergei and his exposer were tried *in absentia* by the Special Commission, each got a quarter—twenty-five years—on three paragraphs of Article 58: 8 (terrorism), 10 (anti-Soviet propaganda), and 11 (counterrevolutionary organization).

"That idiot later learned that he wouldn't have gotten more than ten years for the platinum. And he would have been considered an economic criminal, and not an enemy of the state. He almost went off his nut, chewed his elbows. After seeing him, his wife went to my Lida and said: He's in despair, he begs your forgiveness, he wants to write to the Procurator General, to the Supreme Court, to Stalin himself. And he hopes, the rotten nit, that I'll write, too. Like hell! We have a gentleman's agreement of sorts. I signed what they wanted, and they didn't touch my family and sent me here to the sharashka to use my brains, and not drop dead at hard labor in Vorkuta or Magadan. And what will happen if I start writing complaints? Let him go and write to Stalin, or the city committee, or the board of the society of deaf-mutes."

I liked Sergei the first time I met him. Stately, portly, with wide-open daring eyes under a high brow. He spoke like an educated Petersburger, but was an experienced man, fluent in the languages of the shop and the offices, the tribunal and the provincial beer hall.

"The best Russian painter is Makovsky. Who could doubt that? Just an ignoramus or a snob who pretends to prefer that abstract dabbling.

"Stalin wanted to give Leningrad to the Germans, and it's still not clear who set fire to the Badaev warehouses,* who led Fritz's bombs to them. Stalin fears and hates St. Petersburgers. Because of Kirov.

"Now Kirov was a real Bolshevik! You can't fault him there. A Russian soul. Open. And his head was in the right place. He understood technology and urban construction. He didn't let them destroy Leningrad, mutilate it the way they did Moscow. He wouldn't even let them take down monuments. Alexander III—that cast-iron dummy—was hauled away before his time. But he saved all the others: Tsaritsa Catherine, Nicholas I, and Suvorov. And yet, and I know this for a fact, there were those who were after all of them, they even wanted to toss the Bronze Horseman into the open-hearth furnaces. They said the five-year plan needs tractors. The working proletariat is rich in other kinds of beauty. Shut down the Hermitage, fuck the bourgeoisie!"

He didn't like to argue. Having expressed himself categorically, he waved off any contradictions, sometimes with a curse, other times with a joke or a nasty gibe.

"Ah, excuse me, my mistake. We simple technicians, ignoramuses all, shouldn't dare aspire to the heights of enlightenment. We eat soup with our bast shoes, and blow our noses in our bare feet. Oh, I'm so sorry, a thousand *mille pardons!* I deeply regret that I dared have my own opinion and to have expressed it in such august company. Therefore I shut myself up. And if anyone has any doubts, he can kiss my ass."

We became pals from his first few days there. Sometimes we argued a lot using terrible swearwords, but we made up quickly. His inventiveness awed me and became indispensable to my work.

Panin greeted Sergei very warmly in the first days: "A real old Russian warrior. A brave young man."

He liked the free speech and the whole behavior of the "Petersburg inhabitant." But later Sergei's atheist jokes and disdainful remarks about the Church led to a breach.

---

*On September 8, 1941, during the Germans' most intensive air attack on Leningrad, the Badaev warehouses, holding the city's main food supplies, burned down, greatly increasing the hardships of the besieged inhabitants. (Translator's note.)

"Your Mitya is a holy fool. Holy Fools never died out in Russia. If you tell foreigners about them, they'll crap in their pants, but they won't believe it. I met him on the walk yesterday: he's walking around barefoot, and the ground is frozen. His chest is bare to his bellybutton. All he needed were heavy chains and he could declaim about Judgment Day from a pulpit. I pity people like that, but I can't respect them. I'm a simple man, sad, but psychologically normal. And my healthy soul is as revolted by such spiritual pathology as a mullah is by ham."

Panin and I argued more and more frequently. He was undergoing a difficult spiritual crisis—his first ten-year stretch was coming to an end. But I didn't understand that enough then, I didn't even always notice it, being busy and engrossed in my extraordinary "discoveries." And his asceticism merely amused or irritated me. He worked in the design office, where there were several women. Some played up to the mysterious, gloomy, handsome prisoner. But he forbade himself to even look at them. And if accidentally he did not lower his gaze, did not take his eyes away, then he condemned himself mercilessly. On a day like that he gave away one of his lunchtime fruit compotes or his dinner custard. "Take it! I sinned today. For two—or even three—seconds I stared at a whore. So I have given myself penance."

We finally broke for a completely silly reason. He began arguing that D'Anthès* was a noble, well-brought-up young man, who behaved in a matter of honor as a decent nobleman: he was challenged, and he had to fight (Panin wanted a renaissance of chivalry and especially of dueling). And Pushkin, naturally, was a poetic genius, but an atheist, and therefore an immoral person.

We got into a violent argument. We didn't even say good-bye when he was taken away a few months later.

But five years later, free in Moscow, we met as friends.

My worktable in the acoustics laboratory was in the far corner, by the window. Solzhenitsyn and I sat back to back. Our tables were blocked off from the ones opposite us by double-tiered bookshelves and stands for the filters; we sometimes used them to listen to articulation tests, tuning out various frequency bands. Usually we sat wearing earphones, explaining that we needed to tune out external noise. But while I examined the sound pictures, read, or translated, I could simultaneously listen to music, and on quiet evenings I plugged those same earphones into a special "circuit" that our German radio operator's friends had constructed from a single tube set on a box no bigger than a matchbox, tuned permanently to the BBC.

Sergei had the entire work area directly opposite us on the other side of

---

*Baron Georges-Charles D'Anthès, a young diplomat serving in St. Petersburg, killed Pushkin, Russia's greatest poet, in a duel over Pushkin's wife. Pushkin's political enemies created an intolerable situation that forced the poet to call out D'Anthès. (Translator's note.)

the room. But he was also the speaker-announcer. Everyone liked his marvelous bass-baritone and his very clear, almost actorlike enunciation. For that reason he had to spend hours stuck in the acoustics booth dictating syllables, words, or phrases to the articulation staff. And when local experts or visiting commissions listened to a new channel, he read newspaper articles aloud in there. Dictating to the articulation staff, he had to work under Solzhenitsyn and came to dislike him.

"A boy, a snot nose, and he makes himself out to be a general *en chef*. 'Do it this way! And no chatter!' Take a look at him, he never smiles. All the time, he's so sullen, always huffy. In the whole wide world he's the only person he likes and it's mutual. He even picks his nose with extreme self-respect."

I was the official "phonetics brigade leader," but when Solzhenitsyn got carried away mustering the young free employees of the articulation staff, which included pretty young girls, I kept away, enjoying his assertive skill. I could see that he wanted to show off in front of them, display his erudition and leadership abilities. He had gone to the front very young. And boyish eagerness, youthful ambition, still fermented and boiled within him. I saw myself as a very experienced, mature man, and stifling a laugh, tried not to interfere.

But Sergei kept bringing it up. "I don't understand: which of you is the brigade leader? Who's in charge and who obeys? I for one can't stand being spoken to in a bossy tone. And if some frisky greenhorn sticks his tail up in the air, my first reflex is to send him to hell."

Once he overheard Solzhenitsyn start a conversation with Abram Mendelevich about how the articulation brigade must be turned into an independent organizational unit and that while he naturally would come for advice and consultation as they were needed, he wanted to report directly to Abram Mendelevich.

Sergei told me this angrily, sarcastically: "You should have heard how cleverly he flattered and sucked up, seemingly inadvertently: 'You, Abram Mendelevich, as an officer yourself, naturally know perfectly well the advantage of direct subordination.' And that office sissy, that four-eyes with epaulets, that bandy legs in calf-leather boots, soaked it up; he was practically purring like a cat being scratched behind the ear."

I was amazed, saddened, and hurt. The desire for independence is naturally inseparable from the youthful ambition that I had noted long ago. But why hadn't Solzhenitsyn spoken of it openly to me and had instead, in violation of the unwritten laws of friendship—and even more so of prison brotherhood—gone to the authorities?

I didn't want to have it out; I didn't feel I had the right to give him orders. On the contrary, I was certain that he was managing very well by himself.

But it was hard to hide the feeling of distrust, even hostility, that had sprung up suddenly. And how could I hide it when we were together constantly, twenty-four hours a day? We sat next to each other in the lab, at the same table in the dining room, shared a plank bunk in the cell.

He soon noticed and asked once or twice: "What's the matter, why are you in a huff at me?"

I answered unintelligibly and harshly: "What does 'in a huff' mean? You're not a girl, some broad that I have to court you. Do you know why horses don't commit suicide? Because they never clarify their relationships."

I stopped asking about his work. And when he suddenly—and it seemed to me with deliberate anxiety—asked questions about the testing or brought up political or literary topics, I tried to respond curtly, dryly, refusing to get involved in any arguments: "Well, we each have our own opinions."

The first time he heard that, he pricked up his ears and said that "in work you sometimes step on a comrade's toes." I couldn't control myself and replied that when prisoners work together, one should step a little more carefully and observe certain limits. We have tighter moral bounds than on the outside. His eyes grew dark. "On that score we can have no disagreements. And no one can dare maintain that I have overstepped those bounds."

What could I do? Defend my unfounded pretensions to authority? Pick over petty complaints: who said what to whom, why did he report to the authorities without saying anything to me? I couldn't allude to Sergei's story. He had asked me to keep him out of it. He had eavesdropped on the conversation between Solzhenitsyn and Abram Mendelevich from the acoustics booth with the aid of a simple apparatus he had set up in order to listen in on the authorities. That way he had learned several times who was about to be transferred and who had the godfather's special interest.

For some time our relations were very cool. But gradually our friendship reestablished itself as though nothing had happened, and I never brought up our tiff.

It couldn't have weakened my feelings for him.

He had become too dear to me. He understood me better than anyone else around me, treated my work seriously and with good will, helped me work and think, used my "discoveries" efficiently in the course of the articulation experiments, and applied them sensibly. He was more convincing than anyone else in confirming the meaning of my existence.

And I had taken quite a fancy to him. His strong, questioning mind was penetrating and always maximally goal-oriented. Maximally. Sometimes I was mad at him for not wanting to be distracted, or to read an "unscheduled" book, or to discuss a different topic from the one he had planned. But I was also delighted by the unwavering concentration of will, as taut as a violin string. And when he did relax, he was so unfeignedly sincere and charming.

My only brother—younger—was also called Sanya. He died in battle in September 1941. I had always dreamed of a son with whom I would share everything that I knew, my most cherished dreams and difficult concerns.

Sanya Solzhenitsyn clearly manifested the pain of being fatherless, both in his poetry and when he spoke of his childhood and youth.

In those days I saw myself as significantly older and wiser; I wanted to understand him in a brotherly, fatherly way. And I interpreted our cruelest arguments as "natural generational conflicts."

In those years and for a long time afterward, I trusted him implicitly. I trusted him despite fleeting doubts, despite angry squabbles, despite the warnings from evil-tongued acquaintances. Without that trust my life would have been harder.

In the spring of 1955 Dmitri Panin and I learned the address of Solzhenitsyn, who was in his third year of "eternal" exile in the steppe settlement of Kok-Terek in Kazakhstan.

We began corresponding. He was under observation by oncologists then —he still hadn't recovered from the operation on his tumor. Natalya Reshetovskaya, who had divorced him while he was a prisoner without any particular formalities—for a long time he didn't even know that he was no longer married—had remarried, did not write to him, did not even respond to his request for *chaga,* a white birch fungus that sometimes helps cure or at least alleviate cancer. After his rehabilitation in 1957, however, their marriage was reinstated.

He wrote to Mitya and me frequently, and in some letters revealed the barely hidden depression and loneliness, the anticipation of approaching death, despair. We tried to comfort him as best we could, cheer him up; we looked for a wife for him.

In the summer of 1956 Mitya and I met him at the Kazan Railroad Station. It seemed that he hadn't changed at all, just a bit more austere and with a pale, yellowish "illegal" tan—he was supposed to avoid the sun. We couldn't drink to our reunion—he was on a strict diet. But we talked a lot —then and in other meetings over the next fifteen years; we argued less.

For the three of us, our hopes and conclusions about the country and the world did not often correspond—I considered myself a Marxist (though not a Leninist) up until 1968, and Mitya had changed from a fervent Russian Orthodox to a more fervent Catholic. But we still seemed to agree more than disagree. And the old prison friendship seemed to become even stronger.

In the seventies, however, our paths diverged. But that's another story. And the time to tell it has not yet come.

Solzhenitsyn was developing a theory and method for articulation tests of telephone channels in varying conditions. I read and outlined books and articles on linguistics, phonetics, acoustics, and electroacoustics, on communications theory, the psychology of speech, books by de Saussure, Shcherba, Baudouin, Marr, publications of the Prague linguistics circle, articles in American, British, French, and German journals.

But I read primarily in the evenings. During the day I puttered with the sound pictures, hung around by the spectrum analyzer, recording texts onto a tape, then pulling it onto the disk of the analyzer, obtaining sound pictures and examining them, measuring, comparing.

I had been given a clear goal: to research to what degree intelligibility of speech and recognizability of a voice in telephones of different types is a function of the accuracy of the reconstruction of certain parameters of sound vibration (frequencies, energy, correspondence between frequency and energy in various—and which specifically—ranges of frequency).

All the discussions and arguments that arose around our phonetical-acoustic work and that involved almost everyone developing new telephone systems and individual units had the following main topics:

- How much can be "saved" (cut back) in the frequency range? (In ordinary conversation "from mouth to ear" at a distance of 1 or 2 meters we receive sound oscillations with frequencies of 60 to 15,000 Hertz. The ordinary telephone transmits a limited band of 100 to 2,500 Hertz. But in transmission along "narrower" channels, speech still maintains a certain intelligibility.) To what limits can the channel be reduced? What is better to cut out—the upper or the lower frequencies?
- If it is necessary (in the aims of coding) to transmit speech, breaking it up with filters into separate frequency bands, then what kind of division is the most conducive to intelligibility and recognizability?
- How do differences in energy, that is, amplitude of sound oscillations, affect intelligibility of speech and recognition of the speaker? To what limits can they be cut? To what limit exactly must the differences between amplitudes in individual ranges of frequency be re-created?

These concrete, purely technical questions were inseparable from certain theoretical problems.

- What has a decisive significance in perception of speech: discrete, individual sounds or entire "blocks"—syllables, words, phrases—units of meaning?
- How does perception of a written text differ from perception of speech?
- Which is faster and more accurate? Can these differences be measured?

.   .   .

Sound pictures—that is, spectrograms of sound oscillations—let you see the distribution of energy along a frequency in a range of approximately 20 to 3,000 Hertz. Those sound pictures that were obtained on the AS-2 and AS-3 drew that range with several hundred extremely fine lines. Sergei made an adjustment attachment that could make the drawing thicker or thinner. The degree of sharpness, the darkness of the various parts of each line expressed the higher or lower energy (amplitude) of the sound oscillations of a given frequency and at a given time (fraction of a second). These spectrograms let us reach the secret recesses that had been inaccessible to linguists and acoustics experts, to otolaryngologists and speech therapists.

At first, in both the sound pictures and the simultaneously made oscillograms I found confirmation of the corpuscular theory of speech, which presented speech as a complex construction of clearly discrete building blocks—the phonemes.

Later I became convinced that this was inadequate. A written text from which punctuation and capitalization have been removed is impoverished and can even change fundamentally. However, to use a Russian proverb, "What is written with a pen can't be chopped out with an ax"—the text can be reread over and over until it makes sense. But an uttered word "flies off and can't be caught."

Juxtaposing the possibilities of hearing and vision, I was turning into an "ear patriot," trying to prove that people who were born blind or who had lost their sight early in life were as a rule much more talented and intelligent than those who were born deaf or who had lost their hearing early. This was so because deafness—and the muteness related to it—inexorably suppress reason and consciousness to a much greater degree than weak or lost vision. I thought of Homer and the Muscovite mathematician Lev Pontriagin, but I could not think of a single deaf or deaf-mute genius.

But at the same time, I was growing more convinced that the perception of speech cannot be seen as the work of some superfast ear-brain receiver, which rapidly analyzes the flow of phonemes, as separate as the sounds of Morse code.

For a while I was an adherent of the wave theory of speech. But then I reached a new and final certainty, that we perceive speech as a changeable entity (changeable in time and relative meaning of its various component elements). This entity embraces discrete units (separate sounds) and constant transitional processes as well as the "blocks" of information they both create: words, intonations, phrases.

I finally developed, partly by juxtaposing and compiling what I read and studied, partly by rethinking what I had observed myself, a system of phonetical-physical concepts, which it seemed to me could best help the work of my comrades—the engineers and technicians. I called this system "speech signs of the Russian language."

1. Frequency-energy discrete speech signs, or phonemes. Their physical expression is the formant.
2. Frequency-time and amplitude-time transitional signs of "speech modes," that is, stresses, intonations, expressive dynamics in loudness or melody of speech. They are expressed in amplitude of sound oscillations, transitions from the main tone.
3. Temporal signs: expressive pauses, acceleration or deceleration.
4. Visible speech signs: mimicry, gestures.

Totally engrossed at odd hours, forgetting everything around me, I "invented the bicycle" and "discovered America," as they say, or constructed my own fantastic, speculative schemes.

The sound pictures presented speech in only two dimensions: time (the horizontal axis) and frequency (vertical). The third dimension—energy (amplitude)—was expressed only in the degree of darkening of various segments.

Sergei devised an attachment that gave dotted spectrograms—like the pointillist paintings—so that the number of dots determined the amount of energy, that is, the height of the corresponding amplitude. But he couldn't get sufficiently objective and actually measurable indicators. The more energy, the more dots, and they blurred into spots. He developed an apparatus that analyzed the spectrum in frequency and amplitude. He obtained sound pictures of instantaneous (no longer than a millisecond) segments of separate sounds of speech. The horizontal was the frequency, and the vertical, the amplitude.

I began dreaming of a three-dimensional depiction of speech. And Sergei made several models. About two dozen "profile" frequency-amplitude spectrograms were placed in a row along a time axis, thus creating a piece of a whimsical mountain landscape. But reading a "three-dimensional" word was almost harder than reading a two-dimensional sound picture, and building such models was complicated and difficult.

Besides which, there was no certainty of achieving an accurate objective depiction of amplitude. It depended most of all on the frequency response of the microphones (telephones). These responses had relatively little effect on intelligibility, but differed even in telephones that were similar in all other respects.

When I began more detailed research in the physical parameters of the individual uniqueness of a voice, I came to the conclusion that it was the three-dimensional—the relief—depiction of the spectrum of speech that gives the most accurate determination of the individual characteristics of voice and pronunciation.

However, I was not to undertake such research. Sergei was assigned other work, and then something else again. No one else was interested in it, and no one could have replaced Sergei anyway. He was a design engineer by the grace of God, quick-minded, resourceful, inventive, clever, imaginative, and blessed with "golden hands." He kept inventing new attachments to the spectrum analyzers, and for "reverse checking"—to see how correctly we read the sound pictures—he created the artificial speech apparatus (ASA).

Ten photoelements, corresponding to the frequency filters, ran a loudspeaker. On a long wide strip of white paper Sergei and I drew formants with heavy black India ink on ten "lines." The apparatus pulled this handmade sound picture at the speed of speech; the photoelements "read" it and a hoarse mechanical monotonous voice intoned: *"Zhirnye sazany ushli pod palubu"* [The fat pheasants went below deck]. (We composed that sentence back in the early days of the existence of the acoustics laboratory; it included the extreme formative sounds in terms of distribution.) From morning till night, from various corners of the laboratory, where on stands and on desk panels separate units were mounted and immediately tested, came the announcement, repeated countless times by various voices, sometimes joyfully, sometimes angrily, of the departure of the fat pheasants.

Strangely significant moments. Words were spoken not by man but by his creation. The apparatus pronounced the words from a cribsheet made by our own hands.

With the help of the reverse action, that is, the transformation of sound pictures into sound, I hoped to check, refine, and confirm our ideas about sound signs and their absolute and relative meanings.

Anton Mikhailovich and Abram Mendelevich were very pleased by the ASA at first and listened to my explanations attentively. Anton Mikhailovich grunted in approval when I spoke of the possibilities of theoretical and practical tests. Several times he showed visiting officials "the world's only" apparatus that pronounced words that had never been spoken by a human voice. But soon he cooled toward the idea.

"I see no profit in this toy. We need concrete practical results now. And this is sheer mind play."

6

THE
GRAY MAN

Protruding blue-gray eyes that seem never to blink. The light-brown hair straight and sparse. A long face. Stooped shoulders. He leads with his shoulder when he walks. Long, strong hands. He speaks softly, to the point. Scatters his talk with expressions like "If I dare note," "evinces doubt," "forgive my directness," "the wrong element, so to speak," "takes place." But all mixed in with prison slang, eloquent dirty talk. He quickly switches to a palsy-walsy tone: "Hey, countryman! You keep working away. If I may dare note, even horses die of work. Now I've just finished my sixth year. I have fifteen years plus five of disenfranchisement. I work nonstop. In my field I'm not the least of the specialists. I'm a grade eight metalworker-gauger; no worse as a turner. I can fix machines, any sort; and I'm a universal electrician, I can work on strong or weak currents. Engineers are overwhelmed by me. Extra-class. However, I use my head, without strain. I know how to do it: 'For me—for you—for the boss.' Give me what's due me, and anything beyond that I'll take for myself."

A broad smile that reveals small, strong teeth. His laugh was splintered, throaty; it began abruptly and ended abruptly.

Evgenii G. assembles electrical equipment in the experimental shop. Those who work with him say that he usually knows his business, sometimes corrects the engineers, has improved not only parts, but entire schemes. He has been a longtime ham radio operator. That's what brought him to the camps just before the war. His father, a master at a plant, and his older brother, a military engineer, were also arrested. The brother was shot. The father died in the camps. Former Vorkuta inmates said that father and son were always fighting, and that either Evgenii put his father and brother inside or the father put the sons in, but the decent zeks avoided all of them.

In the cell, G. slept on the lower bunk, and above him, a feisty, noisy engineer from the war prisoners—Kostia K.—kind-hearted and not very bright. Kostia accidentally put on his neighbor's jacket. And pulled out from the pocket a neatly folded piece of paper with a typed text. All the laboratories had typewriters, and G. had changed the type on the war spoils machines several times.

There was no address, but the contents excluded all doubts:

Z/k Semenov uses the evening hours to make cigarette cases, cigarette holders, and brooches out of Plexiglas. Some objects he passed to his visitors, and he also gives other z/ks presents of cigarette cases and holders. He gave (or sold) for personal use to z/ks Izmailov, Bryksin, Solzhenitsyn, Gerasimovich, and he gave (or sold) brooches to z/ks Laptev and Nikolaev to pass during visits. Z/k Laptev passed a letter to his wife during the last visit, giving the address of the site and the daily schedule, which was apparent from her arrival at the fence during a walk. Z/k Nikolaev also passed a note to his wife with the same information, and his minor son came to the fence and even shouted "Papa." Z/ks Panin, Kopelev, and Solzhenitsyn meet every evening during after-work hours in the library, the keys to which are held by librarian Solzhenitsyn, and he doesn't give them to the guards, saying that he bears the ultimate responsibility, and tells the guards that he has urgent work. However, z/k Panin spends most of his time away from his carrel, where he is supposed to be drafting, and I can't hear the typewriter on which Kopelev is supposed to be doing his translations, but I can hear them talking, sometimes raising their voices to argue, or quietly reading literature that has nothing to do with the work of the sharashka, even poetry. As for their discussions and talks, I think they have a political air. Once when I came in for a reference, I heard z/k Solzhenitsyn say to z/k Kopelev angrily: "He isn't great, he covered all of Russia with blood." When they noticed me, z/k Panin said, "*Attendez*, gentlemen," and their faces were embarrassed. Z/k Kopelev said purposely loudly: "No, you're wrong, Ivan the Terrible was a great tsar, he conquered the Volga and Siberia." Then he went on talking as though the whole conversation had been about the tsar. And z/k Solzhenitsyn also started talking about Ivan the Terrible, and z/k Panin said: "Gentlemen, let's not get sidetracked from our work." Z/k Panin always says "gentlemen" to his friends.

Z/k Tolstobrov was talking to z/k Semenov and Izmailov in the cell and extolled German technology and also American technology, and said about our native Soviet equipment: "Our own shit is ten years obsolete!" Gray.

That's exactly how the page found in the pocket of Evgenii G. was signed. Kostia showed it that same day to everyone mentioned in the text. He showed it in turn, secretly, dropping by the labs during working hours. He was brimming over with rapture because he had discovered a secret and had helped us. He asked each of us what to do next. Solzhenitsyn, Panin, and I agreed that the best thing was a public exposure with a "dressing down" (that is, strong curses and threats). A "burned," or exposed, stoolie is rendered almost harmless. Kostia and a few others wanted to arrange a beating in the dark. We disagreed. There was no way of hiding who found the *ksiva*, or secret letter, and Kostia would be the one to answer for the beating. Others argued that no hue and cry should be set up at all; it was enough that we knew, and the *ksiva* should be returned to the owner with an added warning. Kostia was confused by the various suggestions, and by the end of the day his rapture and excitement were gone; he was obviously sorry he had made the discovery, and thinking slowly, angry at his advisers. And suddenly he decided his own way.

We all knew that the prison and laboratory bosses were always getting into arguments, and the clever zeks tried to take advantage of that. Kostia began reasoning: "Who was he ratting to—to the prison godfather, of course. Meetings, talks—the sharashka doesn't care about that at all. He informs to them about work, about the plans, construction, instruments, missing parts. I'll take this *ksiva* to the sharashka godfather, pretending that I think it's for him—here you are, take it. Someone dropped it, I picked it up, I'm turning it over where it belongs, except all this is nonsense, the viper is lying."

We tried hard to talk him out of it. He grew angrier, He had a very high opinion of his mind, his mental ability, his perspicacity—he was as proud of that as of his truly strong muscles. "The old kettle, thank God, boils fine; there are no wise men who are wiser than me."

That's why any careless criticism like "that's nonsense, you'll be a fool," aroused violent, bull-like stubbornness. And this time, responding to the shouts of his unlucky opponents, he ran to the office of the security officer for the laboratory and in a few minutes came out, pretending to be fully satisfied, even though he looked rather sheepish. He had told the security officer everything he had prepared, but he hadn't prepared an answer for the simple question: "Did you show this to anyone?"

"What did you say?"

"I'm no fool you know, I don't answer right away, I drag things out, act dumb—who was I supposed to show it to, the one who wrote it, you mean? But the godfather, though politely, but insistently, says: 'Don't try to cover up, I'm asking which zeks you showed this to.' But my kettle's boiling, thank God, and I've swallowed wiser men than him. So I say that I didn't show it to anyone special, but when I found the *ksiva* I put it on the table, let people take a look and maybe let the person who lost it take it. No one took it, so I brought it to you. No one suggested it, I thought of it myself. He says, 'Oh, you're very clever,' and winks at me like at a whore. I show zero reaction to the winks. Well, 'Go on,' he says, 'and don't gab.' And I say, 'Yes, sir,' and about face."

The next morning G. came to our cell after reveille, as though nothing had happened. He lived in the small one with the engineers—it was called the lords' chamber—and our large, populous one was considered "plebeian." He had a kitten in his hands.

"Catch, countryman, a present!" And he tossed the kitten onto Solzhenitsyn's cot. Solzhenitsyn jumped up.

"What are you torturing that animal for! And anyway, you're Gray, and we're no countrymen of yours."

He hunched down for a second, but didn't even lose his grin. "That's not torture for cats. They jump from the fourth floor. You should know that, gentlemen intellectuals."

Then I began shouting at the top of my lungs in the camp-style dressing down: "We're not talking about the cat. Didn't you hear, you bastard, you're Gray, a stoolie, a rat fink, get out of here, you viper, and I don't want to smell your stink anywhere near here. Go on, or I'll . . ."

Then came threatening curses.

Everyone with camp experience knew: when you're dealing with a stoolie, the best thing is to have an open, angry argument. This immediately devalues his information to "personal accounts." But you can argue only to a certain limit, so that you don't become accused of "camp agitation," "instigation to resistance," and so on.

That's why Mitya Panin, as the most experienced among us, interrupted me, shouting even louder, and moved aggressively toward G. "You torture animals, you scum! The cat's not a toy for you, louse. You throw a living creature around like a rock, you creep! You throw it at a person, carrion! What if it scratched his face? Carrion! Viper! Bastard! Fuck your mouth . . . your soul! Get out of here, you hooligan, before we rearrange your face!"

A few other people who caught on to what was happening picked up the attack. Someone threw a shoe, missing by a very wide, accurate margin.

G. retreated toward the door, slightly paler but still grinning, only his eyes were dark. "Go fuck yourselves. You're crazy . . ."

After that the three of us and a few of our pals did not greet him, we turned away. But this apparently did not embarrass him. On walks and in the dining room his laughter rang out as usual. And he was always in a group. Even from a distance we could hear him telling a juicy dirty joke, an amusing story from camp life, or arguing about soccer, boxing, or technical problems.

When the evening walks were extended in spring and summer and we were given permission to set up a volleyball court, he became captain of one of the teams, playing very well, displaying flashy professional moves and terms. He sometimes tried to strike up a conversation as if nothing had happened with the men boycotting him. We turned away, but he pretended not to notice and tried again a few days later. Quite a few couldn't hold out and eventually responded, albeit coolly and curtly. By the end there were very few of us silent holdouts left.

In 1951 G. was freed before the end of his term as one of the engineers and technicians who were rewarded with freedom and money for the creation of the most perfected system of secret telephony.

Now he was palsy-walsy and joked with the free employees. The prisoners with whom he had worked he either pushed brazenly—you can't trick me, I was one of you just yesterday, I know how to featherbed—or flattered in a buddy-buddy way—don't let me down, help me and I'll help you.

The other zeks, including his former volleyball teammates, he tried not to notice, and if they greeted him, he imperceptibly nodded in response. Meeting me and others who had shunned him before, he stared intently, grinning, waiting for us to talk.

Ten years later he was still working as a fitter in another scientific-research institute, with a few former zeks from our sharashka. In 1960 he even came to a reunion. He shouted louder than anyone else: "Do you remember, guys, do you recall, brothers, countrymen?" He told the sleaziest jokes, danced Gypsy dances. At first some tried to shun him here, too. The organizers of the evening, who worked with him, asked us not to make a scene.

"Fuck him. He seems better now, he works hard, he tries. His only interest outside of work is soccer and vodka, and his wife henpecks him."

He was the only one to have brought his wife to the party. A fat-cheeked, heavily made-up woman with the manners of a saucy commissary manager or waitress in a third-rate bar, she danced with everyone, squealed at all the jokes, and sang the convict songs.

When we had drunk enough, everyone was awash in good feelings. We sang old prison songs, went over our old pals and roommates—who was living where, who died, became a grandfather, retired.

G. nevertheless came over to Sergei K. and me: "May I dare propose a toast. We're countrymen. Everything's water under the bridge. Excuse my directness. Why remember the bad? It's better to think about the good things. Let's have a toast, to our good health!"

It was disgusting looking at his sweaty face, twitching with an ingratiating smile.

Sergei later maintained that I did clink glasses with G. and even took his extended hand, while he sent G. where he belonged. Sergei could be exaggerating. But this time, he may be telling the truth. I had had too much vodka and all I remembered was the general mood, a combination of heartrending sadness and forced, drunken gaiety. From the window of the apartment where we had gathered we could see the fence of the former sharashka. Only a few years had passed, and it was almost impossible to understand how we could have lived there, worked, and laughed. And why did I feel sad now, when everything was so much better than I had ever imagined in my wildest dreams. It was possible that I had gotten so drunk and so soppy that I shook hands with a former stoolie.

7

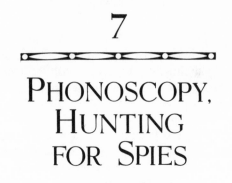

PHONOSCOPY, HUNTING FOR SPIES

There is no dirty work that is not forced on the
contemporary scientist in "progressive" communo-
fascist countries.

—GEORGII FEDOTOV, *New City*

(Drums)—Death is upon us, spy!
. . .
(Drums)—Get to your business, spy!
. . .
(Drums)—Fetch us our answer, spy!
. . .
(Drums)—Bring us deliverance, spy!

—RUDYARD KIPLING, "The Spies' March"

Late autumn 1949. In the laboratories they were only starting to plug in
the equipment and set out their instruments. Solzhenitsyn and I were
spreading out our files, books, journals; several people were hanging
around the metal cabinet, from which the duty officer was taking out the
secret files and the work diaries.

Senior Lieutenant Tolya, one of the assistants of the chief of the laboratory, came up to me: "Anton Mikhailovich wants to see you. Immediately.
No, you don't need to bring any materials."

The large, airy office was carpeted; the wide desk took up a far corner,
and diagonally across the room stood a long table covered in green baize.
Bookshelves. Armchairs. Couches. A round table with a water pitcher.
Everything was festive, gleaming as though lacquered.

Anton Mikhailovich and Abram Mendelevich sat at the long table, with
two tape recorders in front of them and several pairs of earphones—large
ones, like those used on tanks and planes—in a swirl of wires.

Anton Mikhailovich looked up, distracted, aloof. "Hello, hello. I believe
you said that you have ways of determining the physical parameters of an
individual voice. Is that so?"

"Not quite. It's approximate as yet, in the most preliminary approximation. And I don't determine, I guess. With relative certainty I can only say that the uniqueness of a voice lies primarily in the characteristics of timbre, which depend on the microstructure of the larynx, nasopharynx, and mouth. I've managed to observe a few things in the sound pictures, when the same word is spoken by the same person, sometimes loudly, sometimes in a whisper, as a question or as a statement. The spectrum is different each time, but in a few cases, it seems, I've managed to establish constant individual traits of the voice—I call them microintonations and micromodes of speech."

"Fine, fine, that's very interesting. But for now you're swimming in pure theory. This swimming may lead us to a swamp or to the source of a new science. The latter would be praiseworthy and wonderful. Science nurtures youth and brings joy to elders, as the poet said. But you and I are not old yet. Ergo, we need a nourishing science. So, this research of yours has suddenly taken on a new, extremely important meaning. So important, that it is top secret. Here on these tapes is something that requires your especially close attention. What do you say, Abram Mendelevich, shall we take the bull by the horns? Take a pair of earphones and listen to the voice of a certain individual, who chose to remain anonymous. Anatolii Stepanovich, from the top!"

In the earphones through the hissing and clicking came voices, which soon became clear.

"Hello! Hello! Who is this?"

"I told you. This is the Embassy of the United States of America."

"Do you understand Russian? Do you speak Russian?"

"I speak poorly, but I can understand."

"I have very important, very urgent information. Secret."

"Who are you?"

"I cannot say that. Understand! Do you think your phone is tapped?"

"Tipped? Who's tipping?"

"Who, who . . . The Soviet organs . . . Do they listen in on your phone?"

"Oh, I see. I don't know. Maybe yes, maybe no. What did you want to say?"

"Listen carefully. The Soviet spy Koval is leaving for New York. Do you hear? He's leaving today, and on Thursday he's supposed to meet in some radio store with an American professor, who will give him new data on the atom bomb. Koval is leaving today. Did you understand me?"

"Not everything. Who is Koval?"

"A Soviet intelligence officer, a spy. I don't know if that's his real name or a pseudonym. He's leaving today, Monday, for New York, and on Thursday he will be meeting a professor about the atom bomb."

Hissing . . . clicks . . . The four of us listen. Directly opposite me is Anatolii Stepanovich, his pompadoured heavy brow low over thick eyebrows, his heavy chin supporting sturdy lips. Lazily chewing on a cigarette. Listening unperturbedly.

Anton Mikhailovich is sprawled on a chair, covering his eyes with his hands. Abram Mendelevich stands, bent low over the table, one knee on a chair; he listens tensely, moving his lips, as though repeating the words. Noticing me reach for my earphones, he waves his hand—there's more to come.

From the hissing noises comes that same tense, anxious voice: "Hello, hello. I called you before. I was interrupted."

"Who is this? What do you want?"

"I called an hour ago on very important business. Didn't I talk to you? Who are you—an American?"

"Oh, yes, I'm an American."

"What's your job? Your rank? Well, your post?"

"Please, don't speak so fast. Who are you? Who's speaking?"

"Do you understand Russian?"

"Yes. I understand a little. Wait, I'll call a man who understands Russian."

"But who is he? A Soviet citizen?"

"Who's Soviet? I don't understand. Please . . ."

"You must understand, I don't want to talk to a Soviet— Call your military attaché. I have an important secret. Where is your military attaché?"

"The attaché? He's absent. He left."

"When will he be back? When will he be at work?"

"Oh, he'll be here tomorrow, maybe today. At three or four."

"Does your attaché speak Russian?"

"Who? Oh, yes. But not much. I will call the translator."

"Who is your translator? Soviet? Russian?"

"Oh yes, he's Russian. American Russian."

"Listen . . . listen, write this down."

And he repeated: "Urgent. Important! Soviet spy Koval; Thursday; a radio store somewhere in New York or maybe Washington; American professor; atom bomb . . ."

The voice was not an old man's. A high baritone. The speech and intonations of an educated, lively, but not overly intelligent urbanite. Not a Muscovite, but not a southerner. There were no characteristic western (Smolensk, Byelorussian) or Leningrad intonations. The average, characterless talk of a Russian provincial, perhaps with a university degree, who was getting along in the capital.

He was privy to state secrets and was giving them to our most dangerous enemy. He had to be exposed, and we had to take part in it.

We listened to two other conversations. The new interlocutor, an American, spoke with indolent slowness and suspicious indifference.

"And how do you know that? And why are you giving the information to us? And what do you want for it? And why should I believe that you are telling the truth and not trying a provocation?"

He replied in a constrained manner. Once or twice notes of hysterical despair crept in.

"But what can I tell you. Understand me, this is a great risk for me. Why am I calling? Because I want peace."

"Oh, I see." (It sounded almost mocking.)

"But you can check it all. I'm telling you details: he's leaving today, he may have left already. And on Thursday he's meeting— I don't want anything. I'm not asking for anything now. Maybe . . . I'll explain it all later. Sometime later."

(I am presenting these conversations almost verbatim. I heard them over and over many times; the words and intonations are firmly fixed in my memory.)

The last recording was a conversation with the Canadian Embassy. The same heartrending voice asking them to pass on to the American government the information about Koval, the radio store, the professor, the atom bomb.

Anton Mikhailovich plugged his earphones into the second tape recorder.

"And now let's compare the voice of that unknown scoundrel with three others. We might find similarities or comparisons."

A young stentorian voice reporting to a disdainful basso "boss" voice about the delivery or mailing of some documents.

A tired, irritated man explaining to his wife that he would be late, fending off rebukes, giving some sort of orders.

Two young men planning to meet in a restaurant and deciding which girl friends to call. One was a light tenor, not at all similar to the traitor's voice; the other, a high baritone, with something of the timbre—but the pronunciation was pure Moscow, breezy, foppish speech, imbued with deliberately coarse words and expressions, yet with clear echoes of good breeding.

It seemed to me that the voice and speech of the "tired husband" most resembled the voice and speech of the man who had betrayed Koval.

Both young men were ruled out. The loud report still elicited doubts. The completely different character and style of speech could be caused by differences that are clearly heard, but are deliberate, artificial.

Anton Mikhailovich said: "So, from this moment on, you are totally transferred to a military mission. Expose the traitor! The assignment is absolutely secret. You will have to take an additional oath. For your new work we are creating a special laboratory. Without a title, simply Laboratory Number 1. The chief is Abram Mendelevich, the deputy is Anatolii Stepanovich, and you are the scientific supervisor. The staff of the laboratory—I imagine for a start two or three technicians will be enough—will be selected today from the junior officers. You may tell your colleagues that the laboratory is completing a special task in cryptography, developing an extremely stable decoder, and then not another word. There is a room for you already. Get your equipment. Several tape recorders. An oscillograph. And take the second analyzer. Yes, I know the third is better. But we can't strip the acoustics lab. If you need to, you'll work in the acoustics lab in the evenings and at night. Of course, you can analyze pieces of tape there. But so that even half a word doesn't escape. Or we will all pay with our heads. Abram Mendelevich will report to me daily. But this urgent, unscheduled task in no way changes your basic work. Moreover, I am certain that this will merely enrich and speed it up. After all, we are seeking the physical parameters of the individuality of the voice. In completing this military detective mission you simultaneously must solve the same acoustics problems, approaching them from the other end. That's clear, I trust? Then, get on with it!"

By that time I had outlined a dozen books and a pile of articles on the physiology of speech and conducted numerous experiments, trying to determine as precisely as possible the concrete attributes of one voice. Kuprianov, Solzhenitsyn, and I pronounced the same words with various intonations, deliberately changing our voices or imitating a foreign pronunciation or an accent (Georgian, Jewish, German, Ukrainian). Then I compared the sound pictures. Sergei Kuprianov made an attachment for the AS-3 that made "magnified" prints of separate sounds, separate bands of a frequency for analysis.

It sometimes seemed that I had found it—the drawing of a harmonic in the sound pictures for a vowel, and the order of valleys of darker (that is, more energetic) and lighter sections that was characteristic of a given voice. Then it would turn out that the voice pronounced the same sound differently, or, on the contrary, I would find very similar traits in the sound pictures of another voice.

And then hopes, impatient anticipation, and joy were replaced by disappointment, bitter regret, and mistrust of myself.

Now all the striving, research, and suppositions had to be focused, subordinated to a single goal—find the spy.

That very day I began moving some of my books and notes, several enormous files with sound pictures, to the new laboratory. It was a small room, crowded with old office desks and file cabinets, with broken or unopened equipment.

Anatolii handed me a piece of paper, a standard typed text, which had my name and words about an especially important state mission. At the end it read: "In case of publicity or sabotage the undersigned is subject to the gravest criminal responsibility under an administrative procedure of the court." Signing it, I asked how to interpret that. A spark of a smile flashed in his gray eyes. But he replied with his never-changing, glum calm: "That means that if you blab, they'll shoot you without trial or investigation."

· · ·

We listened again and again. First and foremost to the four conversations about Koval and the atom bomb. Anatolii Stepanovich and I listened, selecting repeating words. First I listened, then he, and he also copied the words I selected onto a special tape so that we could later make oscillograms and sound pictures from it. The technicians were three young women, who worked every other day in twenty-four-hour shifts.

I chose words that appeared in the various conversations of the suspects: "Hello . . . hallo . . . I called . . . I called up . . . I'm listening . . . listen to me . . . work . . . working. . . talk . . . very . . . hello . . . yes . . . no . . . why . . ."

Clearly dissimilar were the voice of the traitor and the voices of the "reporter" and "boss"—the men whose voices at first elicited some doubt. They were completely different in basic tone and timbre. This became apparent even in the comparison of the very first sound picture. For certainty we compared somewhat longer excerpts. And I made a confident conclusion—these were different voices. In the four conversations, X's basic tone was sufficiently constant.

That left the "tired husband."

Signing the paper on "administrative responsibility" did not keep me from telling everything to Solzhenitsyn that first day—naturally, so that no one could overhear. He asked questions and cross-examined me. Hearing about the signed paper, he frowned.

"Do you realize that that's not an empty gesture? Don't even think about telling anyone else. In cases like this a third man is superfluous."

I had no intention of discussing my dangerous secret with anyone else. And I had told him not only because I trusted him absolutely, even though that was very important, of course, but also because I needed his mathematical advice and direct help. I had to determine how probable were coincidences of external (visible on sound pictures) manifestations of microintonations and micromodes of speech in different people. In order to do this I decided to "check" as many voices as possible. He suggested studying no fewer than fifty, to get a quicker idea of the percentages of coincidence and deviation.

I made up a text that incorporated the control words with various intonations: "Hello. This is [each reader inserts his own name] speaking. Who is this talking to me? I'm calling you about our work. Will you be working today? Can you hear me? I will work today"—and so on.

Abram Mendelevich agreed that it was necessary to run a mass test. He said several times: "What a bastard. What a lowlife. He can't get away with it. We have to test and retest conscientiously. If an innocent man is accused because of us, that will be horrible. And that son of a bitch will go on spying."

Solzhenitsyn shared my disgust with the man who called the Americans. Privately we called him "bitch," "viper," "whore," and so on.

Anton Mikhailovich agreed that I should test the voices of at least fifty people and use the entire articulation brigade.

"But don't think of explaining anything to anyone. You signed the paper? What will you tell them? 'Imitation of a simple telephone call for a new encoder?!' Well, it's not too clever, but it's believable."

The articulation staff and the speakers were in the hands of Solzhenitsyn, as usual. They all began recording the control text. We got another one hundred "one-time" speakers—prisoners and free employees—and we both instructed them. Then we ran yet another experiment. The text of each speaker took up several sound pictures: they were made up in two copies. One was the control. I fastened the sound pictures for each voice together and then compared them. All the second copies were mixed up and the articulation staff had to handle a pile that represented no more than ten voices: their task was to separate it into individual speakers, determining individual traits visually.

Solzhenitsyn himself participated happily in this game. Abram Mendelevich wanted to use not only the sound picture but the oscillograms as well. We decided to compare on the oscillograms of four conversations all the oscillations of the basic tone of voice, construct corresponding curves (Gaussian, bell-shaped), and compare them with the curves for other voices. Solzhenitsyn suggested studying not only individual absolute meanings, but their relative transitions, too—comparing the rate of change of the basic tone. "Rates, measured in milliseconds, can be an objective mathematical expression of your 'microintonations.' "

We worked intensively. Some days I got no more than four hours' sleep.

The "tired husband's" voice turned out to be identical in all respects with the voice of the volunteer spy. Soon Abram Mendelevich said that he was already arrested and I had to prepare an interrogation sheet for the investigator, one that would make sure that the answers contained the same words that were in the conversations with the embassy. We needed the same simple words—"called," "spoke," "work." But now we would be able to hear words that he had not used in his conversation with his wife: for instance, "the spy Koval," "atom bomb," and so on. Abram Mendelevich and Anatolii with his tape recorder got set up next to the investigator's office, and a small piezoelectric microphone was placed inconspicuously on the investigator's desk. They brought tapes back the same day.

Anatolii told us: "An ordinary guy. What didn't he have?! He was about to go to Canada to work in the embassy in a responsible position. And he tried to become a spy. Shithead! Now he might even get shot."

Abram Mendelevich was excited. And when we were left alone, he said confidentially: "It's simply awful! He was an ordinary Soviet fellow. As they say—from a good family. The father is a member of the Party, in an important job, somewhere in a ministry. And the mother is also in the Party, I think. He excelled at school, an active Komsomol [Communist

Youth League] member. He was accepted into diplomatic school, kept out of the army. He joined the Party there, then worked in the Ministry of Foreign Affairs. They trusted him. He went abroad. And now he's received a major post—second councillor of the embassy. He was supposed to go with his family. The wife is a Komsomol, also worked at the ministry; two children, plus the mother-in-law. And the very day they got the tickets he started calling the embassy from phone booths. He accidentally learned about that Koval and started off. He was selling in advance. Naturally, he figured to defect the moment he got there, like that viper Kravchenko.* Did you read about it in the papers? The information was particularly valuable, and he wanted to get it to them quickly. Now our people will be hurt there, in America . . . I saw him when they brought him in. An ordinary face. And an ordinary surname—Ivanov. Of course, he looks confused and depressed. You can hear it in his replies. And the investigator is a major, very serious, intelligent. They say he is a very experienced criminalist. No, it's simply incomprehensible, how one of our people can do that."

The interrogation, recorded on tape, was apparently not the first. The investigator questioned him slowly, resonantly, showing off his voice, carefully choosing his words: he knew it was being recorded.

"Well, have you remembered at last what you talked about on the phone with the American Embassy?"

Sadly subdued, but obviously familiar, "the very same" voice replied: "I haven't recalled anything. I didn't talk to any Americans."

"We've let you listen to the tapes. Your conversations were recorded when you called the embassy. Our technology is first rate and has allowed us to expose your criminal plans. So I repeat the question: what were you talking about when you called the American Embassy?"

"I didn't talk and I didn't call. It wasn't I who called. I heard it, that's not my voice at all . . . on your machine. No one could believe that it is. I'm a member of the Party, I'm a Soviet diplomatic worker. I've been given a responsible post."

"All right, all right. We've heard all that. We're not investigating your diplomatic work now, but your criminal act. The facts speak against you. Self-evident, obvious facts. Do you know who Koval is?"

"I don't. I don't know any Koval."

"All right. And how do you pronounce it—Ko-*val* or *Ko*-val?"

"I don't know. I don't know anyone by that name."

"But tell me anyway the right way to pronounce it—Ko-*val* or *Ko*-val?"

"I don't see why—"

"You don't have to see, just say it. So which is it?"

"Well, probably . . . Ko-*val.*"

*Viktor Kravchenko, a Soviet trade representative in Europe after the war, defected and wrote several books, including *I Chose Freedom*. (Translator's note.)

(In those conversations he had accented the first syllable more frequently.)

"And now try it the other way—*Ko*-val. And speak up, because I don't hear well."

"Well, all right, here, *Ko*-val."

"Fine, then . . . then who do you suppose phoned the American Embassy?"

"I do not know."

"And who told them—that is, the Americans—about Koval?"

"I don't know. My word of honor, I don't."

"Honor? . . . What is it you don't know?"

"Anything. I don't know anything about this filthy business and I don't want to." (Sobs.)

"Now, now, let's calm down. You mean you don't know who called and who spoke?"

"I don't know."

"What don't you know?"

"Who called, I don't know . . . who spoke, I don't know . . . Not I . . . I swear, not I . . ."

"And where were you personally that Monday at eleven hundred hours? At work?"

"I told you. I don't remember exactly hour by hour. That day I had several errands to run, with the tickets, and the customs office."

"All right. You mean, you didn't work that day? I'm asking you—were you at work?"

"No . . . I don't remember . . . No, I don't think so."

"What do you mean, you think? Did you work or didn't you?"

"No . . . I wasn't working by then."

"So where were you at eleven hundred, at thirteen-thirty, that is, half past one, and at sixteen hundred, that is, four o'clock? Where were you?"

"Well, I don't remember exactly. I was getting ready for our departure."

The investigator still spoke deliberately and clearly, listening to himself, asked questions, playing with expressive intonations of disbelief, mockery, disdain. And the man replied drearily. He told him how he and his entire family were getting ready to leave for Canada, it was all set, and then suddenly he was arrested.

The report on the comparisons of the unknown voices A-1, A-2, A-3, and A-4 (three conversations with the U.S. Embassy and one with the Canadian Embassy), the unknown B (conversation with the wife), and the voice of the suspect Ivanov took up two big, thick volumes. It included the texts of the conversations, detailed descriptions of the method and principles of identification, and appendixes of oscillograms, sound prints, statistical and other tables, and diagrams compiled of the control words.

The report was signed by the chief of the institute, Engineer Colonel

B.; the chief of the laboratory, Engineer Major R.; and me—senior scientific worker, candidate of sciences.

Foma Fomich came into the new laboratory with benign majesty. "A good beginning. Let's keep it up, so the next one will be better, not worse."

Abram Mendelevich began telling him that we were "on the threshold of discovering a new science"—new paths toward scientific criminology.

Foma Fomich nodded condescendingly. "Well, go on, go on, so that with God's help our calf can devour the wolf, as they say."

I was planning to discover the new science and I called it, by analogy with dactyloscopy, "phonoscopy." I imagined a system of exact formal characteristics of the voice that would permit "recognizing" it under any conditions out of any number of other voices, even very similar-sounding ones.

We were finishing up the detailed account of the first phonoscopic attempt at determining the identity of a person through a sound picture recording of a conversation. At the same time, I compiled a preliminary plan for research, necessary both for the development of phonoscopy and for the most precise possible determination of concrete conditions of "recognizability" of a voice, reconstructed after decoding a telephone conversation.

Thousands of experiments were necessary.

In the development of this plan I was helped only by Solzhenitsyn; he outfitted me with mathematical arguments.

Anton Mikhailovich looked through my report attentively, but without any apparent pleasure. "You're reaching far, my friend. Too far! You're being carried beyond the parameters of the possible. At any rate, beyond the parameters of the expedient and prudent! Of course, it's marvelous to dream once in a while, but this is too much. It's all romantic claptrap. What we need is rational, beneficial work—useful and profitable today! Yes. Dreams are sweet, but sweetness is acceptable only in its place, for dessert. You're not doing too badly as a phonetic-acoustic baker. So please concentrate on our daily bread—first and foremost on our systems, on intelligibility and recognizability of speech in their channels. This calls for daily, painstaking work with every new panel, with every new combination of units. Now it's fashionable to speak of 'philosophy' in every context. That's thanks to the Americans. They speak of the philosophy of such-and-such electronic circuit of the philosophy of such-and-such a lamp. I think it was you, Abram Mendelevich, who recently gave an 'elegant' talk on the philosophy of semiconductors. And now we have phonoscopic philosophy! But this is sheer speculation. You can, of course, fool around with it, cook and bake a bit. But I ask you not to leave your main burner. As you must know: 'Theory is gray, but the tree of life is eternally green.'"

Abram Mendelevich did not argue with him, but when we were alone, he was highly critical of our "Anton the Splendid." "A nobleman, a high-society chatterbox! Of course, he's an educated, sensible engineer, he's capable of thinking and inventing. But he's superficial, flashy. He gets fired up over an idea easily—his own or someone else's—sometimes he comes up with original, bold solutions. But he lacks depth and breadth. He digs into one thing and doesn't want to look around. He calls his limitations concentration, direction. But actually he's just afraid of getting sidetracked, afraid of multifaceted research, a wide front of work. He's a gifted empirical worker, with pretensions to scholarship and the flash of erudition. A typical non-Party specialist, even though he wears a colonel's shoulder boards. Of course, he is a lot better than many others. What they call well bred. He doesn't shout, insult, or curse. But if he needs to, he'll betray and sell his best friend."

Abram Mendelevich wanted to save Laboratory Number 1; he said that he was trying for an increase in the staff. We would work on phonetics and phonoscopy, and on some other developments, primarily deciphering speech and voices. Always amiable to the prison workers, he clearly liked Solzhenitsyn and me.

But when I became more than friends with one of our technical assistants (she and I were left alone in the evenings in a room that had to be locked from inside because it was "top secret"), she told me just what Abram Mendelevich said about vigilance at the open Party meeting of the free employees and at the short meetings of the Party group.

"Most of those in our special contingent are enemies of the people. There are those, of course, who have more or less sincerely repented their committed crimes. But special competent organs will be judging that, and we must always keep vigilant, watch over them, so that if we're asked, we can give the necessary information. There are hostile, still-armed enemies, those who barely hide their hatred of Soviet rule. They have to be watched. But as long as they work honestly, are useful, they will be given the right conditions—some will be helped financially and the younger ones, who haven't become set in their ways, might be reeducated. But the most dangerous, the most crafty enemies are the double dealers, still armed and unrepentant. People like Kopelev [he named a few others, people from other laboratories—my 'informant' could only recall Evgenii Timofeev]. They are still in masks, they still hide their true inner selves, they pretend to be Soviet patriots, even ideological Communists. With them, doubled, tripled vigilance is called for. You can't believe a single word of theirs. Positively avoid any conversations that don't pertain to work. Of course, we must learn everything that they know, use their knowledge. And that's why we must not create conflicting relationships, insult them, or speak harshly. But report every attempt at friendliness, and politely but firmly resist them."

Two of my three technical assistants behaved that way. They either didn't "hear" extraneous questions ("Where did you study?" "What are you reading?" "Are you married?") or replied: "We're not supposed to talk during working hours . . . Please don't ask . . . Don't talk, don't or both you and I will have trouble"—and so on. The third one, however, was braver and jauntier and more curious than the others. She was unhappily married—to an MGB colonel. He was away for months at a time—"At home he only eats and drinks until he collapses . . . And he must fool around on the side with no time or energy left for his wife."

A large-eyed, full-lipped, thick-browed, and long-legged daughter of the Moscow suburbs, a thirty-year-old wife of an up-and-coming Chekist, and the mother of two children brought up by their grandmothers, she had worked as a telegraph operator somewhere in the security organs and arrived in our sharashka as one of the "thoroughly cleared cadres." (The majority of these not overqualified free employees were relatives of MGB personnel.) She was sent to our laboratory to work and learn so that she could later replace the special contingent. She turned out to be hopelessly unreceptive to phonetics and acoustics, forgetting the simplest explanations, but she learned quickly to prepare neat sound pictures, listened to them, and cleverly sorted them by eye, and neatly made up all kinds of lists, tables, and so on. And she spoke freely about herself, the bosses, all the comrades, and easily yielded to the blandishments of a prisoner hungry for a woman's caresses.

For a good half year she was my girl friend. The warnings of the boss didn't frighten her: "He's Abram, and the Jews always lie. Don't be insulted, you don't look like a Jew. And there are exceptions: at the technicum I had a friend, Rosa—she was Jewish. I'm talking about the majority. You defended the Germans. Well, of course, there are good people among them, even Party members. But as a nation they are our enemies. Of course, the Poles are even worse. My husband and I lived in Poland for a year—he worked in the embassy there. I saw with my own eyes how hypocritical they are, how they hated us. And my husband always said that they were even worse than the Germans and the Jews."

All attempts to argue, to defend even moderate internationalist views were unsuccessful, just as were appeals to her Party conscience. Almost without contradicting me, she listened more or less patiently.

"Oh, well enough now, you're just like a propagandist, giving me a lecture. Why don't I tell you a joke (or 'a story from life'). No, I believe you, I do. But that's what you were taught, but life can be different."

In the fall she had an abortion.

"I wasn't afraid of having a third child. Where two are full, you can find enough food for a third. But I am afraid of foreign blood. They say Jews even have different skin. Look how hairy you are. No, no, it's impossible for a child with foreign blood to grow up in a family. No!"

However, our relationship continued even after that, as long as the laboratory existed. For a while I was actually in love with her. The joy of our closeness coincided with engrossing work and new hopes. She was the one taking the risk. Exposure threatened more than family problems. Fear, the knowledge of danger, heightened sensuality. But she also had a woman's pity for me.

"Oh, how can it be, for a healthy man to be without a woman for ten years. Horrors! Poor thing! Well, all right, let's do it. No, I'll never leave my husband, he's the father of my children. You can't destroy a family. But we'll be friends, you and I. When you get out, they'll keep you on here. The work is so secret. They'll never let you leave here. Will you forget me then? No?! Well, in a home environment we'll 'do it' even better."

That was her secret expression for sex.

"Do you know, when I hear someone—man or woman—say 'do it,' 'let's do it,' even though I know they're talking about something else, everything inside trembles and I want to very much."

(When Laboratory Number 1 was disbanded, she was transferred to the machine shops and very quickly got herself a new lover, also a prisoner. And until the end of my term—three and a half years—I stayed on the monastery regime.)

So Abram Mendelevich was just a hypocrite, pretending when he spoke to us trustingly, as a pal? And then "immediately reported"? But to whom? He used to warn me about the sharashka godfather himself: "Watch out! The least careless word of yours may reach Major Shikin. His trusted informers work and live next to you. And you should know that he is watching not only the prisoners, but also the free ones. He is watching all of us, including Anton Mikhailovich."

Maybe Abram's calls to vigilance were for his own protection, to preclude the possibility of suspicion or accusation of being friendly with a zek, just in case one of us befriended a free employee and told him about our "nonwork" conversations?

Imprisoned radio technician S. was sentenced somewhere in the northern Caucasus, and even though he spent some time with the *Sonderkommando*, they say even as a chauffeur of the punitive expeditions, he only got eight years. They said that his short sentence was a reward for turning in a lot of people to counterintelligence—he appeared as a witness in several show trials, after which the main defendants were hanged.

He held himself confidently, he even swaggered: all the bosses praised him for his technical knowledge and his "golden hands."

"That's the way I am. I glance once or twice at a diagram and you can put it away in a drawer. I'll mount everything myself and even improve on it. There'll be fewer elements and it'll be simpler. All the schemes I've ever worked on are right here"—he taps his low, broad, wrinkled forehead. "Let them tell me: draw the panel you mounted for Anton last month, and there you go! I just shut my eyes for a minute, remember it, and draw it so that no professor of engineering could pick on it."

His technical abilities were unquestioned. But people who worked with him said that he sucked up.

"Anything at all, and he crouches ass up, like a bitch, he'll lick ass for anyone with shoulder boards."

The more suspicious maintained that he whispered to the godfather.

S. lived in the same room with Solzhenitsyn and me. In the fall of 1949, one morning after prisoner count, when most of the men had left the room, several people in his corner got into an argument over amnesty, and S. said: "Well, I'm sure there'll be an amnesty for Joe's name day!"

A few seconds of tense silence. Then someone asked me: "Hey you, Beard, what do you think?"

Solzhenitsyn and I were in the opposite corner of the room, and I pretended not to hear.

"Hey, Beard. What do you think? Will there be an amnesty or not? You read the papers!"

"What do I think? Back in Butyrki they told me where the word 'ass' comes from: Amnesty—Salvation Soon.* That's what I think."

That same day I was called from my laboratory to see the sharashka godfather, Major Shikin. His office was right opposite that of the chief of the institute, but was separated from the corridor by an open, dark vestibule. The prison office door also opened onto the vestibule. In the vestibule could be found free employees and prisoners, waiting to be seen by Anton Mikhailovich, the office staff, or the godfather.

Shikin was a puffy, large-headed man, with almost no neck; his big, naked forehead protruded heavily over his dull eyes, and his long soft lips disdainfully curved down at the corners.

"Well, how are things? How's your work? Coming along?"

"I'm trying. As for how it's coming out, that's for the bosses to judge."

"But how do you see it: are you giving your all? Showing initiative?"

"I see it as yes. Giving my all! Showing initiative!"

"You, of course, can guess why I called you?"

"Not at all."

"Well, try to remember. You have nothing to tell me?"

"Excuse me, but I signed a special paper: I can't say anything without express permission from my superior."

"Don't evade the issue. I'm not asking about your work. We'll ask about that when the time comes. I have other questions in mind."

As he talked he looked at the papers he was shuffling on his desk, only occasionally lifting his heavy lids. But then he concentrated and gave me a "Cheka stare." "This morning in your room, that is, in the dormitory of the special contingent, there were anti-Soviet conversations. And you personally took part."

"That's not true. There was nothing of the kind."

*The Russian word *zhopa* ("ass") is also the acronym for *zhdushchii osvobozhdeniia po amnistii* ("awaiting release through amnesty"). (Translator's note.)

"What do you mean? Are you trying to say that I'm not telling the truth?!"

"No, not you. You weren't in our room, were you? But the one who told you lied. There were no anti-Soviet conversations that I heard."

"I can prove that you heard Prisoner S. permit himself to speak crudely and in an anti-Soviet manner about the leader of the people. And you responded to him."

"No one can prove anything of the sort."

Realizing what he was talking about, drawing on my rich prisoner experience, I decided to resist intransigently. "I do not keep company with prisoner S. at all. We work in different sections. And I don't even recall seeing him this morning. Our beds are at different ends of the room. You can check."

"And that means you're going to maintain that you didn't hear him discuss the amnesty today?"

"No, I didn't hear him. And I can't hear anything from that end of the room. And I don't listen to other people's conversations. My head is filled with work. I only got in last night from working after two in the morning. And I couldn't fall asleep right away—I kept thinking about serious matters. I could barely open my eyes in the morning—"

Just then the telephone rang. He picked up the receiver. "Shikin here . . . Yes, sir . . . Just a minute . . . Go outside the door into the corridor and don't go anywhere else: we haven't finished our talk."

As soon as I shut the door, I saw Solzhenitsyn coming out of Anton Mikhailovich's office. I called to him softly, and he could tell from my look and my gestures that it was important. I whispered: "Shikin called me in. Interrogation. About a morning conversation in the room. *Seems S. blabbed something anti-Soviet. But we didn't hear a fucking thing and couldn't have heard it. Some bitch blew.* He's on the phone. He'll call me back in. I'll use you as a witness. We were talking. Couldn't have heard anything."

"Exactly. We were arguing about the data on yesterday's articulation. You kept insisting that we had to repeat it and I kept telling you, you creep, that it was precise the way it was."

"Warn S."

"He won't crack?"

"Go warn him."

I heard footsteps behind the door.

"Come on, inside. Well, have you remembered anything?"

"No, Citizen Major. And no matter how hard I try, I can't remember what I didn't know, see, or hear."

"What kind of jokes were you making about amnesty today?"

"Jokes about amnesty? Ah, is that it! Someone gave you the wrong information again. I didn't allow anything anti-Soviet. I couldn't have. Just as I always was and will be a Soviet man. The joke about amnesty is an old, even an ancient one: 'Amnesty—Salvation Soon'. The first letters make a dirty word, which I wouldn't dare say in your presence. But the joke was made up by criminals long before the Revolution. There's nothing anti-Soviet about it. Just a bit of dirty talk."

"You know how to talk. But don't try to talk your way out of it. You brought that joke into an anti-Soviet conversation with S. We have precise information."

"No! That can't be. It's not precise and it's not truthful information. I remember this well: this morning Solzhenitsyn and I had a long talk, we even argued over yesterday's articulation results. And I didn't have any other conversations with anyone else. And that joke I've told many times, maybe even today to someone, I don't remember who—I don't keep rubbish like that in my mind. But certainly not to S., that's for sure—I didn't see him, or hear him, I didn't talk to him. I can give you a formal statement with my signature."

"That's my business, how to formulate your statement. If it's necessary, we'll have a transcript made up and you'll sign it and you'll be responsible for giving false testimony."

"That doesn't frighten me. I didn't lie and I don't intend to."

"Yes? Then why did you write petitions about your case to all the departments—the Central Committee, and the Supreme Court, and even personally to Comrade Stalin—and you keep trying to prove that you are a Soviet patriot, loyal to the homeland and the Party. But you don't want to prove your loyalty in deed, as you have been offered the opportunity, you decline to help the organs. And now here's confirmation. How can we trust your words when you swear patriotism and fidelity, if right now you do not wish to help the security organs?"

"Citizen Major, I have already reported to you and can only repeat it: all my work here, in this scientific-research institute of the MGB, is work for the organs—professional scientific work on creating secret telephony. And I'm not working out of fear, but out of conviction, which is evident to anyone who understands the least bit—"

"I know, I know. I told you we're not talking about your work, but about your moral-political level, about your patriotism."

"I've proved my patriotism with my entire life—at the front I showed it with my blood. With blood, not ink on a payroll or by denunciations."

"Now you're permitting yourself liberties again. That can be construed as anti-Soviet. You call operative signals denunciations."

"I don't permit myself anything of the kind. And I wasn't talking about any operative signals. If I had noticed a threat of sabotage or wrecking, I would have said something without asking anyone's permission. But denouncing, that is, squealing about conversations, whatever they may be, is something I won't do. I refuse. It's not my business. And I'm convinced that there is no threat to the Soviet regime because of that. The conversations are behind bars, in prison, after all. And the signal that led you to call me in right now was a denunciation, and a false one. And that only causes harm. You lose time, increase your stress, and take me away from my work. And I'm working on a very important security task, which I can't discuss even with you."

"All right, all right. You've already talked my head off. Go on. But not a word to anyone."

That same evening S. came up to me in the room. "Give me your hand, brother. Thanks! I found out how you helped me out today. You didn't give in, you didn't crack. You're a brick!"

"I had nothing to crack over. I didn't hear or see a thing. And don't wink at me, like a ruble whore. You'd be better off figuring out what bitch ratted on you and lied at that. And in general, go fuck yourself."

S. wasn't punished at all. The people I told about the interrogation felt that either Anton had defended his "golden-handed" technician, or S. was a stoolie himself and had started the conversation as a provocation.

Anton Mikhailovich was not only the chief of the institute but also the creator of three or four projects for an absolutely secret telephone. Each was being developed in a separate lab.

Some were based on American systems of artificial speech—vocoders. Valentin Sergeevich Martynov, a young imprisoned engineer, invented his own system of isolating and encoding the basic tone of speech, which promised to be significantly superior to the American systems, that is, to the ones that had already been described in American publications; Anton Mikhailovich was interested at first but then decided that it would require major reorganization of the work in progress without a total guarantee of success.

"It's a marvelous idea, but it has a whiff of a hare-brained scheme about it. We don't need to invent bicycles and samovars here. Show me something that's even a bit like it in the *Journal of the Acoustical Society*. You can't? Then get on with the planned work. And don't rush headlong into the fire."

Hot-headed Valentin, who fell in love with each new invention, and was doubly sure of this one, since it had been approved by several serious specialists, started pushing.

"But what is this, really?! All the papers and the radio keep telling us about our priorities, that we can't kowtow to foreigners. And here, when we actually can develop a completely original system, you refer me to the journal. What's in there that I haven't seen? This is real kowtowing, believe me."

Anton Mikhailovich's face broke out in red splotches and he screeched in an angry falsetto: "Cut out the clowning immediately! You've been given an order. You seem to forget where you are! I will not permit any argument!"

The next day Valentin was sent to the cooler for ten days. Abram Mendelevich announced that he had been punished for violation of discipline.

Valentin returned from the Butyrki cooler with a bluish pallor. He had been thin to begin with, and now he was skeletal. Sergei K. said that you could see his vertebrae through his belly.

The German POWs worked both in construction and within the sharashka walls, laying floors in the halls, servicing the boiler room, bathrooms, and even some of the offices. The cellars and the hallways were filled with closets holding the still-undeciphered archives of the Berlin labs of the Philips Company. Among our special zeks were several German engineers and technicians. They, like I, spoke to the prisoners as we passed in the corridors, made appointments for meetings in the cellar. Sometimes we engaged in simple barter with them. We gave them herring and cigarettes (we were entitled to a special ration: category 1, Kazbeks; category 2, Belomors; and category 3, Sever cigarettes), and they knew how to get their hands on vodka, razor blades, and imported socks. I knew some of them by sight, and I answered their questions as befitted a worker on a special project and keeping a state secret: I was a translator, I translated all kinds of scientific literature, and I had no idea what they were doing here. There was no doubt that their countrymen were more frank. In one of our nighttime talks with Anton Mikhailovich, I said: "We're not allowed even to hint at our location to our relatives. We put away every piece of paper in the safe when we finish for the day. Everything's a secret. But what about the prisoners of war?"

"That problem shouldn't worry you. There are people who are concerned with it. Just believe me, they know their work, they have good minds, and they don't need any advice from anyone."

Soon after, one of our Germans told me joyfully: "I saw a postcard with a German stamp with my own eyes today. Remember we had a foreman, a tall blond lieutenant? Last month he was taken away with a whole group. They said they were being sent home. No one believed them. But yesterday some people got postcards and letters. The lieutenant wrote from Dortmund. I just can't believe it. He went home from here, back to Germany."

A few zeks found out about this, and they swore violently. So that was all "state secret" meant!

And there was another nighttime talk with a peaceful and content Anton Mikhailovich. "You know, now we can estimate, give or take a day or two, when exactly American counterintelligence received detailed information about our institute." And I told him about the lieutenant's postcard, which I said I had personally seen.

He frowned angrily and drummed his fingers on the desk. We were alone. "Here's what, my dear trembler. I told you this rather clearly before

—do not meddle in affairs that are not your own. If I, the chief of the institute, am forced to use these Fritzes, that means there is sufficient justification for it. I cannot explain everything to you. You're an adult, you should be able to understand on your own. So, I am giving you an order —do you understand that? I order you to drop once and for all any conversation on such themes. You will bring benefit to no one and can cause a lot of harm, first of all to yourself. I'm not even asking if you understand or not. I'm ordering you!"

I didn't bring it up anymore. I hesitated, wondering if I should write to the Central Committee about it, but I didn't get up the nerve, and I despised myself for my lack of principle.

Solzhenitsyn was running lengthy, multistage articulation experiments on several new models. He worked scrupulously, faultlessly, and conscientiously. He pronounced the "diagnoses," that is, the evaluations of the tested channels, decisively, confidently, in some cases even with an awesome peremptoriness. His youth and army manners were showing.

The model created by Anton Mikhailovich, the "nine," was in last place. Reporting on the test results, Solzhenitsyn didn't miss the opportunity to also note the poor quality of the sound and the significant distortion of the timbre of the voice.

Anton Mikhailovich interrupted his report several times with questions, but Solzhenitsyn did not get flustered.

"So, Aleksandr Isaevich, you've buried the 'nine.' Yes, but what saddens me the most is that you bury it not like a dear departed who was close to many of us, but like a drunken bum who died under a fence."

Sanya recounted this with laughter and pride, for he was right, sure of himself, and doubly pleased—he had shown the "man himself."

But I was worried.

Anton Mikhailovich was usually polite with us, and sometimes jokingly or with regal condescension let us know that he valued our assiduousness, enthusiasm, and education. Dropping in during the quiet evening hours, he would touch on other topics—literature, music, art, history.

Seeing a bell on the table whose sound we had recorded while testing the frequency response of telephones, he said: "A pleasant sound. That's just the kind my grandmother used to call the maids from the servants' quarters.

"And why are you growing a beard? I remember my grandfather the general gloried in his beard, he combed it into two sections, like a swallow's tail. As a child I thought it very handsome. Parted beards at our house were called Russian; short 'Chekhovian' beards, French; and straight smooth spades, German beards.

"Nowadays it's popular to speak of humanism, of love of humanity in literature. Now Tolstoy's a humanist and so's Chekhov, the sweetie. Supposedly they all teach us about humanity. If that was all there was to them, they'd be worth no more than a kopek. What makes them great is that they reveal the real truth relentlessly—without any looking back or around. And all that humanism, ideals of progress, are just empty words. Treacle, and not out of sugar, but saccharine. Words, words, words! In our times what's needed are wolf fangs and tiger claws, not words. Without that, any talent, any genius will perish. Toothless softies are eaten by anyone who's got an appetite. And the one who is strong, full of teeth, you can't eat him, and if he gets hungry, he'll gobble whomever he needs."

Solzhenitsyn listened to such ruminations, too—after all, we usually sat around half the night in the laboratory together. And naturally, I reminded him of that as soon as I heard about the vicious rebuke "buried it."

"Stop trying to scare me. Let the free employees worry about hurting our bosses' feelings—they have something to lose. We don't. They won't put me in the cooler for these articulation experiments. Anton, of course, is a viper, just like Abram and the rest. But believe me, I can tell about people on first sight. He's smart and calculating, and he needs us. He knows that we don't bullshit him, don't pull the wool over his eyes. And he understands that as honest people we are much more useful to him than the toadies who stare into the bosses' eyes: 'What would you like?' No, he knows our value. He'll be mad about his 'nine' for a while and then he'll respect me even more."

"Oh, Sanya, you're reasoning from logic. You want to plan your moves as in chess. But he's one of those who might simply throw the chessboard on the ground. You come up with an elegant move, a friendly check, and he kicks you in the groin: don't beat the boss!"

"You're panicking for nothing, Old Beard! I'd believe it about Foma, but Anton is another breed."

However, a few days later on our walk he told me grimly that Abram Mendelevich asked him who could take over the articulation team, since Anton Mikhailovich was intending to transfer him to "reinforce" the mathematics group, where they were urgently developing a superdependable system of coding. The designers couldn't complete the encoder without it.

This unexpected transfer seemed irrational, but on the other hand, comforting: that meant this was the sole revenge of the insulted Anton.

In the sharashka Solzhenitsyn created something that had not existed before, a scientifically (phonetically, psychoacoustically, and mathematically) based theory and practical methodology for articulation tests. He had become an excellent commander of the articulation team—he was truly irreplaceable. This was understood by anyone who saw his work and could judge it objectively. He realized it himself and had no desire to switch to dreary mathematical drudgery as an ordinary worker alongside more experienced and knowledgeable specialists. He said that Abram Mendelevich felt the same way and promised to intervene.

It was just then that a professor of mathematics from Rostov University appeared, one of the civil consultants in a state commission. Recognizing Solzhenitsyn as his former student, he greeted him with surprise but warmly, compassionately gazing upon his dark-blue prison coveralls. The next day, he called him in for a work conference, introducing himself as the adviser to the mathematics group. Solzhenitsyn, certain that his unassailably rational reasoning would convince the professor, told him out and out that he wanted to work only on articulation, in which he had created quite a few new things, that this was true scientific work, and that the mathematics group didn't suit him for a variety of reasons.

The professor listened attentively, didn't argue, and spoke in a tone that completely soothed his trusting interlocutor. When I expressed some doubt about overdoing the frankness—after all, his respected colleague was still one of the authorities—he merely waved me off. A day later he was called in "with his gear."

I rushed to Abram Mendelevich—maybe it was all a mistake. But he curtly rejected all my pleas and arguments. "Administrative orders."

And that evening, when we were alone, he said: "Let that be a lesson to all of you. Remember: Anton Mikhailovich doesn't forgive anything. Or anyone."

Solzhenitsyn left me his outlines of Dahl,* of history and philosophy, several books, among them a well-worn volume of Yesenin, a gift from his wife with the inscription "Everything that's yours will be returned to you," and—as the greatest "inheritance"—his best friend, Nikolai Vitkevich.

All the outlines survived and were returned to him. This was thanks to Gumer Akhatovich Izmailov. A talented electronics engineer, sentenced to ten years "for POW camp" and also because he had been friends in prison camp with his countryman the poet Musa Jalil† (Gumer learned of Musa's death and newfound fame much later, when he was freed), Gumer was one of seven engineers and technicians released before their time in 1951 as a reward for creating a top secret telephone—the work that brought the bosses medals, university degrees, and Stalin Prizes.

All the released men stayed on at the sharashka as free employees. But only two—Gumer and his friend Ivan Emelianovich Bryksin—maintained truly good will toward their recent comrades, and they did not shy away from us, did not shun us. It was Gumer Izmailov who brought out and turned over to my family all of Solzhenitsyn's outlines and a significant part of my archives.

But Yesenin's book, unfortunately, I had entrusted before that to my girl

*Vladimir Ivanovich Dahl (1801–1872), ethnographer and lexicographer, compiler of the monumental *Dictionary of the Russian Language* (1861–1868). (Translator's note.)
†The Tatar poet (1906–1944) was posthumously cleared of the crime of having been in a German POW camp. (Translator's note.)

friend. Later, when she was working in another section, I accidentally ran into her in the corridor and asked if she had saved it. She whispered in fright: "What book? What Yesenin? Why, that was just tatters. I don't even remember where I stuck it and please forget about it. Forget it completely."

When Solzhenitsyn had told me about his case, he spoke of Nikolai Vitkevich—Koka—his best friend. They corresponded during the war. Vitkevich served as a regimental chemist on another front. Assuming that the military censors were concerned only with military secrets, the friends reveled in freethinking on political topics and used a not-too-subtle code for their discussion of the superiority of "Baldie" (Lenin) over "Mustachio" (Stalin), who made a mess of things in 1930, 1937, and 1941.

This correspondence became the basis of an accusation under Article 58-10, 58-11. They were tried separately. An army tribunal sentenced Vitkevich to ten years and the OSO gave Solzhenitsyn eight.

In early 1950 the prison godfather called in Solzhenitsyn and told him that his "fellow criminal" Vitkevich would be brought to the sharashka soon and warned him: "You will have to behave extremely properly."

Recounting this, Sanya was very agitated: was this perhaps a provocation? Were they planning to bring new charges? He asked me not to tell anyone about it, not even Mitya.

"And you'll definitely like Koka. In his convictions and ideology he's probably halfway between you and me."

When Vitkevich arrived, for the first day or two they spent all their free time together, talking seriously, concentrating. Mitya and I tried to keep everyone from disturbing them. Solzhenitsyn even exchanged his lower bunk for an upper one, to be next to his friend.

Nikolai, who was Russian on his mother's side and Polish on his father's, spent his childhood with his stepfather's family, who were from Daghestan, and he assimilated the manners, world view, and even the psychology of a Muslim mountain tribesman. He spoke with awe and respect of Shamil and the Murids.* He listened enraptured to radio broadcasts of mountain folk songs or the Azerbaijani singer Rashid Beibutov. He was happy that I began calling him Jalil, his childhood name.

Stocky, swarthy, broad-faced, he strode lightly but firmly; he tried to be or at least appear to be imperturbably calm, to suppress his anger.

He described with great emotion his childhood, Daghestan, the front, the camps. He was very good, almost poetic, on his struggle with a wheelbarrow, getting used to it, overcoming his muscles, exhaustion, despair, and how having mastered it, he became healthier, gradually grew stronger. Then, in the taiga, at a logging site, he took primitive joy in a campfire, ready to worship fire.

---

*Shamil ruled (1824–1859) the Muslim Murids in Daghestan and Chechnia and fought against tsarist colonial policies. (Translator's note.)

Sometimes we argued. Jalil considered himself a follower of Lenin, rejecting the ringleader Stalin outright, and he rebuked me for overestimating him and, in trying to be objective, actually justifying his bestial crimes.

I took our political disagreements calmly, but I was very irritated when he called Pushkin Sashka, Lermontov Mishka, Nekrasov Koka, and so on. He rejected all my comments on this matter good-naturedly but firmly. "That just means that I love them. It's just like Volodka Mayakovsky wrote: 'Nekrasov, Kolya, son of the late Alyosha.' And also, 'Aseyev Kolka.' Right? You have an old-fashioned respect: ah, he's great, famous, doff your hats! But for me, if I love someone, I don't have to stand on ceremony with him. That's why Sanya is Sanka or Walrus or Ksandr to me, and you're Levka or the Beard, and as for Yesenin, I'll always call him Seryozhka."

He was just as stubborn in insisting that "a real man" should never marry an actress or ballerina. "They're all whores. How can you allow your wife to be pawed, kissed, grabbed on stage? You can argue as much as you like that it's bourgeois and prejudiced on my part, I don't care. And what's it to you? You're not married to an actress! Drop it, you won't convince me anyway. The only ones who marry them are besotted fools and, of course, directors and actors. But they're whores themselves, without any male honor. They marry and divorce and screw anyone they can. It's all the same to them whether they go home or to a whorehouse."

Vitkevich continued being friends with Solzhenitsyn and his first wife later, when they were freed. In the late fifties he moved to Ryazan, to live and work closer to him.

They broke during a New Year's Eve party in 1964, when Vitkevich began rebuking Solzhenitsyn for getting a swelled head, "thinking himself a genius, forgetting his old friends."

He wrote to me about it then. A year later he was in Moscow and tried to convince me that "Sanka is completely crazy with fame. He won't listen to anyone."

Both Vitkevich and I were good friends in the sharashka for two years after Solzhenitsyn was sent away. He did sometimes refer critically to his old friend, who always "wanted to be first and most important," "the center of the universe," and "didn't care for anyone but himself." However, neither then nor later did he even hint once at the accusations of treachery that were published in 1974 over his signature in a pamphlet by Novosti Press and repeated in 1978 in Vitkevich's name in a filthy little book by a certain Rzhezach.

When the Korean War started, my friend Evgenii Timofeev spent his nights planning a project for an SS (shore-to-sea) torpedo, to repulse a possible American landing. And I egged on two friends—a mechanic and an engineer—to develop a universal self-propelled ack-ack-type antitank gun and wrote a detailed "tactical basis" alluding to our experience and that of the Germans in using ack-ack guns against tanks and to examples of various successful actions by self-propelled guns of various calibers during 1941–1945.

All my arguments with Panin, Solzhenitsyn, Vladimir Andreevich, with German engineers and technicians, among whom were repenting Nazis, the most reasonable broadcasts on the BBC, and the military political articles in American magazines merely strengthened my convictions and faith, which I considered "objective knowledge."

I was not alone in this. For Mitya Panin, Sanya Solzhenitsyn, and Sergei Kuprianov were not my only friends.

Evgenii Timofeevich Timofeev—aka red-haired Zhen-Zhen—a member of the Russian Communist Party since 1919, and the last living survivor of the Leningrad "oppositional center" of 1925–1928, had more consistent judgments in many cases than I. He did not even approve of my closeness to those he considered patent ideological enemies; he avoided Panin and Solzhenitsyn.

Aleksei Pavlovich N.—Halfbeard—was also a former "Leningrad oppositionist." In contrast to Evgenii and myself, he remained a determined foe of Stalin, called himself an orthodox Leninist-internationalist, and criticized Stalin's foreign policy as being imperialist. Timofeev and I, on the contrary, approved of it in every way, maintaining that the expansion of the Soviet borders and Soviet spheres of influence was the path to the world triumph of socialism.

Zhen-Zhen, Halfbeard, and I usually met in the smoking area on the fire stairs, from where we could not be overheard by the supervisors. Sometimes we sang folk and old revolutionary songs there. Vladimir Andreevich and his steady "chitchatters" called us a "Party cell," and there was hostility in their attitude.

However, Igor Aleksandrovich Krivoshein, the son of a minister of Stolypin's* cabinet and a graduate of the Corps des Pages, became a friend of ours. He had been an officer of the old army, then fought with the counterrevolutionaries Denikin and Wrangel, and then emigrated. In France he graduated from an electrotechnical institute, worked as an engineer; after 1940 he joined the Resistance as a scout, and in 1943 was captured by the Gestapo. When the American tanks approached Buchenwald in 1945, the prisoners revolted, the guards scattered, and Igor Aleksandrovich, emaciated and ill, was carried out beyond the gates on a stretcher by his comrades.

Returning to Paris, he read his obituaries. The first newspapers to appear in liberated Paris listed him among the fallen heroes of the Resistance. All the members of the Resistance knew the rule: if the Gestapo gets you, you

---

*Petr Arkadievich Stolypin (1862–1911), Minister of the Interior after 1906 under Nicholas II. (Translator's note.)

have to hold out at least twenty-four hours, after which you can inform to avoid torture. In the twenty-four hours your comrades will have time to hide, to cover their tracks. But even a month after the arrest of Igor Krivoshein, the Gestapo did not appear at any of the apartments known to him or try to locate any of his comrades. And they saw that as evidence of his death.

But he had withstood all the tortures for which the Paris Gestapo was notorious, including the "ice bath," and his fellow arrestee, an antifascist German officer, selflessly and wisely maintained that Krivoshein had played a minor subordinate role. The German was shot, and Igor Aleksandrovich sentenced to fifteen years of labor camps. In the summer of 1945 he returned to his family truly from the other world, resurrected from the dead.

After the war, like many other émigrés, he took Soviet citizenship, his Parisian fellow citizens elected the hero of the Resistance chairman of the Union of Soviet Citizens. And when the Cold War intensified, the French police arrested him and twenty-seven of his comrades. They were exiled to the Soviet Union.

Igor Aleksandrovich and his wife and son (who followed later) were settled in Ulianovsk; he worked as an engineer. But in less than a year's time he was arrested and taken to Moscow. His White Guard past fell under several amnesties. But he did not try to hide the fact that during 1940–1943 he had joined French intelligence, obtained information about the movement of German troops in France and the state of the military industry. Of course, in those years France had been an ally of the USSR, but an honest Soviet citizen should have been helping his own socialist intelligence service, not a foreign capitalist one. The investigators were polite, even courteous, and asked sympathetically about how he had been tortured by the Gestapo and the regime at Buchenwald.

After a few months the duty officer at the prison read him the decision of the OSO—ten years in "general places of confinement."

He was brought straight from the prison to the sharashka. Everything that he had seen and heard in Russia amazed him. He accepted his arrest, investigation, and incongruous sentence with sadness but without surprise. He had expected worse at first. After all, he knew enough about the activities of the Cheka-GPU-NKVD from the prewar newspapers. However, the polite officers at Lubyanka, in their uniforms of the old Russian cut with epaulets, questioned him politely, promised to take care of his wife and son, gave him newspapers, magazines, and books about the greatness of Russian history and the need to overcome "kowtowing before foreigners." All this in light of the still-fresh memories of the Gestapo and Buchenwald seemed to soothe him and give him hope. And an even greater impression came from the general state of the sharashka: clean bed linens, bread on the tables in the dining room—eat as much as you like—food that seemed marvelous after the gruel, and the people who seemed uncoerced and involved in their work, many intellectuals, warm smiles, occasional jokes and laughter.

After we were introduced and I asked him if he was related to the tsarist minister, he stared at me for a few seconds in surprise. "Yes . . . his son. I never expected anyone to remember about Father. The name must sound odious to you, I suppose."

Then I told him that I remembered the name from my childhood. My father, an agronomist, often argued with me when I was a Pioneer, and later a Komsomol, insisting that I didn't know the history of our country, that my Bolshevik intolerance and my brains cluttered with pamphlets and newspapers prevented me from learning the truth about events and people. And every time he would bring up the same story.

"Now, Aleksandr Vasilievich Krivoshein was a tsarist minister; a committed monarchist, a friend of Stolypin's. And for all that he was not only an excellent administrator, educated, wise, and zealous, he was also generous, noble, and truly liberal. I saw that for myself. It was thanks to Krivoshein that I was appointed a country agronomist, even though I was Jewish and considered politically unreliable, having been expelled from the institute. Krivoshein knew his work and knew how to evaluate people. When he toured villages, estates, and experimental stations, nobody could pull the wool over his eyes. He noticed everything in the fields, and in the seedbeds, and in the cattle yards. He visited us in Borodyanka three times. He dined with us and kissed your mother's hand. That tsarist dignitary was better bred, smarter, and better educated than all your people's commissars, and more of a humanitarian and a democrat to boot."

From our first days together I liked Igor Aleksandrovich very much, and soon we grew very close spiritually. And my father's stories about his father seemed like a sign of fate. For prisoners are frequently predisposed to mysticism. Even hard-boiled positivist materialists seriously discussed dreams, forebodings, omens, fateful dates.

Igor Aleksandrovich, gentle, tactful to the point of shyness both in quiet conversations and heated arguments, remained unyieldingly firm in his essence—in his concepts of good and evil, faith and honor, the moral bases of his world view. A Russian patriot, even a nationalist, and a profoundly devout Russian Orthodox, he felt that the Soviet government had become the lawful successor of the Russian empire and naturally the most powerful, most influential, and internationally most significant of all the former versions of the Russian state.

This brought closer our political views as well, or rather, our opinions on the most important political events. We were in agreement about rejecting any form of "Americanism"— from the Marshall Plan and the atom bomb to rock and roll and Hollywood films—and in our desire for victory for North Korea.

· · ·

No sooner had we finished a report on the phonoscopic research in the Ivanov case than we were brought tapes of new conversations with the American Embassy. In both, the same young voice of a sprightly fellow spoke with a clear southern Russian or Ukrainian articulation, which he tried to disguise, struggling to imitate a Moscow pronunciation.

"I can give you precise information on airports, which there are, tank units, where they're repaired, what new construction sites there are. I can find out a lot of other things, too. What do I want for it? Well, you can pay money, but things are better. What kind? For instance, a good radio. Can you give me a good radio? And a camera. But with the right kind of film. You can? And a watch. What kind of watches do you have? Watches, ticktock, with a watchband. And also binoculars. Understand, binoculars? To see far. Well, and of course, some clothing. But not coats. With a coat you can see right away that it's foreign. You can give me good-quality men's knitwear."

The American in both calls was the one who had last talked to Ivanov, lazily indifferent or perhaps suspicious. Still he did agree to meet with him and suggested a railroad station or the Park of Culture.

"What kind of car will you be in? But you can tell right away your car is foreign. Is there a flag on it? A flag, a sign, on the radiator. There, you see! How can I come up to you, then? The pointers will get me right away. You don't know who the pointers are? The GPU, the militia, what you call the police. You come by taxi. And take something with you so I can recognize you. Do you have a large briefcase? A briefcase, but a big one, like a suitcase. What color? Yellow—that's good, I'll see it from far off. So you sort of stroll around, and I'll come up to you. Do you smoke? What —Russian or American cigarettes? A pipe? That's good, too. But you bring some cigarettes for me, the ones with the camel. I'll come up to you to ask for a light, and then we'll talk."

This conversation took two tries. The first time it had been interrupted.

Two other tapes were brought in for comparison: conversations of some kind of workers or foremen with their bosses about rejected or undelivered parts, about metalwork and fittings. In one case the voice seemed similar and the dialect was southern, too.

But the sound pictures of the few coinciding words in the various conversations—"can," "need," "know," and so forth—were not enough to identify the voice. The considerable differences in the microintonations and microtonality seemed "organic" to me. Of course, they could have been explained by an intentional change in the voice and by a head cold (the "worker" sneezed several times). However, after rather detailed study I came to the conclusion that the voices belonged to two different men. The new report fit into one file. Anton Mikhailovich and Abram Mendelevich signed it without any problems.

But a few days later Anton Mikhailovich said, dropping into the lab in the morning: "Your second baby's a mess. That sergeant confessed everything."

It turned out that the conversations with the embassy had not taken place in phone booths, as in the first case, but in the hallway of a military unit, in the shops where they repaired tanks, armored transport trucks, and other army vehicles. SMERSH agents searched the barracks and in the footlocker of Sergeant Petya N., foreman of the fitters, they found his diary, which had information on the location of airports, tank units, HQ, the number of vehicles under repair, and some drawings. After his arrest, he confessed that he wanted "to fake spying," bluff the Americans, and that's why he called the embassy.

I soon received the tapes of two interrogations. Tolya went alone both times; disappointed by the failure, Abram Mendelevich had given up.

Tolya told me about the suspect. "Seems like a regular soldier. Not tall, reddish hair, nothing to look at. But basically he's a fool and a son of a bitch. And he's trying to squirm out of it."

But the sound pictures from the interrogation tapes, which had the same words as those in the intercepted call, did not permit me to definitely identify the voice as that of the unknown fellow who was offering his services as a spy.

The suspect spoke glumly, without any elevated emotional intonations. And the voices didn't sound the same. "But I only called once . . . Yes, yes —twice, I forgot already . . . So I only called . . . I didn't tell them anything. I only called for a joke. You know, to make fools of them. To laugh at them, those Americans. And the stuff in my notebooks, that was to help me remember . . . Well, yes, there are airports there and our units, from where the vehicles come to be repaired . . . No, I don't know anything about a radio. What radio? . . . No, I didn't ask for a camera . . . Well, I admitted right away that I was guilty . . . No, I wasn't planning to go to them. I'm not a fool. And I didn't show the notebooks to anyone . . . No, I wasn't planning to, I just thought that if I had to, I'd tell them things, not what was in the notebooks, but sort of like it. So it would be like it but not it exactly. Just a dumb joke . . . Yes, yes, just a foolish idea . . . but I didn't do any of it, it was just for laughs."

No, this was another man's voice, not the one who was cajoling the indifferent American. But the sound pictures from the interrogation displayed significant differences with those made from the tape of the same voice coming from the shop.

One more zek came to Laboratory Number 1—Vasilii Ivanovich G. Before that he had been a translator of technical documents and literature, part of the library. At the beginning of the war, as a young economics engineer, he had worked as an assistant to the head of a geological or topographical research group. He was drafted. There was a rumor that he had been killed

—he was severely wounded and lost a leg—and some of his co-workers blamed the "fallen hero" for the loss of a large sum of money that had mysteriously disappeared. After the hospital, he was demobilized and worked in Moscow in management. But in 1945 he was traced and sentenced to ten years for "embezzlement" under the ukase of August 7, 1932, a crime that was not subject to amnesty.

Even before the war he had taken correspondence courses at the institute of foreign languages; he was a good translator from German, English, and French, knew the Turkic languages, and was interested in Esperanto. He was a first-generation intellectual, a stubborn autodidact, who had a suspicious and cautious attitude toward the big-city scholars "who thought too much of themselves."

Abram Mendelevich said that Vasilii would be my assistant and that I would have to teach him to read sound pictures, mainstream him into the work with the articulation team, and also enlighten him in phonoscopic and cryptographic work. At first I thought he was a plant.

But Vasilii avoided political topics. "The walls have ears here, and my official sentence is more than I need. I don't want them to add an Article 58 onto it."

He worked sensibly, quickly, though he was too quick to sum up and generalize. "Well, what are you dragging it out for? I've got it by now. Ten tables are enough to show the percentage of intelligibility. But the expletives don't go through. Well, so there's a half. They get mixed up in the high frequencies, too. So why repeat it? Go on, write the summary."

General questions of linguistics did not interest him: "I studied that back in my second year." He was sympathetic to my pet research project and guesses but had no particular interest in them: "You've taken an awfully narrow topic, you know." But he could spend a long time enthusiastically discussing the origin of separate words, about family ties between languages—which borrowed from which, how the same root changed in various languages.

His interest in literature, poetry, history, and music was less than that of my friends and completely different. Our tastes didn't often coincide. He simply did not believe that someone might like the "abstruse verses" that you can understand only after long explanations, and certainly cannot feel something about them.

"It's pleasant sometimes to listen to a good opera or operetta. Even the ballet, though that's more for the 'Messrs aesthetes.' They know if she shakes her leg to the left, that means she loves him, to the right, she doesn't, and if she spins like a top—oh, what passion! But how can you sit for hours at a concert where only the symphony blares, I don't know! Good songs grab your soul. Folk dances of all nations—they're a pleasure to watch, your toes start tapping. But all those Shostakoviches are just jingle jangle, thunder and clanking. No, of course there are people who understand—specialists—but the majority are those who pretend, act smart to seem intelligent. Some pigeon sits there, bored out of his mind, swallowing his yawns, but frowns, squints, moves his lips, pretending to understand and enjoy it."

Vasilii read the sound pictures without enthusiasm, didn't try very hard, and did not take my lessons very seriously. "And why do we have to rack our brains over this, too? If you can see it on a spectrogram, then you can hear it anyway. Well, I can understand using it for decoding, when you have a mosaic telephone. But even then you don't need to bother reading syllable by syllable, spelling it out word by word. You have to determine a code, pick out the filters, and then decode and listen. You have to do things more simply, more rationally. What do you keep harping on science for? There are different kinds of science. Remember how Gulliver ended up among scholars—what do you call them, the Laputans? Well, I have no respect for Laputan science for science's sake, art for art's sake. How do you determine the limits? Well, that can be hard, of course. I was translating American and British articles on physics, mathematics. Pure abstractions, mind games. And it seemed like there'd be no practical application at all. But Anton says that those games of theirs can make cybernetics. Also an abstraction and even a false science. But they use it for ack-ack artillery and someplace else, too. So don't think that I'm against science, I just want to know—each time I want to know—what exactly we're working for. Just like Anton Mikhailovich, who keeps saying all the time, 'We need profit, profit!' And I think he's right. And reading those sound pictures—it's the same stuff over and over, like a psalmbook to a church reader."

They brought in tapes of two other interrogations—two other soldiers, friends of the first one.

The new phonoscopic study was done after Vasilii had joined us. He tried to understand just how I was comparing the voices, kept asking questions; I explained in detail. Sometimes it seemed that he was testing and double-checking me. But soon I was convinced that he trusted me, at least, and if he didn't agree with my conclusions, he said that he wasn't able to judge yet. I forbade myself to suspect him.

Soon he found himself a girl friend, too. One of the two technical assistants who were untouchable fell sick. She was replaced by a tubby, almost conical girl named Shura, who had worked before with Vasilii in the library, helping him with translations; she knew English. She was markedly severe with me the first few days—she even tried to discipline me a few times: "Please drop the jokes . . . explain in a businesslike way. Jokes are out of place. Why are your notes so messy? No one will be able to understand a thing. What do you mean these are notes for yourself? And what if you're sent away tomorrow? All the work will be lost! You have to make notes so that anyone can make them out."

I didn't put up with it for long: I blew up and said that I had to take it from the prison supervisors in prison but I could not do scientific work under the command of a prison supervisor and I would not. And if she did not change her tone and continued nagging me, I would make an official request for either me or her to be transferred to another lab.

At first she just grumbled back at me: "What else do you want! You forget yourself. There has to be order and discipline."

But then she and Vasilii exchanged confused looks, and I realized that they were more than acquaintances. And that her frank dislike for me was probably only a cover-up for her secret liking for him.

He started calming me down. "Drop it, why are you getting angry? No one's picking on you. What do supervisors have to do with it? And if a word is said the wrong way, in the wrong tone, well, maybe the person is in a bad mood or something. You have to be more understanding. You get so official right away. Stop it. And you don't listen to him! He's a scientist, a scholar, but he's also very high-strung."

Later, when we were alone, he kept talking to me, but trying not to give away their relationship by a single word. "You know what they tell them about us, especially those like you under 58: 'Enemies of the people,' 'insidious methods,' 'be vigilant and overvigilant!' And here she sees you: a shaggy hulk, with a black beard, making magic, saying and writing things no one can understand. And you bare your teeth at her, too. Another woman would have been even more scared."

After that we came to an unspoken agreement. I dealt with Shura during the day in a cool, official way, and on those evenings that she was on duty, I spent all the time in the acoustics lab, where I had plenty to do as well, leaving her alone with Vasilii.

And he disappeared during those evening hours when my girl friend was on duty. We didn't discuss it at all, it just happened. But my girl was anxious at first. "Why did he leave again? You told him, didn't you? Honest? And what's going on between him and Shura? You don't know? He doesn't tell you? Not a word, not a hint? Are all you prisoners so inveterate and secretive? But he must guess, if he goes away. Aha, that means that you must know something, too, if you leave when she's on duty. Well, you guess it. That means, he guesses, too. Which means—you can't sew a pair of pants from guesses? But you can make a case out of it. Are you sure that he realizes that if he snitches on us, it'll be worse for him? Well, all right, he understands, but what if she doesn't? She's mean, acts important and intellectual, but her nails are all bitten off and she stinks— she doesn't wash enough. No, no, of course, she's no fool, she won't want trouble for herself. And she and Vasilii do it in here, too, I'll bet. No one else would even look at her. Only someone who's been without a woman a long time. Why don't you make a pass at her, too?"

On the tapes of the interrogations of the two soldiers, one voice seemed similar to me to the voices of the bold caller to the Americans. But under interrogation he sounded hushed and more monotonous.

The investigator—uninhibited and rather crude—played at being buddies, asked them about their girls and about dances. And in between, in a deliberately casual tone, suddenly asked: "So why didn't you smart guys stop Petya when he called the Americans? And it was you who gave Petya the materials about the airports? He's admitted it, that you and Zhora put him up to calling the embassy. Cut out the baloney—Petya's cracked up to his ass, he wrote that you're the gang leader. Zhora and he only followed you. And you taught them how to be spies."

From the tapes I learned that Petya, Zhora, and Senya were buddies, soldiers in the same unit, who worked together in the shop, and apparently the three of them—or perhaps only two of them—came up with the spy game. One called, and another one confessed—the one in whose possession the notebooks were found. Perhaps there were other considerations here or preliminary conditions that prompted him to take the blame. Under interrogation he didn't "recall" right away that he had had two conversations with the embassy; he spoke of only one, and he didn't remember well what they had talked about. But he stubbornly insisted that he had done it all alone and no one else knew anything about it, no one helped him, and Senya and Zhora were just pals, to party and drink with or to beat at dominoes.

The persistent investigator repeated over and over: "They've both broken. They confessed that you lured them into it, gave the orders, sent them to spy."

But he replied each time: "Oh no, that can't be. They didn't know a thing about it. No, no, Zhora and Senya have nothing to do with it. I did it all alone."

The tapes of the interrogations were of poor quality technically. One of the less-experienced technicians went down to record them this time, and no one asked us for a crib sheet for the investigator. Comparing the sound pictures of several more or less similar-sounding words, I guessed that it was Senya who made the calls. Judging by his voice and speech, he was older and more educated than the other two. Vasilii and Abram Mendelevich came to the same conclusion, but not with great certainty.

These three blockheads did not elicit as much revulsion in me as the diplomat—they were immeasurably less dangerous and certainly less guilty. I could have insisted on a detailed study of Senya's voice and tried to expose the real caller to the Americans. That way, probably, we would have confirmed the effectiveness of our phonoscopic methods. But the miserable Petya had taken all responsibility, even though both his pals were already under arrest. Perhaps they really had only been playing a stupid game like dumb nitwits. Perhaps this had been a serious idea, a stupid helpless attempt at spying.

Either way, Petya behaved courageously and selflessly, What would my evidence have done by overturning his confession and exposing his friend? It would only have worsened their fate. The notebooks and confession were enough for the tribunal to find Petya and his friends guilty. An additional "scientific" exposure would only strengthen the prosecution's case and prove a conspiracy. Any "collective," especially in the army, was always considered a dangerous crime.

And I wrote once again that "the present sound pictures do not permit us to identify either of the control voices with the one that . . ." and so on.

Anton Mikhailovich ordered me to include an additional paragraph saying that the evidence did not allow us to conclude the contrary either, since the parameters were not established for the possible differences of audible and visible manifestations of the same voice.

He heard out my report grimly. "So. Obviously, your method is unsound. For this and that are indisputably one and the same voice: this is the fool they were interrogating. And yet there are obvious differences. I know, I know, there's noise, a cold, different intonation, a different telephone. I understand. But that will always be the case. You will always have to compare conversations that took place under different circumstances. This means that Abram Mendelevich and I ballyhooed your epoch-making discoveries in vain. We've embarrassed ourselves with your phonoscopy!"

"It doesn't exist as yet, Anton Mikhailovich, our phonoscopy. It hasn't been born—it's only being conceived. That's what I've been reporting to you all the time. Phonoscopy is not yet a reality, it's only a possibility. But it's a realistic possibility; I'm firmly convinced of that. Even today I can determine with sufficient certainty the identity of a voice in various recordings. I can say: these and these details on the sound pictures, and such and such statistical data are evidence that at these different times the same person spoke. And I can explain why I am certain of that. However, I know almost nothing about the possibility of changes of the same voice, I do not know the limits within which it can vary, be distorted, intentionally and accidentally."

"In other words, you can use all our acoustics technology the way a Gypsy can use a deck of cards or some tea leaves?"

"Not at all! On the contrary: I strive for a precise, objective analysis, not necromancy. I can give a positive answer under certain conditions even now. But a negative one, as you see, is dubious. And I can't be certain of negative answers until we determine the limits of deviation. And for that I must run thousands of tests."

"And where will you find the time and the means for thousands of tests? My friend, you're full of schemes and fantasies. But I'm not Jules Verne, not Wells, and we don't need science-fiction projects. Please concentrate not on the seeds of unknown sciences but on real work. Ever since we got rid of that . . . Solzhenitsyn, the articulation experiments have dried up completely. Now the 'seven' and two other circuits haven't been articulated in over two weeks." He turned to Abram Mendelevich. "You would think there was nothing so complicated about it, even in the olden days they knew how to test telephones by ear, but your workers, Abram

Mendelevich, it turns out, don't know how. Are you going to tell me again about Solzhenitsyn's irreplaceability? I do not accept that or understand it. We do not have and must not have irreplaceable people. You and I will be replaced, if necessary." And then back to me. "So, my respected Lev Zinovievich, please start reorganizing the articulation tests right away, today. Naturally, without a break in your basic work. Study the physical parameters of the intelligibility of speech and the recognizability of voices. I doubt you'll have to run any more criminological tests. The security officers are quite unhappy with our expert evidence. Worse than that—they're laughing at it. You have proven scientifically that it's not the same voice and that the suspect is innocent, like a lamb. But he's confessed himself: 'I was a spy, I made the calls.' "

"They found the notebooks in his possession, that's why he confessed. But someone else could have made the call!"

"It's possible, anything's possible. But these Sherlock Holmes puzzles are not for us. We played a bit and that's enough. Let's return to our basic work. You'll get back to articulation."

8

"THE BEGUM" AND OTHER CAPITALISTS

Nikolai B. took his time going over some three dozen worn books—our first library stock. And finally he chose a small book with a red cover and faded gilt lettering: Jules Verne: THE BEGUM'S FIVE HUNDRED MILLION. He read it a long time, almost a month.

He worked in the machine shop (he called himself the head machinist). As soon as he came into the cell in the evening, he took the book from his nightstand. His bed—one of the few "ordinary" ones among our bunks— had a metal net bottom. The others lay on boards. Instead of the standard-issue pillow, stuffed with lumps of stiff cotton, his bed was graced by several personal down-filled ones. Lying on his luxurious bed, he munched on cookies or smoked and concentrated on *The Begum's Five Hundred Million*.

"Why can't you finish it? The book is a slim volume, but you're in your second month with it."

"What's it to you? What do you mean 'slim'? It's a very deep book. You think just because it has pictures it's for kids. Let me tell you, this is a profound book, with significance for real life. I've never read anything like it. It's very educational."

"What's so special about your *Begum?*"

"When we go for a walk, I'll explain. That requires serious talk, not off the top of your head. And so that no one who feels like it can overhear."

Nikolai was a little over forty. He was of medium height and build and had a radiant urban face, with a high forehead and a widow's peak. He was polite and steady with everyone, without that prison familiarity. He addressed both his bosses and his comrades amiably, softly, and apparently trustingly. Even when asking about the weather or what was for breakfast, he spoke softly and tilted his head meaningfully, as though the subject were an intimate secret. He put off our talk several times: either there were too many people around on the walk or there wasn't enough time. Finally, he did open up about it.

"I don't see why you don't understand. You're educated, a docent or something. Obviously, you're lacking one kind of education. This book is a sort of fairy tale, you know, made up. But only sort of. Actually it shows what the most important thing in life is. You don't know what? The important thing is wealth. Now, you're more educated than I and you've read scientific books and know various languages, but I understand better than you what's important in life. I understand because I lived through it myself. And you don't even know what there is to understand. That's what you think, isn't it? Yes, that's what they taught you in the Pioneers and the Komsomol. I know, they taught all of us that way: the person with wealth doesn't want to work, only stuffs money in his pocket; he's a spider, a bourgeois, a crawling viper, greed choked in his craw. I used to think so, too. I studied political science at the technicum, I was a Komsomol member. And two of my uncles are in the Party. My father, though, isn't. He was a master in a machine shop. He taught me to do metalwork and woodwork. I can work any machine, a planing machine. I respect all kinds of work. When I was a kid and got into the shop for the first time, I wanted to be able to do it all. I studied, worked hard, and greed choked in my craw.

"So, who am I? The working class! A proletarian from my roots, my grandfather, my great-grandfather. Understand that? Well, I'm confessing to you—but don't tell anyone, not your best buddies—I was just like that begum. You don't understand? I was a millionaire, twice over. You laugh, go ahead, but listen to my story."

And Nikolai began telling me in a low voice, without rushing, with long digressions . . . sometimes saddened, sometimes angered, sometimes gladdened by his memories. He recounted his story over three or four evening walks. When someone came near, Nikolai would go on talking in the same low voice, with the same intonations, but about something else entirely—telling a long anecdote or a "story from life."

Before the war he had worked in Slaviansk, a small town in the Donetsk Oblast, as chief machinist at a small plant that produced simple instruments and construction equipment. When the war began, the plant received orders to devise an evacuation plan, but it was to be top secret—no one was to know. The German troops entered Slaviansk unexpectedly—there hadn't even been any battles in the area.

"The bosses from the regional committee and the regional executive committee managed to get away. But many residents stayed. My director had run off. The plant stopped working, the workers went home—they didn't know what to do. And their families were hungry. And I thought: 'Why should the goods and the people perish?' And it came to me like a hammer blow to the head. I went to the German commandant. The *Oberleutnant* was along in years, solid, intelligent, wore glasses. His translator was a young German boy, fair-skinned, also polite. So I said to them: 'Give me the plant; well, rent it to me, or sell it to me. I'll give you an advance of as much as I can scrape up, and then I'll pay as you say, a tax or whatever. What will I make? I think I'll start with carts, you know, wagons, and then later traps. I know that's what's needed. All the cars and tractors are standing around the villages; there's no fuel, but people have to get around, have to transport things. You can hitch a horse to a cart and, at worst, even a cow.'

"The commandant understood right away, asked a few more things, and said: '*Sehr gut.*' He didn't take an advance. 'You have to pay your workers,' he said. 'Instead, we'll give you a loan, to help you start up.' Well, I'm going to tell you the honest truth—I swear right now, may I go a century without freedom, may I never see my children if even a word of this is a lie—in just two months, by Christmas, I had over a million of my own money. And I didn't exploit anyone. I paid a higher salary than under the Soviets, some fifty percent higher, and the good masters even a hundred and fifty percent. And I didn't figure percent the way the newspapers do, when on paper you have total overfulfillment of the plan—hurrah!—but nothing in your pocket and nothing but a grain of corn in your oven. No, I figured out what could be bought with that salary. I had one hundred and fifty to one hundred and sixty people working for me, and all in the shops, doing real work.

"There were only two in the office, me and the bookkeeper: a little old man so honest and so neat that he watched every kopek, every paper and tack. Then I got a partner. His name was Misha; he was a mechanic, but he used his head better than his hands. A businessman. He was so clever that he could twist ten Jews or Armenians or Gypsies around his finger and buy and sell them and they'd give him a bonus for it. So the two of us were the supply and the demand. And the following year I rented a bicarbonate-of-soda plant in Lisichansk. The Lisichansk commandant—a captain—and ours were buddies, good friends. The captain really liked Ukrainian embroidery. '*Prima,*' '*Kunst,*' he called it—that means art. So Misha and I would bring him wagonloads of shirts and towels and table-cloths. So he let us rent the plant. There were several tons of unsorted soda in the warehouses. We hired girls right away to package it, ten-gram and fifty-gram packages—we let them work at home. People paid in money and in kind. When we sold a cart or a trap or so many sacks of soda in a village —we sold to Germans, too, who had farms—we accepted not only money, but flour and potatoes, an occasional pig. By spring I had three million, and Misha, a million plus.

"Then we started up auxiliary farms in Slaviansk and Lisichansk, like sovkhozes—vegetable gardens, cows, chickens, ducks. Food for us, and we sold it at a good price to our workers. They were so thankful: our prices were way lower than the market's. So they gave us bride-price back. Greed choked in my craw. I got myself a ZIS one-and-a-half-ton truck, then I bought a bus from the Rumanians. If I had wanted to, I could have gotten a car as well. But I realized that a car could cause me problems: the Germans maintained strict controls on gasoline. Of course, they had those who sold on the side, too, and the Rumanians, Italians, and Hungarians, even more so. With those, everyone who could worked his own little business: give and take. But I didn't want to risk it. Both the truck and the bus ran on gas, on chocks of wood, or on briquettes. But on the other hand, I had passes whenever I wanted them. The commandant and I were friends. At Christmas, New Year's, and Easter I gave him presents; not just anything, but in a cultured way—a gold cigarette case, a solid silver samovar. Misha got him a fantastic lamp, bronze and silver, with those statuettes: naked girls, real beauties, practically alive, you wanted to feel their titties . . .

"Of course, we had some losses at the plants—either through rejected material or because sometimes someone would take the goods and then not pay. But our profits were unbelievable! We lived high on the hog for over a year. And then came Stalingrad. And Soviet planes were flying overhead. The commandant said: 'Have to go back.' I managed to put away a few things. I sold the whole plant to two fences. They cleaned the place out, took all the lathes, the instruments, everything. I sold it cheap—forty thousand marks—in a hurry. Misha and I loaded our families in our buses —he had a bus, too. We loaded the truck with chocks, briquettes, and some other stuff, and set off. I had hoped to reach my wife's family in Zaporozhie, or Misha's family somewhere near Kiev. But the retreat was so fast that we couldn't go anywhere. Sheer panic! We hadn't even gotten as far as the Dnieper River when they threw us off our buses. The Germans are fascists, after all. They shouted '*Raus!*' and waved their machine guns around. I lost Misha at the river crossing. And all I held on to was my family and the truck. I saved them through luck and cleverness and because I didn't spare anything. I gave those fascists what marks I had, and gold bracelets, and rings, and silver spoons. I took the wheel myself. And thank God that some man taught me to shout when stopped, '*Polizei, SS Sonderkommando.*' Well, they were afraid of the SS and let me through. They let me cross the Prut River and therefore get across the border. I wept with joy there. Believe it or not, but I was always a patriot, even a patrician. What's the matter, don't you know that patrician means a real patriot? What do you mean that's wrong? Well, maybe I got it mixed up with Rumanian . . .

"All right, call it what you want, but I always loved and respected my homeland. And here we were in Rumania and I suddenly learned what breathing free was. What had I known before that? Labor discipline! Socialist competition! Sabotage! Shock labor! Fulfill the plan! Fulfill the counterplan! Fulfill another percentage! Then the war and the Germans. Well, one commandant or two treated me like a human. But all the rest were fascists, damn soldiers put their machine guns at your bellybutton: '*Russe, Schwein!*' They robbed me blind, we were lucky to be alive.

"But here everything was free. People lived however they wanted. And the countryside was heaven. Gardens, vineyards—such wealth just for the taking. We reached Bucharest. A beautiful city, with luxurious houses and rich stores. Everything piled high in the markets, especially all kinds of fruits. But the prices were decent. And when we traveled around, they practically gave it away in the villages. And I had a dream right away in my mind, well, just like the begum—this was a sure thing! I made a deal with a Rumanian—he had a vegetable stand—to get a pass from the police. I left him my wife, mother-in-law, and children as collateral—he gave me credit and I exchanged whatever marks and rubles I had left into Rumanian lei. I got behind the wheel and the two of us drove around the villages, buying up grapes, apples, pears, plums. We brought them in and sold them in a day. Well, there's nothing to talk about: a month later I had five trucks. I rented a garage and found a boyar to be my partner. A real intellectual, a lawyer, the highest chic. We don't have types like that here. A handsome man, pomade on his hair, you can smell his cologne a hundred paces away, has a gold toothpick. So he was a lawyer and his brother was a big shot in a ministry. They couldn't do the selling themselves. The lawyer spoke all the languages, German and French and Russian, too. Not very pure, but understandable. So we came to terms. They came in as partners, but secretly. I had my five trucks and the boyar brothers added another six. We set up a garage in their house. For all the dealings with the police, the authorities, and clients they had a procurer—that's like a secretary—called Mitru, a young fellow, but a dealer. He got from them and from me. He had a wife and a mistress, a house and a dacha—they call them villas—on the Black Sea. And he was always merry and did everything sort of jokingly, with a laugh and a song.

"Through my friendship with him I had twelve trucks by spring and bought myself a nice little house, not large but decent and furnished. And the boyars got their share, too, of course. From Mitru and me they made a lot more than from their law and ministry. They had two town houses in the city. They were more of an expense than profit. Well, I set up a restaurant in one, getting cheap peasant wine and simple but fresh food. I hired Gypsies with violins, tambourines, songs and dances. Every evening we made a full bag of lei. Enough for everyone. And in the other house, where the garage was, I set up a repair shop in the basement. To repair our vehicles and other people's. Profit again. And on the first floor a store —inexpensive village fruits, vegetables, grapes. The main occupant was a grocer who had helped me out when we started out. His name was on the sign. He almost wept, and told me that I was more than like a brother to him. He had been in business for ten years and all he had scraped together was enough for corn mush and wine. But with us he got his own house in one year and a store instead of a stand. And what a store—three windows, one with running water pouring from above to keep the fruit fresh.

"I began taking orders for shipping more than just fruit. I carried different freight both for companies and private individuals and the state. I employed drivers and mechanics and metalworkers—over twenty people, Rumanians, Russians, Moldavians, even two Jews. They hadn't been as exterminated in Rumania as in other countries; they managed to pay off

here and there, and the Rumanians are a kind people—they hid them from
the Germans. And the office was small again: including me, we were three.
The other two were a bookkeeper, a local Russian, elderly and very honest
—you could leave all your keys with him—a godly, churchgoing man, a
church warden; and a Rumanian secretary, a dark-haired beauty who could
type fast and knew shorthand and made the telephone calls. She understood Russian and was also my translator. And that was my staff. We
worked hard, to tell the truth, but we were free—no one was on our backs.
In Rumania people made big business deals, and right in the office, like in
a restaurant, they drank coffee or wine or cognac. And almost no paper-
work. If you say so, then do it, turn over the money, no receipt necessary
if you respect the person. In less than a year I had two million in the bank.
Understand—I had come with nothing, and in ten months I made two
million. There's your begum!

"And then the Soviets came—that is, our people. But I went on with
the business for almost a year after the war, until fall. I called myself Nikola
Nikolescu. The boyars did advise me to split—they promised to set me up
with their friends in Austria or even Italy. But I didn't want to leave my
cars, the house, the shop, the store—greed choked in my craw. I was a
dumb cluck. Everything seemed to stay the same in Rumania—the king,
the police, private enterprise. I transported various cargo for them, and for
the Soviets, too, and repaired their vehicles. I kept to the side, so that only
the drivers and mechanics dealt with them. But they got me nevertheless.
One senior lieutenant brought in an Opel to be repaired. And he seemed
like a simple, pleasant fellow. We talked and drank. I tried to talk with
difficulty in Russian, looking for words. He says: 'Where are you from?'
I say: 'Moldavia.' He was so fair, pug-nosed, a pure Russian you would
think. I didn't think of him in any other way. And then he goes and asks
me something in Moldavian. Well, I couldn't say boo or understand a word
of it. He seemed to laugh. And then two days later another lieutenant came
by for repairs, also with an Opel Captain. He brought vodka; we drank,
then he asked me to come look at a three-ton truck. He said: 'It needs an
overhaul. It doesn't go at all. It broke down not far from here, in the middle
of town on the boulevard.' I didn't want to go at first, but then I thought:
What is there to be afraid of in the middle of Bucharest, surrounded by
Rumanians? The police are Rumanians, and the boyars know me, we're
partners. I went, like a fool. And never came back. They shoved me into
an alley. Hit me so hard that I didn't even have time to shout. And tossed
me into a Studebaker. And the rest you know—ten years, and five years'
disenfranchisement.

"It's been three years—I still can't find out where my wife and children
are. And if they got any of my millions."

Anatolii M. worked as a fitter technician. He worked honestly, sensibly,
but he "didn't bust his gut."

"Let those who hope to get out early keep their nose to the grindstone. They can kill themselves. But I'm an experienced bird. I had a university education in prison camp, and did my graduate training in Vorkuta. And I know this for sure: the more you hope, the more it hurts when you're back with your nose in the shit. There's a golden rule: don't push to be first and don't be left last. Because in front they hit you in the forehead and behind they kick you in the ass. It's best in the middle. That's why they call it the golden mean."

Even in appearance he was—he tried to be—unnoticeable. He never started a conversation, he kept to himself in the cell, he didn't take part in discussing gossip and rumors, but read, darned, or napped with his earphones on.

He grew animated only in the spring, when they set up a volleyball court in the yard. They got a ball and the games began. Anatolii became captain of the Iron Will team. He played well, but his team always lost to the undisputed champions—the Falcons. Their wild and daring captain was the engineer Aleksandr K., a tall, round-faced "looker," an athlete. A native Muscovite, the son, grandson and I think the great-grandson of engineers, he graduated from the institute in the spring of '41. He kept asking to be sent to the front from the first day of the war, and his uncle the general helped him through the red tape. In August near Vyazma, he was surrounded and taken prisoner. He escaped twice, almost starved to death. And finally, he joined Vlasov.* He was commander of communications on the shore of the English Channel. In the summer of 1944 he was captured by the Americans. A Negro convoy soldier struck him with the butt of his rifle. He got mad, ran off, joined up with a German unit, and fought for a few more days. Then he found refuge with French peasants, who thought he had escaped from a German POW camp. He went east with the first echelon of repatriates. By then he had learned that his uncle had attained a very high position. In the processing camp he tried to insist on his rights, and demanded to be sent to Moscow as fast as possible. But they took him to prison, and the investigator informed him politely that he was to be tried for betraying his homeland and that he should be ashamed for dishonoring the glorious name of his ancient line. The great nobility, of which his grandmother was proud and which his parents did not like to recall, was once more an asset. His mother told him on a visit that his uncle was very angry, shouting that he was ready to shoot the traitor with his own hands, but still agreed to arrange things so that he could expiate his guilt in the most comfortable surroundings.

Aleksandr was given ten years and brought straight from Butyrki Prison

*General Andrei Andreevich Vlasov (1900–1946), a Soviet officer who was captured by the Germans in 1942 and who with their support led a Russian "liberation army" against the Soviet regime during World War II. After the war he was turned over to the Soviets by the Allies and executed for treason. (Translator's note).

to the sharashka. (A gifted inventor, he was one of the men released early, in 1951; after that, he avoided meeting his former prison comrades. He drank hard. And died young.)

He chose his volleyball team carefully and trained it rigorously. During the game he gave fierce, concentrated orders, as though on a battlefield. The Falcons usually won, and then he smiled condescendingly—it could be no other way. But any loss, even a dropped ball, could bring on a fit of frenzy: Aleksandr grew pale, his eyes glazed over, his mouth twitched uncontrollably. It seemed that he was capable of hating the miserable player, ready to beat him, kill him. If he himself missed, he either fell into a depression or he picked on the others even more.

Anatolii played with as much enthusiasm but not at all in that style. The team's name, Iron Will, was a joke based on the fact that his team continued to exist even though it usually lost and its members kept changing. Anatolii took anyone who wanted to join. Panin and Solzhenitsyn and I played with him several times. Our captain played daringly, easily, merrily, without acrimony. And that's how he trained us. He explained to Panin that he played beautifully, bravely, but he hit the ball too hard, not caring where it might go. He asked Solzhenitsyn not to scurry up and down the court, not to give orders instead of the captain, and not to intercept his partner's ball, worrying that he might miss it. And he rebuked me: "You're a born volleyball player—you have the height, the stroke, the jump. But your reactions are delayed. You're always a half step behind: you wave your arms when the ball's already behind you."

I left the team without glory. But the captain and I remained good friends.

Anatolii was a Muscovite, the son of a worker who became a master, a shop foreman; he finished grammar school in 1940 and studied at a technical institute, wanting to become a radio engineer. He was an active member of the Komsomol, secretary of the school organization, spent a lot of time on athletics—he ran, jumped, took part in citywide games. In June 1941 he went on vacation to his sister's in Grodno, wher her husband worked in construction.

"They had just begun building fortifications on the new border. My brother-in-law, an engineer, was there day and night. I didn't see him when I was there. On the third night we were awakened by gunfire. War! My sister and the children managed to get out. The families of our commanders were taken out immediately by truck. I rushed off to find the military recruiting station of the city committee of the Komsomol. I wanted to volunteer, get right into the action. But everyone was in a panic, no one knew where anything was. They collected a bunch of boys like me and sent us to dig antitank ditches and foxholes. We were still on our way when the Germans rolled into the city. The only weapon I had was a shovel."

Anatolii and the other POWs were taken west. He ended up in Belgium; first he worked in a mine, underground, and then as a metalworker and electrician. The Belgian workers sympathized with prisoners from the Red Army and brought them food and cigarettes.

Anatolii had studied English at the institute, and he remembered a few words from his school German. Having made friends with the Belgians, he soon spoke and wrote French. The soldiers guarding the prisoners of war—not very young reservists—often shouted at them crudely, were capable of poking them with a rifle butt, but they almost never interfered with their conversations and trade with the Belgians. Handy POWs used wire, lumps of coal, shards of glass, and sticks to make amusing trifles, Christmas tree decorations, and wall hangings. Some of their convoy soldiers even traded tobacco and canned foods for them. Anatolii drew "portraits" from life. The head of the convoy, an elderly asthmatic *Oberleutnant*, liked his drawing and paid for it with several packs of cigarettes and a bottle of beer.

Anatolii's Belgian friends helped him escape on a truck transporting goods to a local grocer. He left for Brussels, where he was expected by the brother of one of his new friends—the owner of a small shop where they repaired teapots, irons, hotplates, and radios.

The shop and the apartment were located in a small house on a quiet street. The owner had two apprentices working for him before the war. But they were drafted and then taken prisoner to Germany. The owner's friends got Anatolii the documents of a Belgian youth who had died of stomach ulcers. And he worked without hiding, creating an attractive window display, drew a sign, came up with clever decorations for the equipment; with a piece of linoleum, a cylinder, and homemade paints he manufactured humorous advertising leaflets, which he posted on other streets. The owner, his wife, and two daughters—the elder was finishing Gymnasium—came to love the sensible and cheerful worker. Two years later Anatolii married Cecile, and his father-in-law proclaimed him his partner.

The girl friends and classmates of his wife introduced Anatolii to underground members of the Resistance. He made two radios and a duplicator to print leaflets for them. When the Germans began their retreat, he worked with his new comrades to disarm the rear-guard commands of arsonists and miners—partisan sappers who mind certain buildings, roads, and bridges. Anatolii's unit took over a large warehouse of the German communications battalion. And as a present for his father-in-law, Anatolii drove up a truck filled with radio apparatus, and other equipment and instruments.

Not long before the victory, his son was born; they naturally called him Victor. The shop expanded quickly. They had to rent a nearby house. The old apprentices, who had returned from POW camp, were promoted to master technicians, and they helped find fifteen good workers of both sexes. They all got on well with their young boss.

"Basically, I became a Belgian. I often even thought in French—well,

1

1. The sharashka in Marfino
on the outskirts of Moscow;
formerly the church "Ease
My Sorrows"

2. Ivan Emelianovich
Bryksin

3. Gumer Akhatovich
Izmailov

4. Aleksandr Isaevich
Solzhenitsyn, as drawn by
Sergei Ivashov-Musatov, a
fellow prisoner

5. The author in the
Marfino sharashka, 1950

6   7

6. Dmitri Mikhailovich
Panin, 1960

7. Sergei Grigorievich
Kuprianov

8. Valentin Sergeevich
Martynov

9. Evgenii Arkadievich
Solomin

8   9

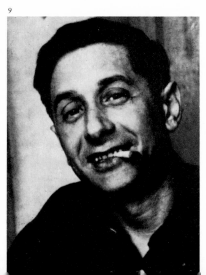

10

11

12

13

10. The author caricatured
by Alekseev; a birthday
present from friends in the
sharashka, April 9, 1952

11. Valentin Efimovich
Levin, military engineer,
third grade, January 1941

12. Maria (Musya) Zinger-
Levina

13. Inna Mikhailovna
Levidova, 1952 (During all
my years in prison, she sent
me letters, magazines,
poetry)

14. Nadezhda Kolchinskaya,
the author's wife, 1949

15. Their daughters, Maya
and Lena, 1948

16. Sofia Borisovna
Kopeleva, the author's
mother, 1950

17. Zinovii Yakovlevich
Kopelev, the author's father,
about 1954

14

15

16

17

18

18. The author in the
sharashka, 1948, drawn by
Viktor Denl, a prisoner

19

20

21

19. E.V. Semyonova,
Nikolai Semyonov, and
Natalya Reshetovskaya-
Solzhenitsyna, 1962

20. Evgenii Solomin with
his wife and daughter,
Ukhta, 1963

21. Igor Aleksandrovich
Krivoshein (in profile);
photograph by Igor Palmin

22

22. The author in the
sharashka, winter
1950–1951

when I was thinking about something near me, going on just then. But my memories were in Russian still. No, I didn't want to go home. My mother had died a long time ago. My father had started a new family long before the war. And my sisters and brother-in-law would only have trouble from a relative like me: a former prisoner, now a capitalist. I had never been interested in politics. Well, I studied what I had to and how I had to. I sang 'Broad is my native land,' and revered Comrade Stalin. And I joined the Komsomol consciously. Of course, my activities were more along the sports line. But, of course, I believed that socialism was marching from victory to victory, that all our temporary difficulties were mere piffle. And capitalism was tottering and dying, and so on. But prison camp and the war and my life in Brussels—how can I put it—had such a powerful effect on me that my brains were shaken up. Willy-nilly, I began remembering. How we used to stand in lines. How we lived hand to mouth. How in the communal apartments and in the barracks there were five or six to a room. I remembered other things, too—about the class struggle, about vigilance. We had a neighbor, an old Bolshevik. Under the tsar he had been sent off to hard labor, he'd fought in the Civil War; he held an important position on the city committee of the regional committee, but at home they didn't have an extra plate. All their wealth was in books. His son and I were in the same class; we dreamed together of running off to Spain, to the International Brigades. And then his father was taken away—an 'enemy of the people.' And then the mother—a wonderfully kind old woman. Worked in the library. And also a Bolshevik through and through. And then my pal was taken away—he wasn't even sixteen yet. And his sister, tiny. I got a letter from him from a colony in Kazakhstan. My mother was still alive then, sick. She was very scared. She wept and begged me not to respond or I and all of us would be arrested for having ties. Well, I didn't respond. There were other stories like that. I wanted to forget, but I kept remembering. In the camp and then later. In Brussels, life was not at all the way we had learned and read, not at all the way it was at home. Well, I decided to stay Belgian. I thought—sometime later I'd go visit Moscow, find out how my sisters and father were, visit my mother's grave. But later, much later . . . We lived well, happily, my wife and her family. In the fall—this was in 1946—I was walking in the daytime down the street and saw some Russian officers. One of them, a first lieutenant, was Mishka, an old classmate. He might not have noticed me, but I hailed him. Well, this and that. We talked. They were from some commission on former POWs and free Soviet citizens. Helping them return.

"I told them briefly about myself. And told them I wanted to stay the way I was—with my wife and son. They laughed: 'You've become a factory owner. From the Komsomol to capitalism.' But without rancor; they even seemed envious. They asked if I didn't want to drop a line to my family in Moscow. They had opportunities, without any red tape, whereby no one would find out. We agreed to meet that evening in a fancy restaurant. They explained that they weren't permitted to go just any-where—they had to go to one or two of the most dignified establishments. I arrived as we had agreed. There was another man with them, a captain. He said that he was leaving for Moscow that night and would take a letter for me. Well, I immediately wrote a short note, gave him the address of my father and youngest sister. I wrote that I was alive and well but living another life and asked them to understand and forgive me. And I asked them to write at least once or send a message with the comrade—the captain said he would be returning soon—telling me how they were and about the other relatives.

"He took the note, wrote down my address and telephone number in his book. We were drinking and eating. We drank to victory, to the homeland, to our families. They laughed that this was the first time they ever drank with a capitalist, especially a former Komsomol. And I replied that I would definitely support the Belgian Komsomol and Communist Party, and when I made a million francs I would return to Moscow. Then we got ready to leave. I realized I was drunk. My legs were rubbery. They said: 'Let's take the side exit, our car is there, we'll drive you home.' We went into the alley and all I remember is being hit on the head. I came to in the car. We were driving. My head ached. A terrible taste in my mouth. Unfamiliar officers on either side of me. The captain was in front. And I was wearing a military greatcoat with epaulets and a cap. I wanted to ask a question, but the one on the right punched me in the stomach: 'Shut up, motherfucker! One word and we kill you!'

"I don't remember how long we traveled or where we stopped. By evening we arrived in some German town. A large courtyard, soldiers walking around. They brought me to a cellar: 'Strip.' They took my papers, money, watch, pen. Even the picture of my wife and son. They shoved me into a cell. There were Germans and Russians in there. Most of them POWs and some criminals. The supervisor gave me a piece of black bread—full of roughage and spotted with mildew. And a tin can of wheat gruel. I took a sip and almost threw up. But it was then that I fully comprehended it: 'Hello, homeland!' "

Nikolai and Anatolii were the first capitalists I ever met.

Walther R., an engineer and doctor, worked in the chemical lab: he prepared radio ceramics. The chief couldn't praise him enough. "You couldn't find another like him with a lamp in daylight. I think he only lives for his work. He keeps inventing new compounds; he constructs kilns himself and goes into the machine shop himself to do it. And he keeps testing new methods. Every day he improves something. He's a capitalist, you know, but such a hard worker—our Stakhanovites could learn a thing or two from him. To look at him, you'd say a skinny old man, a breeze could blow him over, almost nothing to hold body and soul together. But he's double-sinewed when it comes to work. Once he sits down in the morning, he doesn't straighten his back all day. Sometimes I have to remind him ten times to go have lunch. My other old man, Fritz, is also assiduous, and he's also a capitalist—but he's Walther's second fiddle, an assistant. And he listens and obeys him. Walther comes up with ideas and gives orders, and the other 'jawohls' him: '*Jawohl, jawohl, Herr Doktor . . . sehr gut, Herr Doktor.*'"

His laboratory head, Evgeniia Vasilievna, did not trust her own German and called me in several times to translate Dr. R.'s new proposals when she discussed them in the laboratory. That's how I got to know him.

He was very thin, which made him seem taller. An elongated, thin, elderly pink face, almost without wrinkles, a gray crewcut, intense light-blue eyes, a thin, strong mouth. His smiles were rare, miserly. But he didn't seem huffy or grim or sad, merely concentrating seriously. He spoke with a light but noticeable Austrian accent.

In 1945 he began working in a large chemical laboratory near Moscow, under contract. He spoke kindly of his colleagues there. "Professor Ki-tai-go-rodsky is a very good chemist. His foam glass is a very interesting invention. It presents a multitude of possibilities. In the West, of course, he would be a millionaire. A good chemist and a good person."

In 1945, Dr. R. managed to find his relatives by mail: his daughter and her husband and his younger son were in Vienna, his older son in Switzerland. Through them he asked the Austrian government to consider him a citizen of Austria—from 1919 to 1939 he had been a citizen of Czechoslovakia—and he received an affirmative reply. His contract was up in 1950.

"Professor Ki-tai-go-rodsky offered me another contract for another five years. Another manager came and asked me to see an even higher administrator. They offered me a higher salary, five thousand instead of three, promised me a new large apartment, promised to send me to a resort in the Crimea or the Caucasus: in the five years there I had only taken two weeks off. I lived in the woods in a nice little house, called a dacha. Good food, fishing . . . But I hadn't seen my sons in almost ten years, and my daughter and grandchildren, in five. I did not want to sign a new contract. I'm a citizen of the Austrian Republic, a sovereign neutral state. They already had an embassy in Moscow. I wanted to go to my family. I had to settle several estate and financial questions. Professor Kitaigorodsky understood me. He was sorry—we had worked well together, he liked my methods—but he sympathized. The most important chief talked to me politely but with irritation. And he kept arguing: 'Think about it, think; you must stay here, things will be good for you, otherwise you may cause trouble for yourself.' But I didn't understand that. What harm could there be in going back to your family? A month before my contract was up I went to Moscow to the embassy. I spoke with the ambassador himself, filled out some forms, papers, came up with a date for my departure.

"I came back and the next day I was called from the laboratory, and two officers took me to Moscow, to Lubyanka. The investigation was short. I told them what I had said in the embassy and what I had written on my application. And the investigator told me that I shouldn't have revealed where I had worked those five years and what I had been doing. I replied: 'I work in a civilian scientific institution, I have no part in any secret projects, and besides I did not give any details in either the forms or in my conversation with the ambassador.' During the investigation another officer came to see me, apparently a very important one. My investigator, a lieutenant colonel, spoke to him as his subordinate. He offered me another contract in the same laboratory. I refused flatly. He grew angry. He threatened that things would be bad. Then the investigator made the same offer a few more times. But I couldn't accept—and I couldn't believe the threats. For I wasn't guilty of anything. I worked honestly according to the terms of my contract, I hadn't broken any laws. I was certain of my righteousness. But then they took me to another prison. The duty officer of the guards came with a translator and read me the text of the sentence from a piece of cigarette paper. That was how I learned I was sentenced to twenty-five years of espionage.

"But that was absurd! First of all, I never did any spying. Second, I'm almost sixty. How can I be sentenced to a quarter of a century of prison. I can't possibly live that long. Totally absurd!"

I helped Dr. R. write a few complaints and appeals to the Procurator General, to the Presidium of the Supreme Soviet, and personally to His Excellency Generalissimo Stalin. And so our friendship developed, so to speak. We took walks alone or with his colleague and assistant, Dr. Fritz B., a sharp-faced, milky-gray, stoop-shouldered old man, extremely polite. Whatever the question, he replied with a courteous smile and even a giggle. The owner of one of the largest chemical pharmaceutical firms, he had been a member of the Nazi Party since 1930, for which he had been sentenced to twenty-five years.

"All I did was pay the dues. It was my sons-in-law and youngest son who dragged me into it. They assured me that their Führer would save Germany from a crisis, from the Versailles dictates. My son is an idealist, a romantic. And my older son-in-law is a businessman, and he maintained that the party would help the firm succeed, and I never understood anything in politics. I love chemistry, music, and wood carving. I don't think there's anything in the world greater or more beautiful than Bach . . . Ah, what a collection I had of ancient wood carvings. Almsot all of it was lost. A direct hit by a one-ton bomb. The fire reached the cellars where I had everything hidden. There were statues from the twelfth and thirteenth centuries, carved cabinets, trunks, marvelous boxes, utensils. Priceless treasures. I regret them more than the ruined and confiscated factories. Yes, some of our enterprises survived. In the American and French zones. I'll never see them. But I hope that my grandsons are taken care of. My older son-in-law was killed at the front, my son is a prisoner of war . . . Our firm could bring a lot of good not only to Germany. Before the war I had contacts with all the continents; and we exported several millions' worth to Russia every year."

Dr. R. recalled that he, too, had traded with many countries. Of course, the Soviet Union bought less than the others, sporadically, and he thought, only laboratory vessels and industrial glass.

"But to all the European countries, America, and Japan, I sent dozens of tons: sets of dishes of every kind—formal, elaborate, everyday, toy. My factory is still working. The Czechs nationalized it. First they wanted me to stay on as owner and the state as co-owner. The Czechs hid me from your people in a forest lodge. Among my workers were both Czech nationalists and Communists. But we had good relations, almost familylike. The Prague Communists helped yours, they put them on the trail. They came after me in the forest, a whole truckload of soldiers. They took me to the airport and straight to Moscow. And there they announced that my factory had been nationalized, and they gave me a choice: a contract or prisoner of war camp. This was right after the war. Austria didn't exist then. That's when I agreed.

"I hope that the factory is working well now. Real craftsmen remained. I'm certain that they will maintain the good name of our firm. It has existed since 1701. The same age as the Prussian kingdom. And it has outlived it. The first owner-manager was my great-grandfather's great-grandfather, a glassblower and potter. In our area, they made glass as early as the thirteenth-fourteenth centuries. He worked as an apprentice in Italy—Venice—and Nuremberg. He returned to our village a master. We celebrated the anniversary of the founding every year on the first Sunday in September. Yes, next month it will be exactly two hundred and fifty years. My children will celebrate, naturally. They've started a small shop in Styria. And they've begun manufacturing some dishes and radio ceramics and industrial glass."

Through the prison supply clerk I got a box of good cigars. And with the permission of the foreman of the gardeners I picked a bouquet of asters and chrysanthemums. On the morning of the anniversary I formally congratulated Dr. R. as he came in from his exercises. Whatever the weather, rain or snow, he exercised for at least fifteen minutes upon arising and then ran and jumped in place.

He thanked me in a few words, with calm dignity. He repeated, "I'm touched, I'm very touched," a few times, in his usual low, slightly creaky voice, but with an unusually soft, slightly vibrating tone.

That evening on our walk he began a detailed story.

"Bohemian glass has been praised for many centuries, and part of that fame is due to our family. My grandfather was proud of it, and my father, and I hope so will my grandsons. This has nothing to do with national pride. This pride we share with the Czechs. My family is Austrian. We called ourselves Bohemian Germans. The Nazis called us *Sudeten,* but I didn't recognize that. I'm a Bohemian German or simply a Bohemian. In our family we never had problems or hostility with the Czechs. Perhaps that's because in our area the Czechs are Catholics, too. There were no religious arguments.

"I had over a thousand workers and technicians in my factory. Approximately four fifths were permanent workers. You might say they were related to our factory, to our family. They lived in their own houses. The village is conveniently situated in the foothills—beautiful scenery, healthful air . . . In two hundred and fifty years we never had a strike or a single conflict with the workers. Maybe that is why we suffered less than others from economic crises. True, the family chronicles do have sad notations. In the beginning and middle of the last century many European countries raised the customs duty on Bohemian crystal, and German and Russian factories began luring away our masters. However, our family survived that. And as far back as my father personally remembered, the family knew no anxieties. For even in economically troubled times people buy dishes for themselves and as gifts—for weddings, anniversaries, birthdays. And they always celebrate Christmas, and there are always buyers for toys. Neither my father nor I ever had to fire workers or cut back production. Naturally, we had a union. And there were left-wing young workers. They celebrated May Day. And red flags were seen on other days. But political problems never interested me.

"We knew many of the workers personally. And we met with many not only at the factory and in church, but with our families. Our office knew the birthdays and other important dates in the lives of all our workers. I, my wife, and my sons were often asked to be godparents. And on our birthdays the doors were never shut in our house. Entire families came with flowers, homemade gifts. And naturally, as is our custom, choirs sang congratulatory cantatas. In the summer several tables were set, and we feasted and danced until dark. In bad weather or on cold days and in winter my children and our servant offered wine and cakes to our guests on trays. Only the family and a few invited guests—relatives, close friends—sat at the table. It was not our custom to invite workers or employees to the family table: we couldn't accommodate them all, and selecting one or two meant insulting the others.

"The factory was inherited but never by primogeniture. The owner had to name one successor—this could be his son or a nephew, son-in-law, or adopted son. The only requirement was that he be honest, sensible, and generally a worthy man. And that he know and love the work. I was third of four brothers. Father had taken us all to the factory as soon as we could walk. He introduced us to the masters, the workers. He encouraged our playing glassblower. But my older brothers weren't interested. One became an architect, the other a physician. Only my younger brother and I began studying chemistry as our father wanted. And while still students, we had to work at the factory. That was an inviolable tradition in the family: the owner had to start at the bottom. Coming home for vacation, we'd haul sacks, mix the clay, do all the errands the masters wanted. They knew at the factory that we weren't to receive any breaks. And we were paid just like all the other unskilled workers. And we didn't dare be late in the morning by even a minute or leave before the others for lunch. After that first summer we had to work our way through all the areas and shops. And the masters who trained us were more demanding of us than of their other apprentices. Father said: 'This is demanded both by family tradition and the real interests of the firm. The future owner must know the work thoroughly.'

"By the third year my younger brother began reminding him of other traditions—our grandfathers had gone to study in Paris and Dresden and Venice. He was tired of the same old shops and the same old people. And then the war broke out. We three oldest were drafted. I was promoted to captain of the mountain artillery. I was heavily wounded in the Abruzzi. I limped for a long time afterward. I went home. Mother and Father had aged a lot. My second brother died—he had contracted typhus in his own field hospital. My oldest brother was a POW in Italy. And my younger, my colleague, freed of military service, had married a painter, developed ties with her family—Venetian businessmen—and bought and sold stocks; he didn't even want to hear about our factory, 'that crow's nest in the sticks.' But my very first questions to my father were about the factory, the people. Some of our fellows had served in my regiment. This was the first time I had seen him so agitated. He was a very controlled person, no sentimentality, none of that Austrian *Gemütlichkeit*—he was cool, even severe. But scrupulously fair. He had never struck or slapped any of the children, but he had never once hugged any of the boys, either. He sometimes did pat our sister on the head or kiss her forehead. But if he praised one of us, he would slap us on the shoulder, and if we were parting for a long time, he would shake hands. But this time, hearing my questions, he grew so excited tht it seemed he wanted to embrace me—there were tears in his eyes. And he said formally—I had never heard such words or that tone from him before—'My son, you have made me extremely pleased by your concern, I am happy to see before me a worthy heir to our ancestors.' He had prepared his will earlier: the factory went to me; my brothers and sister got specific amounts of cash and also equal shares of ten to twenty percent of the annual profits. The percentages depended on the level of profit. If it was too low, their share would not be paid at all.

"Father died soon after. He was finished off by the fall of the empire. No, he wasn't political or a nationalist, our family never cared for that. In the Austro-Hungarian Empire, enlightened people and good Catholics had a certain supernational breadth of world view. The military and the bureaucrats served the state, the crown, the dynasty. The industrialists, the scholars, and the businessmen worked for the common good of all the tribes of the empire. Only empty fools, demagogues, greedy or ignorant provincials tried to glorify their local interests, their language, their customs and myths above others. My grandfathers and my father revered the emperor, God's anointed. We spoke and thought in German. But our Czech neighbors and Czech workers were just as close to us as our fellow tribesmen, and much closer to us than the northern Prussians or even the neighboring Saxons. Closer, more understandable, and more *simpático*. And if we did have a national dislike, then it was for the Prussians. They were the ones who destroyed Austria. My grandfather was wounded in 1866 by a Prussian bullet near Königgrätz. And during that war even our most extreme conservatives hated Wilhelm. And even many socialists liked our little old *'kaundka'** Franz Josef out of family feeling.

"Of course I read *Schweik*. A jolly book, even though quite undignified in places. However, there is no hatred for the emperor in it. Just not enough respect. There was that. Have you read Joseph Roth—*Radetzky's March?* He's a Jewish Austrian of Galician origin. And he wrote with such love about our homeland, the dynasty. No, the old Austria-Hungary was much much better than the way it's depicted by satirists. Better than Prussian Germany. And now, after the Nazi thousand-year empire, that should be apparent to everyone.

"What did you say? 'What we have, we don't cherish; when we lose it, we weep.' A wise proverb. Yes, that's just it. But life in Czechoslovakia wasn't bad either. Yes, the ancient national contradictions became more acute there. Naturally, the Czechs had a completely just dislike of the Deutschmaster's imperial powers. And the Slovaks had a right to be insulted at having Hungarian authorities and landed gentry. But just dislikes and ancient hurts often give rise to blind vengeance and irrational chauvinist pretensions. Sigmund Freud, a great scholar even though the Nazis denounced him, wrote about the inferiority complex. And it's that complex that gives birth to chauvinist prejudice. And to a maniacal hatred of foreigners. That's how the German hatred for the French, anti-Semitism, and disdain for Slavs came about. Yes, yes, you're right, those are also Austrian diseases. Hitler was Austrian. A typical Viennese plebeian, a bourgeois turned lumpen. From the Bohemian dregs. But the Czechs had their own maniacal chauvinists. And it was among my countrymen that those 'white stockings' developed—the *Sudeten* Nazis. Even in our village before Munich, flags with swastikas were to be seen. Some young fellows ran around in white stockings, shouting the 'Horst Wessel Song.' But in our family and among our friends and the core workers of our factory there wasn't a single Nazi. I don't know what the new Austria will be like. I hope that it won't turn completely red or black. And of course, not brown. I would like it to become multicolored. In the old way—red-white-red—and rainbow-colored in a new way. Without the Prussian blackness. Monotony is

*K und K = König und Kaiser.

always bad. In art and in life. And for countries and nationalities it's dangerous. Now your great country—I always considered Russia a country of great culture and great spirit—suffered badly from color monotony."

There was another real capitalist in our sharashka, Gustav H., a Berliner, the owner of a small transformer factory. The son of a worker, he had spent twenty years himself working for Siemens. Before 1930 he had voted Communist; losing his job, he decided to start his own place—his relatives helped him out—and from a tiny shop that rewound and repaired transformers he created a small but substantial plant in just a few years. He exported transformers to the Soviet Union and to America, he supplied the Wehrmacht and aviation. For this he was sentenced to ten years as a war criminal.

Red-faced, stocky, and solid, he was sociable, jovial, knew a multitude of dirty poems and dirty jokes. He had no interest in other forms of literature. He didn't want to discuss politics.

"It's like hammering empty straw. But sometimes you can make a strong rope for a scaffold out of straw."

He worked just as fiercely as our other capitalists. Once he came to me, angry and upset.

"Please, I'm asking you to help me. Here, translate this. I've written a petition, a protest. It's disgusting! I've developed a completely original system for winding compact transformers. We never had anything like it at our factory. And here I've done it all from beginning to end. And I've been robbed—two others have been named the inventors. At first I agreed, fool that I am, to have them as co-inventors. First they added the boss, a captain. I couldn't argue there. He's the chief, an officer. But the second one was another prisoner, the engineer Sergei R., but he's not a political prisoner—he stole state funds. Other Russian colleagues told me that he's a stoolie. They explained to me that I'm a practician and he's a theoretician, that I do everything by eye, by intuition, and he calculated it all. They said the patent had to be in all three names. But today I learned that the captain got a medal and Sergei got a bonus of three hundred rubles and the first category of nourishment, while I got only a hundred rubles and the second category. I was told that in the report of the work of our shop I'm not mentioned at all. This is a monstrous inequity, this is vile swinishness! I thought, I worked night after night. I invented it all by myself and calculated it myself. They say I don't have a diploma. I wouldn't wipe my ass with their diplomas. I wouldn't take engineers like that uniformed fellow and Sergei as apprentices: they're lazy, they gab, and they make a mess . . . I've written a protest. I don't care if they send me to the camps, the mines, Siberia! I work here conscientiously. I follow orders like a soldier. I've never been criticized, only praised. But I have my self-respect, my work honor. I will not put up with such injustice, such humiliation."

I translated the complaint, having convinced him to tone down the very harsh expressions. He was raised a category, and the chief confirmed his authorship in the presence of the entire shop. It didn't go beyond this oral confirmation. Gustav continued working as conscientiously, but he became glummer and quieter.

9

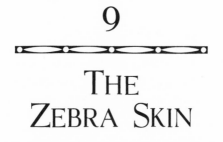

THE
ZEBRA SKIN

The soul should also have a skeleton that will not permit it
to bend under the slightest pressure, that will give it resistance
and strength in action and counteraction. The skeleton of the
soul must be faith (religious in the direct sense of "convictions"), but the kind that people are willing to die for, that is not
subject to the sophistry of immediate practical considerations,
that tells a person its "I can't." And not I can't because something is either beneficial or harmful practically, from the point
of view of immediate gain, but because there is something in me
that will not bend in that direction.

—Vladimir Korolenko, *Diary*, December 5, 1917

Old prisoners have a saying: "Our life is like a zebra skin—black stripes
alternate with white; when it's black, bear it, don't droop, and when it gets
light, don't relax!"

In the summer of 1950 the black stripes thickened. Panin and Solzhenitsyn were taken away. My phonoscopic work wasn't going well, and my
related hopes dimmed. My girl friend was sick, but she had time to tell me
that her husband was returning from a long business trip and she was "so
afraid, so afraid."

Technician S., because of whom I had been called in by Shikin, had been
sticking close to me persistently since then. He either told me dirty jokes
or kept trying to box, waving his gangly, angular arms. One morning in
the cell, as we were making our beds, S. "playfully" crept up behind me
(bent over the bed) and pushed me so that I struck my forehead against
the wall over the hot-air furnace. The pain and the unexpectedness of the
attack angered me. I whirled and stuck my fist in his grinning mug.

He fell on the neighboring cot. "What's the matter with you? I was just
joking, and you start fighting, you viper. Kike face!"

He grabbed an empty soda bottle standing on the night table, but I
picked up a boot and before they pulled us apart I managed to hit him once
or twice on the hand holding the bottle.

Vitkevich, who was first to get between us, said that I shouted all kinds
of things that I didn't remember—I called S. a fascist, a stoolie.

The next day we were moving to a camp that had been emptied of its
last prisoners of war. In a small rectangular area that bordered the grounds

of the sharashka stood two or three small houses—a dining room, a steam-bath, warehouses, an office, the guardhouse, and two rows of round ply-wood yurts, each pair connected by short, wooden entryways.

The head of the prison, a phlegmatic lieutenant colonel, who observed us as we dragged our stuff over, called me over. "You had a fight with someone in your cell yesterday. I'm not asking you who started it or who finished it. You should be ashamed. Serious grown-up men. You're not boys, you're not thieves, but you fight, you hit with boots. You should be punished severely for that. The cooler. But we have urgent work here at the sharashka. And I don't have a cooler on the premises, so that you could spend nights there and do your work during the day. I'm announcing your punishment: you're being demoted back to the second category. You are deprived of your next scheduled meeting. And I'm also issuing a strict warning . . . the next time the punishment will be more severe."

The two yurts of the first category had ordinary cots. All my friends moved in there. But Vitkevich, who was still new, and I were sent to a distant yurt, filled with wooden four-tiered bunk beds. I had been in the first category for over half a year, smoked Kazbeks, got eggs for breakfast and two pork chops instead of one for lunch. But as punishment I had to return to Belomors and wheat cereal—"the blonde."

Abram Mendelevich was unhappy.

"You're so uncontrolled. A fight—just like that! No, I believe you, I believe you. That S. is a highly antipathetic person. But he's very highly esteemed. You can count masters like him here on the fingers of one hand. And he knows how to sell himself, when to toady. Compare Sergei Grigorievich, Valentin Sergeevich, or Evgenii Arkadievich—what fine specialists! Much more experienced than S. and more intelligent. And are just as skillful. But they are treated significantly worse. Because they argue and always make it clear that they see flaws in the management. And when S. thinks something up, he fawns: 'I think I understood your thought, I thought through everything you told me, I was convinced that you had a great idea and here, it seems to be working out well.'

"But the others are always looking for an argument: 'Now you say one thing, but I came up with something else, and look which is better.' And Valentin Martynov gabs like a parrot. In technology, you might say, he's a mature talent, but in life, he's just a kid. That's why he ended up in the cooler. Lucky for him the comrades and I managed to keep him from being sent away permanently. That's what Solzhenitsyn was taken away for—he kept insisting on doing things his way. Anton Mikhailovich appreciates and values, but only to the point when he feels personally rebuffed. It's lucky for you that you're considered irreplaceable. You're the only reader of visible speech in the Soviet Union. But the important thing is that he likes you, he says: 'He's eccentric, sort of a holy fool, but he's useful for the project.' And I hope that everything isn't lost with the phonoscopy, even though Foma Fomich is very angry. He was told off at the MGB.

He'll probably have you on the carpet, too. Keep in mind that he's very crude, and I advise, no, I ask, that you control yourself, don't drop any careless words. Or it might end badly."

Anton Mikhailovich's voice in the telephone receiver was cold, distant: "Come by. Immediately."

He was sitting at his desk, going through papers. And Foma Fomich Zhelezov stood by the long table; he barely nodded at me. "Sit down," he said. He continued to stand and look down at me with dull eyes that seemed to express nothing.

"What came over you to start a fight?! Have you forgotten where you are? Maybe you think this is a rest home for hooligans? I do not wish to hear explanations. And your work is fucking shit. You've invented all this phonovision and sound reading. It's fifty percent wool over the eyes of the most blatant kind. You managed one security task so-so. And you covered yourself with shit with the second, so that the whole institute is covered with shit. The security officers laugh at us as though we're fools. We're lucky it wasn't considered sabotage. Because you wouldn't be able to prove that you didn't lie consciously, that you weren't trying to cover for spies, enemies of the people. You couldn't have proved it! Your work is shit, you permit yourself forward conversations with the security officers. You lie shamelessly. And now hooliganism— Silence! I'm not asking you, I know."

The most frightening thing was that he wasn't shouting. He spoke almost indifferently, in a monotone. His voice sometimes rose to a squeal, but he didn't shout or bark once.

Anton Mikhailovich kept trying to interject comments, sometimes "reproachful ones" directed at me: "How could you— I didn't believe it, when I heard— Disgusting." Sometimes placating ones: "Foma Fomich, this was the first incident— The atmosphere there must be unhealthy— And scientific work can bring on nervous exhaustion."

"Scientific? All he's learned is to pretend to be a scientist, and he grabs a boot like a vagabond. He's shit, not a scientist. A hooligan and a shit. Do you yourself understand that you're shit, or don't you?"

My throat contracted in dreary, impotent hatred and fear, vile, paralyzing fear.

"Why are you silent? Don't you understand what I'm saying?"

"I don't understand how you can . . . insult a person who can't argue with you."

For a second he looked at me with the same silence, the same dullness. A second of terror.

"A person? He pretends he's a person?! If he dared argue, tomorrow he'd be shipped off to the back of beyond. To the uranium mines. In six months his beard would fall out, all his hair and his teeth, too. And then he'd die like a rat. You don't appreciate the conditions that we've created for you here—you've grown insolent. Playing scientist . . . Anton Mikhailovich, who gave him permission to wear a beard? He's the only one in the entire place. It's intolerable. We know what a beard means with them—vows! Anti-Soviet vows!"

He spoke only to Abram Mendelevich now: "And you, a major [that is, Abram Mendelevich], defended him, you didn't even allow him to be sent to the cooler. Now, you say there's new work, that you need him. I'm granting you a concession for the last time. Let him be grateful to you, and let him know whom he owes and for what. Let him justify himself with his work. Next time it's the uranium mines for sure. And now he's to be reduced a category, until he proves he's worthy. And he must shave that beard today. He's shown off enough. You will report to me."

And to me, over his shoulder: "You may go."

Lunch had started. The new dining room was also in the camp. After eating, I went to the yurt, took a pair of scissors from Jalil and a razor, and scraped off my beard, which was still all black then, with only a few gray hairs.

To the amazed questions and gibes I replied curtly: "The boss's orders! I was sick of it! Hard to wash up . . . I felt like it . . . Get off my back . . ."

My girl friend stared at me in wordless fright. When I told her about it that evening, she clucked over me, asked if they wouldn't keep a closer watch on me now. Then she started to console me. "Oh, now it's like having another lover. What's your name, mister? Don't get fresh, or I'll tell the bearded one, and he'll hit you with his boot."

The new project, to which Anton Mikhailovich referred in order to spare me more severe punishment, was an acoustical study of fine wire intended for recording sound in bugging devices. This wire was manufactured in another sharashka, and chemists coated it with a special compound.

The chemistry laboratory was headed by Captain Evgeniia Vasilievna K., the daughter of intellectual merchants and a former investigator of the industrial section of the NKVD.

Panin had been at school with her older sister—"they were both beautiful, and of irreproachable morality, of the highest order. I can't understand how such a young lady could have turned into a Chekist."

She was still good-looking. Intense gray eyes, reddish brown hair parted in the middle and drawn into a round bun in back. Her face, though grown coarse, was still pretty. But her mouth, with its perpetual cigarette, was compressed into a cruel line. Her figure had gotten rather bulky, heavy around the hips. Her legs were a bit too short, but well proportioned, muscular, and she strode heavily, solidly, like a man.

She had been widowed a long time ago, was bringing up two children who were finishing school. She did not mince words with certain prisoners who worked in the chemical lab or with the free young women employees.

"What are you staring at? I can see what you're looking at! Clara, adjust your coat! And you'd better console yourself with masturbation."

She liked the looks of Sergei. She would take him into her office in the evenings, complaining that she was starved for affection.

He used to say: "She looks so rough, like a pushy bitch, a female tank. But it turns out she's unlucky, unhappy, falls in love easily . . . But she's awfully insatiable."

She also had a need for ordinary friendship, for serious "heart-to-heart" discussions. Zhen-Zhen, who worked in the chemistry lab, became her platonic friend and Party mentor. Preparing for political studies, she conferred with him, "an old Party member and educated Marxist."

But he was unhappy with his life in the sharashka. His specialty was shipbuilding. In the war years, after Solovki,* he was put in a sharashka, where he constructed submarines, first on the Volga, then in Baku. Released in 1947, he worked on a wharf in Rybinsk, had time to marry. (His first wife was shot in 1937.) A year later he was arrested again. The investigator filled out the usual protocol on "determination of identity." When the suspect asked about the case, the charge, the investigator shrugged in irritation.

"You're an adult. Do you read the papers? Then why do you ask? You should understand."

There were no more interrogations. The OSO sentenced him again to ten years under the same article and same paragraphs: 58-8 (terrorism), 10 (anti-Soviet propaganda), and 11 (anti-Soviet organization)—the usual "Leningrad selection."

In the chemistry laboratory he supervised all the electrotechnology, was in charge of the documentation of the experiments, and designed kilns for firing small ceramics.

The coating for the sound-recording wire was prepared by prisoner F., a doctor of physical sciences, a former co-worker of S. L. Vavilov, the president of the Academy of Sciences.

F. had been sentenced for "high treason and espionage" to twenty-five years, and he had been brought to the sharashka straight from Lubyanka. At first, he was afraid of everyone. Of medium height, stoop-shouldered, swarthy, with poor vision—he wore very thick glasses—full-lipped, and with a marked Jewish accent, he gave everyone a badgered look: "Don't. Please, don't. Don't ask. I don't know anything. Please, don't. Forgive me, I don't remember a thing. Which article? I don't remember. Yes, yes, twenty-five years. Excuse me, please . . . excuse me, let me pass. No, no, I can't. I don't know, don't . . . Please . . ."

They dubbed him Br'er Rabbit. Soon after his arrival we had a bath day.

*A group of islands in the White Sea with the Solovetskii Monastery, one of the first forced-labor camps after 1917. (Translator's note.)

Three times a month we washed under hot showers in a stone shed not far from the guardhouse and washed our laundry there at the same time.

When Br'er Rabbit shuffled under the shower, the general rowdy chatter quieted down for a minute. His back, shoulders, buttocks, and thin calves were striped and blotched with dark blue, almost black, and fading reddish ridges.

Someone tried to find out: "Where did they do that to you? You wouldn't confess for a long time, eh?"

He grimaced under the stream of water and whispered, almost crying: "Please don't . . . It's nothing . . . Please . . . !"

But others stopped them. "Leave the man alone, idiots! Can't you see for yourselves?"

In the following months and years Br'er Rabbit did not become more sociable. He went on walks rarely; he hurried back to the laboratory and his desk from the dining room. Zhen-Zhen and Jalil, who worked near him, and his chief, Evgeniia Vasilievna, said that he was a very well-educated and talented physical chemist. He worked primarily on the phenomenon of fluorescence, developing glowing coatings for measuring equipment and for televisions. He labored with frenzied diligence.

When the first variants of the sound-recording wire were prepared, I had to check the degree of intelligibility and recognizability of recorded voices. Sergei created a new attachment for the analyzer that permitted making sound pictures from wire.

The device, loaded with rolls for two three-hour recordings, fitted into a case about the size of ten matchboxes. The most difficult part was getting rid of stray pickup, "cross talk," on the recordings. The more coils—that is, the longer the recorded conversation—the more persistently the sounds were jumbled. And a few days later it was even more difficult to listen to. Some words sounded against a background of others, which had been pronounced later. For more than a year the chemists searched for newer compounds that would make the wire sensitive enough yet at the same time sufficiently isolated and protected from pickup.

New coating methods were constantly being developed. And each time we had to do acoustic testing "by ear" with the articulation team and visually with the sound pictures.

Br'er Rabbit worried, lost weight, and when responding to questions from the bosses muttered almost inarticulately: "Have to test more. Yes, yes, please. I'll try. Of course, I must. It doesn't depend on us. We need another core."

Evgeniia Vasilievna pitied him and fiercely argued with Anton Mikhailovich and Abram Mendelevich that in her department both chemistry and physics were at their peak and they had to improve the manufacture of the wire itself.

And we were being pestered by the designers. They were supposed to develop a device so small that it could be placed into a car or a hotel room unnoticed. The acousticians had to come up with a circuit that would be activated only at the sound of a voice and not by footsteps, the shuffle of a broom, or street noises. Sergei began working on a switch that responded only to speech. But the main obstacle was the requirement for small size.

Anton Mikhailovich at first persistently asked: "What's new today? Well, how's the new coating? You haven't gotten rid of the echo yet? Well, come on, don't drag it out!" But gradually he grew cool to the unyielding wire.

I don't know the eventual fate of these developments. They were turned over to another sharashka, along with all our materials.

"But we still won't bury our phonoscopy. Just the reverse. But this is strictly between us."

Abram Mendelevich came in joyously excited and spoke in a friendly, confidential tone: "They're creating a new institute. I had wanted to develop our laboratory into a section. But Anton Mikhailovich considers something else more efficient. He said—you know, how he likes to joke a bit—'I want to follow the old peasant tradition of setting up the oldest sons. Let them farm on their own.' He says 'like a peasant,' but actually he's a lord, a bourgeois. He can't stand rivalry or comradely competition. Well, let him! The better for us. The Directorate has already prepared the orders. I will be named head of the new institute, and Vasilii Nikolaevich will be my deputy. Another ten free employee engineers and technicians from here will be transferred and naturally you, Sergei Grigorievich, Valentin Sergeevich, Evgenii Arkadievich, Vasilii Ivanovich, and another two or three people. We will create conditions for you that exist nowhere else. We will work on phonoscopy, and decoding, and the development of new telephones. I've already spoken with Valentin Sergeevich. His system of distinguishing the basic tone is excellently conceived. Anton Mikhailovich sent him to the cooler that time, but what he was proposing was a very very promising thing. You'll see, we'll work marvelously. And all your prospects will be optimal."

I wanted to believe the lavish promises. But even Valentin, the youngest of us all, the most trusting and easily enthused, had doubts. "He promises a lot. The lady doth protest too much. But what will come of it? It's not serious somehow. Anton may give him the people. But where will he get the equipment, apparatus, rooms? There's plenty of everything here. But he needs more power than he's got to set up a sharashka in an empty lot."

Abram Mendelevich suggested we think about plans, projects, and details, compile lists of equipment, instruments, and attachments. "The Directorate's order is precise: supply us with everything necessary. I'm certain that Anton Mikhailovich won't be stingy. For he knows that I have complete information on what's available at the institute, what supplies we have of war-spoils equipment and what materials we have that were not yet debited. We'll take the analyzer that's newer. And then Sergei

Grigorievich and Arkadii Nikolaevich will develop an even newer and better one. The library here will supply us with books and journals. This is spelled out in the order and we have agreed on it. We'll be moving in two weeks or so, three at the latest."

But a few days later he had lost his merry tone. "Unexpected complications have arisen. The prison wardens. They say that the building there isn't equipped. It's in the middle of town; there are residential houses all around. I simply don't understand; there's a similar small institute with a special contingent working right on Bronnaya. Now the question will be decided at the highest level. At worst, you'll have to live here for a while. They'll transport you from here to there. Breakfast and dinner here, and we'll arrange lunch there. That's still less complicated than our arrangements. Yes, yes, I realize it will be worse for walking for you, less time in the fresh air. But we'll arrange that with time, too. At least the work conditions will be much better. Unlimited opportunities for creative initiative. When we move and start working, you'll see."

With every day he grew less radiant. He spoke with less confidence, covering up his irritation. "The wardens are stubborn. They have their own rules and regulations. You can't live here and work there. Apparently you'll have to move to Butyrki or Lefortovo for a while. But understand, it's just for sleeping. And, of course, with special conditions. And in terms of food, we'll arrange it for the highest category. And you'll have more frequent meetings with your families. Now you see them only once every three or four months. There we'll make arrangements for monthly visits or even more. Yes, of course, and for walks and fresh air. But at least early release is much more likely. I know you don't feel like going back to prison. I realize it's very difficult. But that's only in the beginning. When we present the first concrete results of our work, we'll fight for the best living conditions."

Sergei took me into the farthest part of the yard on our walk. "Do you understand what he's come up with? Back into the cell with the latrine pail. Door locked. Go outside—hands behind your back and don't turn around. Walks—a half hour and watch it, don't talk. And where do you walk?— on asphalt, between the prison walls. Breathe deeper with your nose. If you don't like it—you can die early. And are we going to go there willingly? To earn him another star for his shoulder boards? Another Stalin Prize? Are we going to be silent cattle? Wherever they herd us—the pen, the slaughterhouse—we go without a moo? What can we do? Well, let's think what to do!! I think we should go straight to Anton and say: 'Look, you brought us here and we're trying hard—we work, invent, research, solder, and rivet. And we're prepared to serve you not out of fear but out of conscience. Why the fuck are you getting rid of your faithful servants? It's a loss for you and ruination for us. Have pity on us, Your Honor, Your Highness, I'd like to fuck your mouth! You're so wise, so all-knowing, you must understand. For that, Mendelevich, our brains will only go at half-speed. But for you each of us works like two men.' No, joking aside, we have to resist some way. You know that Mendelevich and Anton are like cats and dogs. And Anton will try to louse him up in any way he can. But if they mess him up, he'll shake it off, and we'll drown in the shit."

Anxious days passed drearily. Anton Mikhailovich was either sick or away on business. We didn't want to talk to anyone else. Abram Mendelevich occasionally dropped by the laboratory, gave a falsely hearty hello, and hurried to leave.

Captain Vasilii Nikolaevich M., his deputy in the acoustics department and appointed deputy head of the new institute, was a businesslike, courteous, almost shy man, who was rarely angry; when he was angry, he didn't shout or curse, he chewed you out in a boring, squeaky tenor. He usually avoided "extraneous conversations." However, persistent Sergei managed to find out from him that the prison administration of the MGB considered it impossible to use the special contingent at the new site because it lacked the necessary conditions; the doors and windows opened onto the street, and in accordance with the building's location the "norms" called for so many guards that they would outnumber the staff of the institute. They would require a special guard building. And there was neither the space nor the money for all that.

When it was explained to Abram Mendelevich that he would not be given a single prisoner, he replied, either out of despair or in the hopes of winning a concession, that he had to refuse the directorship of the new institute and in general consider its existence inefficient and a poor idea without those cadres.

But the order for the creation of the institute had already been signed by Minister Abakumov. At the Directorate someone said: "So that's what that Jew is like, eh? He pretended to be a great specialist, wormed his way into the laureates. But it turns out he can't take a step without his prisoners."

In all the sharashkas it was the prisoners who earned scholarly degrees, orders, and prizes for the Chekists who were listed as scientists. But discussing that aloud was just as forbidden as discussing who made up the major work force at the "great construction sites of communism." Therefore, the order was rescinded, and the unfortunate engineer major was demoted and demobilized.

The last time he came to the sharashka he was wearing a baggy civilian suit. His thin neck stuck out defenselessly. His glasses glinted sadly. He stood for a few minutes by my desk. "Anton Mikhailovich turned out to be even sneakier and more perfidious than I had thought. He couldn't get me through work. As an engineer I'm no worse and maybe even better than he. I'm more familiar with modern technology. And I think faster. They know that in the Directorate. And then, I'm a Communist, while he, after his Promparty business, ended up without a party. So he couldn't act against me openly. So he invented a clever shunt. And like a fool, I fell for it. But nowadays—and this is strictly between us—with a name like mine you can't be the head of an institute. No achievements, no Party seniority will help. There is a cadre policy! So the arguments of the warders was just a formal excuse. Rather, they chose a building that would elicit the arguments. My comrades told me that a long time ago. But I didn't understand fully. Well, I'll work in civilian life now. And let this be another lesson to you. All my best."

He shook my arm by the elbow and left with a crooked smile.

The top secret phonoscopy Laboratory Number 1 was simply disbanded, and Vasilii and I were turned over to the mathematics group, which was developing codes and systems. We were supposed to use sound pictures to determine the relative stability of secret telephones. Besides that, Vasilii, on the orders of the technical information group, was also translating articles from British, American, and French journals. I was also subordinate to two sections, because I continued running the articulation tests, participated in several research projects of the articulation lab, and in the evenings taught English and German to young officers, training them to translate technical texts.

The evaluations of the systems of secret telephones we were testing were expressed in fractions. A constant numerator stood for one minute of coded conversation. The denominator was given a two- or three-digit number that represented the minutes spent on decoding or determining the circuit of the decoder and the code. The larger the denominator, the more stable the system and code. The "grades" of the various telephones fluctuated between 1/120 and 1/600.

But gradually I became convinced that the speed of our guesses, which should have determined the objective characteristics of the telephones, changed markedly for various reasons. In the mornings, we decoded faster than by the end of the day. The guesswork was slowed down by any discomfort—a toothache, a bad cold, an upset stomach. And on those days when I was in a foul mood because of an unhappy letter from home or an unpleasant conversation in the cell, Vasilii quickly overtook me and bragged jokingly: "See what nerves of steel can do? My grandmother was right when she said unhappy thoughts breed lice."

Group leader Major Konstantin Fedorovich K., a dry, elegant, narrow-faced man, with a wise cold gaze, was inevitably polite, but kept his distance. "Extraneous conversations" were deflected coldly and firmly: "This issue has no direct bearing on our task."

But he talked at length, enthusiastically, about a tricky mathematical problem that came up for the encoder designers, both with the chief mathematician of the group, Aleksandr L., and with other specialists. They said: "Even though he has shoulder boards, he's a serious mathematician and a conscientious engineer."

Aleksandr Mikhailovich L. was sentenced because he had been a POW.

He got to the front from, I think, his first year of graduate school. An intelligent Muscovite, a mocking skeptic, and a bit of a snob, he was in love with mathematics—"the science of sciences"—and with music. When an upright piano appeared in the free employees' "red corner" [room for cultural and recreational pursuits] at the sharashka, he tuned it and was therefore given permission to play it Sunday evenings. Other zeks were forbidden by the prison warden to attend—"not allowed, it's not a concert for you." But when the screw on duty was in a good mood, some of us managed to sneak in.

Aleksandr played Beethoven sonatas, Chopin's preludes and mazurkas, and Tchaikovsky's "seasons" by heart.

And then time went either very slowly, almost stopping, or else speeded up enormously. Joy and sadness either alternated or blended—joyous sorrow, when you're on the verge of tears, barely holding yourself back. A fleeting instant of happiness, piercing your heart to the point of pain, when the whole world is beautiful and all people are good. And then the suffocating realization—where you are and what they've done to you.

Aleksandr, a prisoner, "a traitor to the homeland," behaved properly, even rather punctiliously, and in some cases almost haughtily with anyone in authority. But when he spoke with Major K., they both seemed to melt, and argued casually, sometimes even joked, laughed, happy over a successful solution.

At first, Aleksandr barely noticed me. Once, when we were talking about the fact that I was a confirmed Marxist, he noted that that was natural, since I wasn't a Russian.

"No, no, I'm not anti-Semitic at all. I had Jewish friends at school and in the university. But in twentieth-century Russian history, the Jews played a rather unattractive role. It's enough to recall Trotsky and Zinoviev.* You of course may counter with Levitan, Rubinstein, Ehrenburg, violinists, pianists, and mathematicians. Einstein's a genius, of course. Every nation has its good points and bad. And at different periods either the good or the bad predominate. Even the Germans had great people. I know, I know, I don't need to convince you of that. I heard that you were sent up for an overestimation of the Germans. But when Hitler came to power, the German flaws became dominant. And everyone forgot about Bach, Beethoven, and Schiller. I'm sure even you shouted: 'Kill the Germans!' And if you didn't, then I can only be surprised that they didn't put you away sooner."

Another mathematician was a student from Riga, the Zionist Peretz G., whom they called Don Perez, very young and even younger-looking than his years, but already balding, pointy-faced, self-confident, making categorical judgments about everything and everyone.

*Grigorii Evseevich Zinoviev (1883–1936), an associate of Lenin, shot after show trial in 1936. (Translator's note.)

Aleksandr and Peretz greeted Vasilii and me coldly. Soon I realized that they suspected us of being plants. Vasilii was not a political prisoner; he had worked alone in the library before that and, they said, avoided fifty-eighters, and then the two of us worked in some special top secret group. And I shamelessly proclaimed my Communist convictions and that meant I could only be an accomplice of the bosses.

While considered part of their group, we frequently went off to the acoustics lab or the library; that meant that we could drop by the security office with a report. I had noticed that conversations broke off when we came into the room when there were no free employees in it. One morning Vasilii started talking about the latest news from Korea—we were worried about the North Koreans. Aleksandr interrupted in an almost bosslike tone: "I would like to ask you not to distract us with talk. Some people here are using their brains. Perhaps gabbing helps your divinations from those pictures, but it bothers me."

The group leader came in from time to time; his assistant, a senior lieutenant, a slimy four-eyes, simple-minded and lazy, was supposed to be there all the time. But he was always going out for a smoke with his friends or to flirt with the girls from the design bureau.

He treated Vasilii and me with respect, having no idea of what we were doing. He considered the mathematicians his colleagues, and tried to be buddy-buddy with them, even though he looked up to Aleksandr Mikhailovich. Sometimes he'd sit by him to get help with his homework; he was taking a correspondence course in the graduate department of a communications institute.

The senior lieutenant often amused us with stories of sports events, robberies and thefts, and family dramas among his neighbors and friends. Once he started to tell us how in the last year of the war he was traveling from Tashkent, where he had been studying in an evacuated institute.

"I had started there before the war. Not that I was particularly interested. But they gave a military deferment. I didn't want to live in barracks. And I wanted to go to the front even less. Well, life in the institute wasn't so bad, though we were hungry and they kept pulling us away—to go to the railroad station and help load and unload, or go pick cotton in the fields —at least you stayed whole, graduated, earned shoulder boards, and went into the security organs to work. My father did enough fighting for all his sons. He was even with the partisans. His whole chest is covered with medals and awards. And now he's back in the security organs. He went into the border patrol when he was still in the Komsomol. Now he's a colonel of very secret stuff—no one, not my brothers, not my mother, knows what he's in charge of; we only know that he's got a general's position. So, when we were coming back from Tashkent to Moscow in 1944 we didn't have a lot of money. And what could you buy with money? But I had a pal, a Muscovite, who knew the ropes—he was taken into the security organs later in communications. Well, he came up with this idea:

we bought two pails of salt—there were these salty places along the way, I forget what they're called. We made a deal with the conductors and at the other stations we traded the salt for fish—smoked and fresh. We took them by the sack, and then farther down we traded the fish for vodka, tobacco, milk. We even got rich on it."

Aleksandr and Peretz encouraged him with sympathetic responses. But I was angered and ashamed: an officer, a Komsomol member, bragging about how he speculated. He probably thought that's just what criminals like us wanted to hear.

After several carefully worked out experiments of sound picture decoding of mosaic telephones, I came to the conclusion that all our "fractional" evaluations were not well grounded. The amount of time we spent was the basic criterion for evaluating a telephone system. We—two not young and not very healthy prisoners—worked conscientiously, tried not to be distracted. But it was easy to imagine that the enemy—those Americans from whom we had borrowed the technology for visible speech—had plenty of young, well-trained decoders. And for them the differences between more or less complex forms of mosaic systems were negligible. With the appearance of spectrum analyzers this kind of encoding becomes unstable—it's easily and quickly read.

Vasilii did not agree. He maintained that comparisons were more important than absolute coefficients of stability. And we were checking the same compared systems several times. And the results each time were if not identical then at least close. And it had never happened that one of us considered best a system that the other had considered worse than others. Even though the size of the fractional indexes fluctuated, the sum of the comparisons more or less corresponded.

I relayed my thoughts to Konstanin Fedorovich. We argued hotly but not acrimoniously. The chief asked many questions, listened frowning, and chewed on the filter of of his extinguished cigarette.

"Well, all right, it's now clear that nothing's clear. Try to put this into written form in the work notebooks."

(Each of us had a workbook—a large notebook with numbered pages, sewn with a cord and fastened with sealing wax or a lead seal. We were supposed to write down everything we thought about that day. They were kept in the safes, along with secret documents, circuits, and blueprints, for the night.)

Aleksandr had overheard our argument. After work he asked me: "Do you realize that you're sawing the branch you're sitting on? The bosses don't like to be shown that they're gold-bricking and passing shit off as gold. What are you, tired of the sharashka? You want to go fell timber or dig in the mines?"

I said that I didn't want to participate in featherbedding, no matter whose idea it was; you couldn't expend state and national funds to manufacture telephone systems that we knew wouldn't work.

He listened with a suspicious smile. He must have thought that I was playing at being very "honest," hoping for special favor from the bosses, and therefore a fool, or hoping to insinuate myself into the trust of my comrades, and therefore dangerous.

Soon Konstanin Fedorovich said: "We've examined your thoughts on the matter. When it's said and done, you're proposing to bury mosaic coding without a ceremony and as fast as possible. You've presented certain reasons." He was using almost the same words Anton Mikhailovich had used to reproach Solzhenitsyn, but without bitterness, disinterestedly. "However, reality is much more complicated than your theories. Mosaic telephones are still needed in the army and in the security organs. They are much cheaper than our latest system will be. They prevent direct wiretapping. The tapped conversation can be decoded only under laboratory conditions. Therefore great stability of the codes is still important. And we must conscientiously determine the relative merits of the various systems. Vasilii Ivanovich has had sufficient training and I imagine will be able to manage on his own. Anton Mikhailovich is taking you back in the acoustics lab."

That same day I began hauling my books, note pads, and pile of sound pictures back over there. I said to Aleksandr: "Our love was without joy, parting will be without sorrow."

But it was from that moment on that he warmed up to me noticeably; he even invited me to take the evening mathematics courses he was giving to the free employees. And I became his diligent listener. I enthusiastically drilled Fourier series and the theory of probability, recalling long-forgotten quadratic equations, elementary trigonometry, and the basics of differentiation and integration.

The "prodigal son" was taken back merrily in the acoustics lab—I was given Abram Mendelevich's old desk in the far corner by the wall. There, behind the shelves, I could read and write again, hiding behind a pile of sound pictures. Once again I set up my homemade receiver tuned to the BBC.

In the mathematics group all the desks were open—all surfaces in view —and every task precisely defined; you couldn't get sidetracked.

In the fall of 1949 our best workers came up with a television set with a large mirrored screen and remote control in the form of a rubber bulb on a cord. It was mounted in a mahogany chest, upholstered in blue velvet; a silver plaque was engraved with the information that this was a gift "To the Great Stalin, the Beloved Leader of the People, from the Moscow Chekists."

And a few months later they began work on something even more luxurious for their Minister of State Security (MGB) Abakumov. By the summer of 1951 they had completed an electronic console that combined a wide-screen TV, a radio, and a tape recorder—in those days the only such piece of equipment of its kind.

It was almost more luxuriously mounted than the gift for Stalin. It had to be put together on the spot. Early in the morning several master zeks, along with the disassembled gift, their instruments and tools, were loaded into a special van and sent in a special convoy straight to Abakumov's apartment.

They dragged the precious cargo to the doors themselves. But there was a search under way at the apartment. The security officers, tired from their long night, didn't realize right away who had come and for what, and what all the equipment was for. Twelve years after Yezhov* they had forgotten how to arrest their own ministers.

The television console was never installed. The prisoners were ordered to keep silent, not to breathe a word, a half word, to anyone.

But by lunchtime Sergei, Zhen-Zhen, and I were discussing the implications of the arrest and what awaited us: "Tightening or loosening."

We zeks with no rights learned about the fall of the all-powerful boss of the security organs before many members of the government. There was nothing in the papers in the following months and years about it.

The free employees let loose rumors that he had either missed some conspiracy or made a mess in Yugoslavia and had been arrested on the personal orders of Comrade Stalin. That's approximately what the commentators of the BBC said. But there was another rumor—a latrine rumor, born of prisoners' dreams: he was being punished for excesses, just as Yezhov had been. And that meant that things had to get better.

A week passed, then another, and some of the participants in the development and construction of the system of secret telephony that seemed most perfect were released early. The engineers I. Bryksin, G. Izmailov, A. Kotikov, and L. Feinberg, the designer S. Protsenko, and the technicians N. Stepanenko and E. Genishta left "with their gear" and returned a few days later as free employees.

It was then that we learned that the ukase of the Presidium of the Supreme Soviet on their early release had been signed a year ago, but had lain all this time on Abakumov's desk. Either it had been forgotten, or the minister wanted to keep them out of his private considerations. One of them, N. Stepanenko, who had already done five of his eight years (he had been sentenced under Article 58-3 for working in a private radio shop under the Germans), had submitted a petition for pardon in the winter. And he was refused by the same Presidium of the Supreme Soviet that had freed him by special ukase just a few months earlier.

*Nikolai Ivanovich Yezhov (1894–1939?), chief of the NKVD (1936–1938), who administered the most severe stage of the purges; he disappeared in 1939. (Translator's note.)

Our joy for the comrades who had earned their own freedom gave birth to new hopes and strengthened old ones.

But that delay of one year—a delay in executing a state ukase on the whim or forgetfulness of a minister! And a refusal to pardon someone who should have been free a long time ago! That meant that even up there, at the very top, in the MGB and in the Supreme Soviet, those who were in charge of our fates and the whole country were simply indifferent, crudely indifferent toward people, and law, and their own ukases!

But perhaps these were simply exceptional, unique outrages? After all, the minister had been arrested.

All the zeks were convened in the dining room. And Anton Mikhailovich's new deputy, Major K., climbed up on a chair and read the ukase of the Presidium of the Supreme Soviet on the early release and the resolution of the Council of Ministers on awards for the people released: financial prizes ranging from 5,000 to 15,000.

Then the security officer, Major Shikin, climbed up on the chair, panting, and read an order from the MGB on awards for workers of the special contingent of our institute. Over 300 zeks received awards from 100 to 1,000 rubles. At the time the sharashka had about 400 zeks. Many had arrived quite recently. All the workers of the acoustics laboratory and the mathematics group received awards except for two new ones and me.

Then next day Captain M. told me: "I heard that you weren't given an award. But we had proposed your name. The list had been made up a long time ago. You were presented for the maximum sum. Anton Mikhailovich signed it; you were crossed out at the Directorate. You know, Foma Fomich was displeased with you."

After a hiatus of a year and a half, I was finally granted permission for a meeting.

Lefortovo Prison. The investigator's office. Mother and Nadya on one side of the table.

The screw on duty was at the head of the table. "Don't shake hands. No embracing or kissing. Not allowed."

My mother had aged considerably and looked ill. Her entire face was in wrinkles, in folds of faded skin. If I had met her on the street, I wouldn't have recognized her.

Nadya tried to be cheerful, smiling. Her dear tired face. Sad eyes. Slumped shoulders. Tormented smiles.

She told me about the girls: their grades, what they were reading. Getting ready for Pioneer camp. My father was on a business trip. They brought greetings from relatives and friends. One was sick, another married.

"Finish up. You're five minutes over already."

I hugged them. The screw grumbled, but not too zealously. "You were told you can't do that. You're breaking a rule. Do you want to be deprived of visits again?"

On the way back in the van, chewing my mother's shortbread, I tried to think only of tomorrow's work.

In the summer and fall of 1951 the optimistic rumors multiplied.

The rumors imagined an amnesty for the fiftieth anniversary of the Party —that is, by 1953—or even earlier, as soon as peace was concluded with Germany and Japan. And certainly by Stalin's seventy-fifth birthday in 1954. But I didn't allow myself to dream or hope. I understood that I would stay in "until the bell," to the end of my term. And then, at best, I'd stay on here as a free employee, highly secret, that is, a serf in essence. But at least I'd be living at home with Nadya and my daughters. Maybe they'd let us live closer to the sharashka and in a larger place than our 18-meter room—all six of us, including my parents.

And of course, I'd go to the theater, concerts, museums . . . When I got a vacation, I'd go to Leningrad, stroll along the embankments of the Neva and Fontanka, through the rooms of the Hermitage. Or to Kiev—I'd go up on Vladimirovskaya Hill. And for my next vacation I'd go to the Crimea and swim in the sea or maybe I'd finally see the Caucasus; before I had only been to Essentuki and Kislovodsk, from where on a clear day I looked at the sugar-white caps of Mount Elbrus.

These were my most secret, most daring dreams.

I consoled myself by reading the Stoics, Chinese and Japanese philosophers. I didn't know anything concrete about existentialism then. The magazines and newspapers wrote that this latest reactionary semifascist philosophy rejected class struggle, tried to "replace politics with ethics," and Fadeyev called the existentialist Sartre "a hyena with a typewriter."

But ten years later, like Jourdain, who suddenly learned that he had spoken in prose all his life, I discovered that in prison I had become an "essential existentialist."

Despite the fact that then I wanted to be a consistent follower of Marx, Engels, Lenin, and Stalin. Even Stalin's semiliterate thoughts on linguistics did not shake my faith. Moreover, I convinced myself that in dilettantishly repeating certain ABCs of linguistics, crudely berating Marr but affirming the nonclassness and superclassness of language, Stalin was in that way opening new paths for a new movement toward the creative development of Marxism-Leninism. It would no longer be hampered by a simplistic sociologizing "class approach." I tried to prove to myself and to others that these random and, at first glance, primitive statements of Stalin on language, even incorrect in some particulars, still gave us an opportunity to examine in a new objective light the history of a nation and modern national problems, which after the war turned out to be so unexpectedly complex. And in blatant contradiction to all our former class and dialecti-cal-materialist concepts.

The war raged on in Korea. Regiments of Chinese volunteers hurried to help the North and push back the UN forces—Americans, Turks, Aus-tralians—"the united forces of international reaction." Vietnamese and Algerian rebels fought with French colonizers. Indonesia and India be-came independent states, and powerful Communist parties were active there. In Greece the communists fought, defending mountain strongholds.

Only Tito was in error, enjoying arbitrary rule, stubbornly refusing to come to terms with us and other fraternal parties.

The sudden death of Dimitrov and the trials of Kostov, Rajk, and other "Yugoslav agents" in Bulgaria, Hungary, and the GDR elicited unhappy doubts. Was it happening again, the same thing we had in 1935–1938, when they tried Zinoviev, Bukharin, Piatakov, when they hunted for enemies of the people?

Zhen-Zhen and Vasilii Ivanovich saw things about the same way I did. My constant opponents were Sergei Kuprianov and Semyon P., a young Moscow engineer, the son of an important old Bolshevik, who had been a political prisoner in tsarist times, a Soviet official, and then disappeared in 1937.

Semyon had been brought in right after Solzhenitsyn and Panin were taken away.

He had graduated from the Moscow Energetics Institute with such flying colors that he was accepted into the graduate program, despite his "bad background"; he was preparing to defend his dissertation on gyro-scopes. In 1949 he was visited by a former neighbor and classmate, whom he hadn't seen since grammar school. (He had left for the front directly from ninth grade.) The young captain was on leave from the occupation forces in Austria and was looking up his old friends in Moscow, drinking with them, asking them to find him a bride, talking, asking questions.

Semyon, telling him about his future dissertation, drew him a picture of a gyroscope on a piece of paper—the kind of illustration you find in school physics textbooks.

The merry captain went back to Austria, and a month later Semyon was arrested and a sleepy investigator at Lubyanka accused him of espionage.

It turned out that the former classmate worked for American intelli-gence. His contact with the Americans, an Austrian engineer, had been found out, and they discovered the captain's report about his trip to Mos-cow and a list of people he had supposedly enlisted and given advances to —rather large sums. Among the appendixes to the report was a pencil drawing of a gyroscope.

The merry captain was imprisoned. At first he confessed that he had enlisted his school comrade and bought a blueprint of the military equip-ment from him for cash. Later, at a face-to-face meeting, he recalled that he didn't come out and enlist him, but merely hinted; he had been convinced of the anti-Soviet attitudes of his old friend, was convinced that he had understood him, and that's why he made the drawing of the important piece of equipment. He actually gave him less money than he had indicated in the report; perhaps he didn't give him any cash at all, but bought drink, food, and other treats. He didn't remember exactly, he had been very drunk.

The investigation moved fast. The captain and his Austrian resident apparently were real spies; they "broke" readily and were happy to help out the investigators, satisfying and oversatisfying their expectations.

The stubbornness of Semyon, who did not confess or repent, still did not destroy the generally successful course of the case. He did not deny, after all, that the captain had come to see him, had brought cognac and schnapps and some canned goods, or that they drank and talked for a long time, that they told jokes—including anti-Soviet ones—and that he had told his guest about his dissertation, that gyroscopes were used in warplanes and warships.

He did not deny the facts, he merely disputed their interpretation. The investigators were indulgent. Semyon was not beaten. Twice, to shake him up, they put him in the cooler, depriving him of receiving packages. And then the OSO sentenced him to fifteen years for "participation in espionage," and as a specialist he came straight from Lubyanka to the sharashka.

Despite his youth, he reasoned calmly and was gently mocking in ideological arguments.

"You maintain that your views are scientific. But in reality it is not scientific knowledge, but faith. Others believe in the immaculate conception, in self-renewal of icons, in the supremacy of the Aryan race, in shamans, and you believe in in dialectical materialism. And all the faithful refer to *Das Kapital*. I studied it; it was boring, but it seems convincing. And I got an 'excellent' in my Lenin, even though *Materialism and Empiriocriticism* is boring and unconvincing. More berating than arguments. And there's so much wrong in *The Short Course*!* And how they lied before the war about Poland and Finland! And during the war they lied, and after. No, let's not argue about it. You can believe it if it's better for you, but I prefer this."

He was reading Schrödinger's *What Is Life?*

"It's a small book, but I feel that there's more sense in it than in the multivolume editions of your classics. Then could you explain why they're attacking Morganism-Weismannism† now? After all, biology is a science;

The Short Course of the History of the CPSU, the Stalinist version of Soviet Party history, the official text in schools from 1938 until the mid-1950s. (Translator's note.)

†Named for Thomas Hunt Morgan (1866–1945), the American geneticist who received the 1933 Nobel Prize in Physiology and Medicine, and August Weismann (1834–1914), the German biologist, it is the doctrine of the noninheritance of acquired characters—the direct opposite of the theory held by Trofim Denisovich Lysenko (1898–1976), who was in charge of Soviet genetics under Stalin. (Translator's note.)

in science you argue with facts, experiments. It's philosophers and political economists who bombard one another with quotes and abstract formulas. But when you're talking about harvests, cattle breeding, you can test all that in practice. Why ruin institutes, shut down laboratories, and deprive scientists of their work? If they're wrong, that can be checked and demonstrated. The Americans aren't idiots. If Morgan is given major funding there, that means there is some profit from his studies. You can't possibly believe that the Americans are paying millions for a pseudoscience just to make Soviet Academician Lysenko unhappy. Or that they're bankrupting their biology, their agriculture, in the hopes that we will ruin ours by following their example. Say, do you believe that they're dropping the Colorado beetle onto our lands from planes and submarines? It's all baloney. Why don't we listen to the radio instead—Gilels is playing Beethoven sonatas today."

Trying to persuade myself and my friends, I came up with what seemed convincing arguments. "We're all traveling on a single train. You and I are unlucky: the bastard conductors and idiot ticket takers stuck us in the prison car. They could have thrown us under the wheels. It's bad for us, but we can't blame the engineer or the railroad for that. If most of the crew are jerks, bastards, and crooks, does that mean that the station we're headed for is bad? That the tracks are laid incorrectly? There are millions of passengers like us. Immeasurably many! But there are so many more who have different fates. Of course, they're all traveling in different ways, too —some in luxurious sleepers, some in heated freight cars. But we're all moving in one direction, toward one goal—socialism. And along the only possible path."

Sergei countered metaphorically, too: "We're not moving anywhere. We're mired in shit. We're up to our ears in it. And you're arguing that it's not shit, it's honey."

Of course, both he and Semyon were less radically negative than Panin. For them, just as for me, the rightness of the October Revolution and the greatness of Lenin were unassailable. And we argued more about how much our society had decayed and degenerated and whether there was hope for its healing. And what we could expect—state slaves without rights.

More than once I recalled Turgenev's prose poem "The Threshold," about a young Russian woman selflessly performing a fatal deed, about which no one would ever learn. Two voices follow her: "Fool!" "Saint!"

After the fighting started in Korea, Zhen-Zhen thought more resolutely. The war in the Far East required his expertise. He started writing petitions to the Central Committee, to Beria, to Stalin, insisting that he must work in his specialty.

His chief, Evgeniia Vasilievna, sympathized with these feelings and suggested that he write to Malenkov, too—"He's Comrade Stalin's main assistant now"—and she passed on the letters herself.

When Zhen-Zhen was finally shipped off, he left her the inheritance of our friendship.

Evgenii Timofeevich Timofeev, who dreamed of designing new submarines and torpedoes for North Korea and China, was taken away not to another sharashka, as even Evgeniia Vasilievna had thought, but to Magadan. There, as someone who had come from a "special object," he was sent to a special camp. The drunken director greeted the transported group with a short welcoming speech: "You damned fascists, what do you think, why are you here? You think to work? You're right, you'll work here, you'll work hard as long as you breathe. But do you think you'll ever get out of here? Fuck you, fascists! You came here to die. You'll die here. Know that now." Stubborn Zhen-Zhen still managed to be transferred from there to a camp near a wharf, where he repaired cabotage vessels. In 1956 he and I met in Moscow. He had been rehabilitated, they reinstated him in Party seniority as of 1919, he was working as a leading engineer until the last days of his life. He died in 1975.

The experiments with the wire continued. I had occasion to be in the chemistry lab, to report to Evgeniia Vasilievna on the results of our tests. And the brief reports were followed by long chats, sometimes quite trusting.

She was so lonely that she shared her female sorrows and dreams with a prisoner pal. The former security officer knew that she could trust people like Zhen-Zhen and me more than her comrades, with whom she was in the same party, the same "Chekist subdivision."

When Gumer was released, Evgeniia Vasilievna took him to her apartment and later complained to me: "I love him, the four-eyed devil. Do you understand: love him! I'm not a girl anymore. I've seen a lot in life; I should know you men well by now. But I'm in love; I could cry, beat my head against the wall. There's no joy in it. He's a year younger, actually, two. No, no, don't argue, it makes a difference! The first day he was out he ran to me, like a gentle calf. And now I see that it's all over. He says that he loves me but can't marry me. Because his parents won't allow it. They're supposed to be insisting that he marry one of their own, a Tatar. You see how old-fashioned, and with a tinge of bourgeois nationalism. And he thinks I'll believe that he obeys his papa and mama like that! The man is almost forty. No, he just doesn't love me. He stopped loving me. And he's making up excuses—so stupid—with a nationalist underpinning. Don't try to console me; what do you mean 'he loves you but can't,' 'a son's duty is stronger than love.' I was younger when I broke with my family, went into the Komsomol, the university. And it's harder to do that for a young girl. No, I didn't leave for love. Though there was love, of course. But the most important thing was ideals. So you think it's easier to break with your family, with your parents when you're young? Well, of course, what ideals do he and I have? He just finally got his hands on female flesh, tenderness in a soft bed, after all those prison years. And I, stupid fool, believed that it was love, passion. He's so handsome, so amiable. I melted, and now I'm suffering. We live as though in a railroad station . . . day and night, another twenty-four hours gone. I'm waiting for his parents to find him a Tatar girl, and then it's good-bye forever. No, I'd be better off throwing him out now. I'll bawl for a week—and then I'll be over him. I wish there was a way of not seeing him anymore, because every look of his is like a gimlet in my heart.

"No, there aren't any of our troops in Korea. Everything that needs to be done is being done by the Chinese there. You can't even count how many of them there are. Enough for ten Koreas. Well, we give weapons, of course. But they're capable, they learn fast. And their discipline is like no one else's. If the order is to go, even into fire, they'll go without batting an eye! With soldiers like that, even the atom bomb isn't scary. They're better than the Koreans, sort of like the Japanese once were—samurai. The Japanese have gotten fat and lazy. But the Chinese have starved for centuries. And they're highly idealistic, too. They're not afraid of anything.

"We have political education tomorrow: 'Comrade Stalin on Problems of Linguistics' and its significance in general. I have a few theses on that. Evgenii Timofeevich and I worked them up last year. But now, probably there are new materials. You follow the papers and magazines. Here, take this notebook, but carefully, so our plants don't notice. And make some additions, on a separate page. Tomorrow we'll be checking our wire again, bring it back. All right?

"How does my fellow behave in the lab with you and others from the special contingent? Is he acting very conceited? Yes, yes, of course, he's tactful, well brought up. Well, he shouldn't allow himself anything beyond that. That's right. It's so easy to land back in there."

Naturally, I didn't let Gumer know that I knew about his adventures in the free world. It was very strange sometimes to talk to him just an hour or two after listening to the sorrowful stories of his girl friend.

He told me he had visited his parents in Kazan, and that he had really liked a very pretty young girl there.

Time passed; back in the sharashka Gumer had shown us a newspaper article about Musa Jalil—the hero executed by the Hitlerites.

"And yet my investigator had shouted at me: 'Your Musa is a traitor to his country, a fascist viper! And you're his helper. You should all be hanged.' "

10

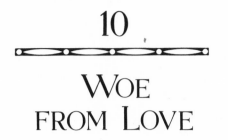

WOE
FROM LOVE

Several people at different times had noticed that engineer Sh. secretly chewed on wads of cotton soaked in alcohol that was used to wipe up equipment in the labs. He chewed and smiled blissfully. They saw him greedily sniff the alcohol bottles. Not tall, narrow-shouldered, he seemed a morbidly aged youth, almost a boy. Pale narrow face, surprised pale-blue eyes, pale reddish-brown hair in thin strands, thin pale-pink lips; a shy smile. He spoke with exquisite old-world politeness. Some camp workers even thought it servility. However, those who had worked with him said that that was not the way he argued with the authorities. "He's quiet, but stubborn. He looks like a baby chick, but he works like an eagle." The specialists maintained that he was an excellent radio engineer. "He takes one look at a circuit and he's at home with it."

A neighbor in his cell, celebrating his birthday, gave him a half cup of diluted cologne. Sh. got high immediately: he laughed, chuckling and squealing. "Ah, that's good! Marvelous! Thank you, my dear fellows, thank you, my dear fellows! I never dare get any cologne, in order to avoid temptation. What joy, so unexpected! I know, I know, it's dangerous. Green serpents and pink elephants! That's what got me in here, you know. Yes, yes, vodka did it. I'm paying for my sweet minutes and hours with bitter years. No, no, of course not! I'm not capable of hooliganism. And as a child I was as still as water. I am meek, like a lamb. And vodka merely intensifies my meekness. The one problem is that I get uncontrollably chatty. Don't you judge me too harshly, don't complain about my gabbing. No, no, I wasn't sent up for gabbing, either. What could I say bad even at my drunkest?! I'm a true Soviet patriot in mind and at heart. Vodka let me down in a completely different way. In a way that's hard to believe. Excuse me, is there another sip on the bottom? Thank you, my dear friend! I'm eternally grateful to you!

"Yes, it let me down, how can I put this precisely, by being both a catalyst and a developer of my feelings—truly deep feelings, but in the wrong circumstances. Yes, yes, love, it was love. But not the kind that you imagine, I think—not romantic, not adulterous, not jealous love. No, no, pure patriotic love for Comrade Stalin! Yes, I know that sounds paradoxical, even unlikely, but I swear it's the truth. I landed in prison because— how can I put this—I love Comrade Stalin too much, because I expressed my love in the wrong way and . . . the wrong place. That was it, inappropriateness. And that was the fault of the vodka. The green serpent! Just one drink, and I can't control my feelings. Right now, for instance."

He spoke, smiling humbly, not noticing the mocking looks, the mean voices: "Is he a psycho or a son of a bitch?" "He had a kopek's worth to drink but he's acting up a ruble's worth, the good citizen fag!" "What are you whistling about, you fucker—if someone snitches that you've been sucking up cologne here, even Stalin won't help you."

"I've loved Comrade Stalin since childhood," he went on. "Even in grammar school, I adored him, you might say. I read him, watched him in the movies, listened to him on the radio, and saw him personally three times—at demonstrations. He stood on the Mausoleum, smiled and waved at us. During the war years I read all his speeches and orders over and over from beginning to end. I was a student then. I asked to be sent to the front —they wouldn't let me go. My health was bad and my myopia was minus twelve. And they needed radio engineers. I began loving even more then. After all, he's the one who saved Moscow, saved Russia, and the whole world. I love him like my own father. No, probably more. My late father and I had a complicated relationship. He used to drink heavily and sometimes beat me, and even Mother. Even though he was from the intelligentsia. He was a pure man, didn't care about money. And when I got acquainted with vodka, he reproached me more than anyone one else, he cursed at me with real curses. I loved him, of course, loved and respected him, but I saw his shadowy sides. And Comrade Stalin is light without shadow, the pure light of wisdom and goodness! And sometimes I worry about him so—he doesn't spare himself, take care of himself. He's alone, and the enemies are innumerable. I have a drink, like now, and then suddenly fear grabs me by the throat: here I am enjoying life, cooling off, and he's in the Kremlin, tireless, ceaselessly working, not husbanding his strength, suffering for everyone, everything. And maybe, just at this moment the enemies are creeping toward him, and naturally somewhere conspirators are meeting, evil wishers.

"About two years ago, in a group of friends, we were talking just like this—we had drunk too much, and, can you believe it, I don't even remember how, I ended up on Red Square. They told me later that I had knocked on the Spassky Gate, weeping and begging to see Comrade Stalin, to tell him how much I loved him, how worried I was about him. They took me into the guardhouse in the tower. In the morning I woke up remembering nothing and not understanding where I was. They checked my documents, called my place of work. Then a colonel came—a serious fellow, very proper. He asked substantial questions: Who, what, from where. No official records, but his adjutant took notes. At the end he rebuked me severely—it wasn't right or proper to try to get into the Kremlin drunk in the middle of the night. But I knew that myself. I was so ashamed, I couldn't find the words for it. I apologized. Promised.

"But a few months later the same thing happened. And again I had no recollection of doing it. I woke up in the militia station—in the regional division for my neighborhood. I had my passport. The militia authorities were not so courteous. They threatened to send me to court, to take away my Moscow residence permit, to send me away from Moscow. And I had trouble at work. I was called into the special department in personnel, to a meeting of the local committee. But what could I tell them except that I loved Comrade Stalin with all my heart. And as you know, what's on a sober man's mind comes out of a drunken man's mouth. Naturally, I admitted the impossibility of my behavior, I repented, sincerely. But even less time passed. During the October holidays I grew chilled at the demonstration. I grew hoarse, singing songs and shouting hurrah. It was fun. I felt part of the group. Then I dropped by a friend's house to warm up. I had decided firmly, I resolved: two shot glasses, no more. And I remember I was planning to go straight home. But they wouldn't let me into the metro—they noticed that I was tipsy. And what happened next I don't remember. And I woke up in the box cell at Malaya Lubyanka."

I had heard all this several times from Sh. All he needed was a sip of spirits on a quiet evening or a holiday, and he began telling the story, almost in the same words and same intonations. And his eyes, wide in fright, glistened the same way. And every time at this point the people around him—both those who knew the whole story and those who were hearing it for the first time—laughed. Some laughed in disdain or maliciously, others with pity, commiseration, but all with a certain sense of relief—at last! And every time he stopped in fright and confusion and then also laughed. And went on about the same thing in the same way.

"Yes, yes, in Lubyanka. They conducted an investigation. They said that I had come back to Red Square, pestering the guards again. And they charged me. You'll never guess with what. Terrorist intentions. Can you imagine? That's even frightening to think about and wildly incongruous. But the investigator demanded that I name the instigators, co-conspirators. At first I was interrogated by a senior lieutenant, a young man, totally without an upbringing, crude. He hit me in the face . . . several times . . . and put me in the cooler. But I couldn't lie! I couldn't be untrue to myself. I couldn't calumny other people. Another investigator—a captain. He was older, more polite, and had such sneaky manners. But he tormented me no less than the other. He'd take out a bottle of vodka or cognac from the safe, pour a glass, and smile: 'Sign it, I'll give it to you.' Spasms began in my throat, in my chest, and here in my stomach. One time I even lost consciousness. But I didn't give in to my pain. The last time he announced: 'The investigation is over, and even though you resisted, the charge remains. The court will decide.' I said: 'Your terrible accusation is the greatest sorrow of my life.' And he replied with a Mephistophelean

smile: 'Well, you've heard of woe from wit, you have woe from love.*
There was no trial; they took me to Butyrki, and two weeks later an officer
called me in—I think, the duty officer for the prison—and showed me a
paper, the decision of some special commission: 'Condemned to eight years
under Article 58, paragraphs 8 through 14'—that meant, for intent to commit terror, for intent. What madness! You laugh, but it hurts me. Sometimes, it seems unbearable, the hurt. It would be easier to die. Yes, yes, of
course, I complained. I wrote to the Procurator General, and to Comrade
Stalin. They naturally don't deliver those letters. I get the standard replies:
'No grounds for review.'

"Ah, if he only learned the truth! If he only found out what kind of
inequities occur in our country. But they keep that from him. And I think
it's fair that they do. He has to be protected. His time and spiritual strength
have to be protected like something holy. He can't be upset, or depressed
by individual outrages. The whole country, the whole world rest on his
shoulders."

Sh. elicited my pity and sympathy, but also dismay and irritation. The
bizarre story of his "case," his drunken exaltation was a parody of my case
and my stubborn adherence to the Party. Panting with excitement, gulping
convulsively, about to break out in tears, he spoke of his great love, of the
wise leader of humanity, free of any flaws.

My friend Sergei disdainfully kept his distance. "Soft-boiled shit! Not
a man, but a teary, snotty blob. And a fool to boot. He thinks Stalin doesn't
know anything. And don't you act the fool, either. Don't you realize
anything: of course they told Stalin about this psycho. And of course Stalin
made the decision himself. How do I know? Why don't you move just one
ridge of your brain, and then you'll understand: What's his name? Whose
relative is he?"

Sh. was the nephew, with the same name and surname, of a famous
figure in the arts,† who was under attack once again for lack of ideals and
"formalism."

"They didn't send up his uncle. The whole world knows about him.
He's export goods. He was washed in the trash, beaten, and they spat in
his eyes. But that's not enough. They had to give him a scare, so he
wouldn't think of acting up. So he wouldn't forget to repent. And the
nephew came in handy. He's naïve, to put it mildly, and as civic-minded
as a young Pioneer; he'd climb into fire and an asshole for his beloved
leader. But he's the one they sent up. And that was done with the Great
Leader's knowledge. Probably, on his direct order. A hint to the famous
uncle. One of Stalin's practical jokes."

*Woe from Wit by Aleksandr Sergeevich Griboedov (1795–1829), an extremely popular play.
(Translator's note.)
†Dmitri Shostakovich. (Translator's note.)

11

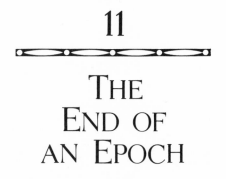

THE
END OF
AN EPOCH

When they bury an epoch
The graveside psalm does not sound . . .

—ANNA AKHMATOVA

Evgeniia Vasilievna told me: "Our new minister, Ignatiev, used to head the personal bodyguard of Comrade Stalin. He often lunched and dined at the same table with Comrade Stalin. He understands him with just a half word. The most important link now is intelligence and counterintelligence. The Yugoslavs have become too brazen; they've solidified their relationship with the Americans. They send their agents into Poland, Hungary, and Rumania. We have to take decisive steps. The MGB is taking a new battle course. And our institute is being handed over directly to the Central Committee. They've set up a special Directorate for Secret Communications. We'll be subordinated personally to Comrade Beria or Comrade Malenkov. There'll be a new director. Anton Mikhailovich is a very wise engineer, but he doesn't belong to the Party. And our institute will be the main site of the new Directorate; a site of special importance! Now everyone will have to shape up. A new broom . . . Because some people have relaxed quite a bit. Everything is familylike, homey. The officers and the special contingent will be shaped up. So keep your eyes peeled."

The new head of the sharashka was Lieutenant Colonel Naumov—neither an engineer nor a scientific worker, simply a lieutenant colonel. They said that he "made his career in operative work."

Anton Mikhailovich stayed on as his assistant in scientific work and as head of the acoustics laboratory. But he was also appointed scientific head of the entire Directorate, and therefore, he did not visit us as frequently as before. The acoustics lab was still headed by the very quiet and polite Captain Vasilii Nikolaevich.

Naumov occasionally dropped by the labs and shops, and when he did, he seemed not to notice the prisoners. A stocky, round-faced, and short-necked man, with regular features on his fat face and a dull cold gaze from under his dark reddish brown hair, carefully combed into a semicrewcut, he never smiled, spoke softly, unhurriedly, and passionlessly.

In the very first days he gave a few orders "to strengthen discipline and bring about strict order."

Vasilii Nikolaevich, without raising his eyes from the paper, dryly and briefly read the new rules for work. From now on no one from the special contingent could have access to the cabinets with secret documents and apparatus. We couldn't even put in our own workbooks ourselves. Only through the officers. Each of us was assigned to one of the free employees and from now on the employee was considered responsible for the actions of the "assignee." Previously, all the texts of scientific consultations, report notes, technical projects, and so on that had been compiled by the prisoners were signed by the authors: engineer or candidate of sciences so-and-so, followed by the signatures of the heads of the work group, laboratory, and institute. That was the way the signatures read on our reports about the study of the word makeup of Russian speech, Solzhenitsyn's reports on articulation tests, my reports on phonoscopy experiments, and so on. Some zeks had received patents and could hope for royalties in the future.

On Naumov's orders the prisoners could no longer sign anything, could not be considered authors or even coauthors. The documents of the institute could no longer refer to the work of the special contingent.

We ceased to exist.

Another order called for the immediate removal of homemade television sets from all laboratories and living quarters. Only the vacuum lab, where television tubes were manufactured, kept two sets out of the need to test tubes, but it was strictly forbidden "to use them for aims other than technical testing."

The orders elicited confusion, fear, bitterness, and despair. Our TV sets had been made in our spare time from rejected parts. Now the bosses would take them for themselves. Some men were already preparing to turn them over docilely. But in others anger was stronger than fear: "Fuck them, the vipers, they won't get to use our goods."

The order read "take apart." And the television sets were dismantled with such alacrity that some parts got lost or broken in the rush.

Sergei Kuprianov and I tried to prove our "right to cultural rest."

Anton Mikhailovich listened to our convincing speeches impatiently. "I understand, I do. But it's not my order, and I can't rescind it. So don't waste your oratory. And I can't help you in any way. I can't! And I won't explain anything, either. The order was signed by the head of the institute. You want to address him? I don't recommend it. But I strongly suggest that you calm down. Yes, calm down. You need your nervous energy for work and for life. Yesterday you worked under one set of conditions, today you must do so under other conditions. Tomorrow they might change again. To a great degree that depends on yourselves, whether things change for better or for worse. But you must work under any conditions. On that cheery note I end this fruitless discussion. Sergei Grigorievich, show me what you've come up with for the new analyzer. And you, Lev

Zinovievich, please articulate in three regimes today what our neighbors dished out. And then study the spectrograms—which bands have the worst noise."

Some complained about the new orders in whispers, others out loud. "They only make things worse. It'll be harder to work. Fucking vipers, they spit in our faces and expect us to work harder after that. That Naumov is a jerk—a foolish boor!"

Sergei and I decided to see the new director ourselves.

Anton Mikhailovich's old office seemed darker, grayer, and emptily roomy: the bookcases had been removed and the drapes changed.

The lieutenant colonel lifted his head slightly from the open file. "What's the matter?"

Standing at attention (he was an officer, after all, he had to appreciate my manner and style), I began to report: "We request permission to leave at least one of the homemade television sets in the yurts, since they allow us to pass our leisure hours in a cultural way. And this adds to the increase of creative energy of the engineers and scientific workers."

"And who gave permission to set up these television sets?"

"I don't remember who did it personally; however, it was known to the authorities of the institute and the prison."

Sergei jumped in, complementing my "military" official report with a trusting tale of a simple-hearted worker. "They're all put together out of rejects, garbage, as they say, stuck together with snot. But in making them, people trained, experimented, tested their serious technical ideas. They're rough drafts, you might say. Test runs."

"They are valuable equipment. They used materials that belong to the state. This can be viewed as misappropriation. And they were made during working hours. That means a crude violation of discipline. I was indulgent; I didn't start an investigation, I didn't call in the guilty. I merely ordered you to get rid of the illegal television sets. And the order must be obeyed."

"Citizen Director, we ask this as an exception. We used to have movie shows. And now this is the only form of relaxation we have, and at the same time it's cultural and ideological education."

Sergei picked that up, too. "You know how hard we work here. Fourteen to sixteen hours a day we work, not out of fear, but out of conscience; we invent, think, we've had major results. Most of us have received awards and bonuses."

"Who gave you permission to talk to me?" he asked without raising his voice, looking past us.

"We always applied directly to the director."

"Because you have forgotten where you are and who you are. This will not be repeated. You may apply only to your immediate supervisors. And only about your work. Questions of regulations are decided by the prison administration. You have permitted yourselves a gross violation just now.

For this first violation, I am giving you a verbal reprimand. From now on, I will punish severely. Go."

On the stairs, we had a smoke. Sergei's fingers were shaking. "What a viper, fuck his mother in her wormy heart. Did you see those eyes? They're not human, they're like a toad's. A guy like that should be an executioner in a cellar shooting people with his Nagant, and he's head of a scientific lab."

"A sack of cold shit!"

A few days later in all the labs they began weeding out "noninventoried apparatus and incorrectly filled out secret documents." An especially important state commission was due. The apparatus and papers that had not been included in the inventory description that had been added to the official document of passing the sharashka from the MGB to the Directorate of the Central Committee were to be destroyed.

Vsevolod R., a vacuum engineer, an ironic Odessite, a tireless raconteur of dirty jokes and a fan of the Rumanian monarchy (he had worked in Bucharest during the occupation years), said in confusion and fear: "Listen, they've gone crazy over there! We had a Zeiss microscope, with two eyepieces. A unique model! Made on special order for Philips Labs. Before the war it cost seventy thousand marks—real ones, gold. And they ordered it destroyed and thrown in the pit. Did you see the pit they dug out behind the boiler room, by the garbage dump? That's for equipment and parts. And all the documents, blueprints, circuits, patents, and detailed descriptions of technology—hundreds, thousands of files—all into the boiler! The Americans or British would pay millions for them. We had hoped to save at least the microscope for later; we packed it in cotton and a crate and carried it to the pit. But Major Shikin and two jerks were there—workers from the machine shops with crowbars and sledgehammers. They saw the crate: 'What's this? Whose idea? Sabotaging the orders of the commander?' And they broke it to smithereens with the sledgehammers! I tried to explain, and he threatened me with the cooler. You should see what's been thrown into that pit! The most expensive measuring apparatus. Philips equipment! And so many of our unfinished projects . . . whole panels. And first everything is smashed, so that no one would think of unearthing it later. Can you believe it, I almost wept like a woman. This is madness. Who says sabotage? No, if they wanted to sabotage, they'd be sneaky about it. This is just some psycho in command here."

During those days I learned that all the material on my phonoscopic work was thrown into the fire—thousands of sound pictures, hundreds of pages of descriptions, calculations, diagrams. They had been "incorrectly made secret" and were subject to destruction.

Only the notes in my workbooks remained.

A pitiful consolation was the fact that I didn't have to participate personally in the destruction. Junior Technician Lieutenant Valentina Ivanovna

P. was putting my work archives "in order"—that is, choosing the material to be destroyed and signing the documents. She became the official author of everything I had done before and of all my future work.

A pretty, red-haired, plump woman, with gray eyes and fluffy lashes, and apricot fuzz on her cheeks and a birthmark near her plump lower lip, she looked at me with sadness and commiseration, and when no one was around, would whisper: "Ah, how I understand you. It's so sad, so sad. It's your work! You probably hoped it would help you get an early release? It's so painful. But what can you do? Orders. Lieutenant Colonel Naumov is a very strict boss. He reports personally to Lavrentii Pavlovich [Beria] every week. But you know, you were in the army, weren't you? Orders! Will you help me with my English today? I have to pass my language requirement next month. It's so hard! And Vasilii Nikolaevich also said that you would help me write the proposal for my dissertation. I still haven't picked out a topic."

Anton Mikhailovich was grim in those days. Finding a minute, I tried to talk to him about the materials on phonoscopy. Using my old workbooks, I could try to repeat the research, re-create at least part of what had been done—this was all work that was indispensable for the basic theme of the institute; without them I couldn't manage to re-create individual characteristics of a voice after superdependable "impulse" coding.

He frowned angrily. "I've heard all that. More than once. I don't want to hear any more. I do not discuss orders. Understand? You have precisely defined tasks. You are required first of all to study intelligibility, then the conditions for re-creating a voice in each special concrete case. I don't think I have to tell you that our institution does not belong to the Academy of Sciences. The work conditions have changed now; you must understand that. Therefore, I suggest and order—note, I could order, but first I suggest —that you cut out the discussions. They're useless. I stress: all these discussions, tsk tsks, complaints, and grumblings are absolutely useless and even harmful, first of all for yourself. Work. Good-bye."

But still Sergei and I wrote to the Party Central Committee: Sergei about the barbaric destruction of equipment, and I about the bizarre, and in the final analysis, harmful depersonalization and elimination of the creative role of the prisoners and the doing away of the materials on phonoscopy.

Knowing the traditional antagonism between the authorities of the prison and of the sharashka, we decided to send the letters through the prison.

After easygoing Shevchenko, the new security officer of the prison was Colonel Mishin—a well-fed, obnoxious dandy. He paraded around in well-cut uniforms, dressing up as a pilot, or tank driver, or artillery officer— the officers of the security organs wore the insignias of the most varied armed forces, either for greater secrecy or so as not to frighten the inhabitants of the capital with the growing number of Cheka personnel. Two or three times a month he handed out letters, transfers, and bulk mail. The mail-call recipients were either named at the morning check or their names were posted at the medical yurt.

At mail call, he tried to recruit stoolies. The first time he tried to convince me almost gently. He knew that I was a Soviet patriot, and he was in much need of precise, conscientious information. But that time and the next I told him the same thing I had told Shikin and his other colleagues in a similar situation: if I find out about something dangerous to the sharashka or the state, then naturally I will sound the alarm immediately, but I do not want to, cannot, and will not eavesdrop, spy, or suck up to those who express opinions that are alien to me. As for reporting arguments and conversations, I consider that both unworthy and simply unnecessary. For no matter what words are said in prison, they can cause no harm to the government—every talker is already being punished, already incarcerated.

"Now this conversation of yours is anti-Soviet. It can be construed as agitation against vigilance."

"Excuse me, Citizen Lieutenant Colonel, but who would believe that a prisoner tried anti-Soviet agitation alone with an officer of state security, a security worker of such rank?"

He was silent, smirking and bugging his eyes out at me—practicing his iron-hard gaze. But I knew the antidote—calmly look at the bridge of his nose and try to think about something else, distant.

"Go!"

At morning check the duty supervisor announced that from now on we would write only to our immediate relatives—parents, wife, children, or brothers and sisters. And that very day we were supposed to bring the security officer a list of all our correspondents, giving their exact age and place of birth.

I brought the list, but I couldn't remember the exact name of the little settlement in the Donbas region where Nadya was born—Aleksandrov, Aleksandrovsk, Aleksandrovka, or Aleksandriia—and I didn't know what it was called now.

Mishin looked through the list and gave me an almost jovial look.

"I won't accept this, this is useless. How could you have gotten married without knowing anything about her, where she was born?"

"Getting to know someone you don't study her passport."

"So, you found yourself a wife in a whorehouse?"

"Citizen Lieutenant Colonel, you do not have the right to insult my family. I insist that you take back your words!"

"What else?"

He rose from his desk and smirked a different way now, maliciously: aha, got you where it hurts!

"What are you allowing yourself to say? I ask you and you must answer.

I want to know in what whorehouse you got married since you don't know the origins."

"Apparently, you're the one who's accustomed to dealing with people who marry in whorehouses. Until you apologize I will not come to see you no matter what you call me in about, not even to pick up my mail. You can have me dragged in by force. But even then I will not talk to you."

"What is the meaning of this?"

But I no longer saw or heard him. Feeling my nape turn to wood from cold fury, afraid I would blow up, I turned sharply and ran from his office.

The usual line of mail recipients stood in the hallway. Some of them told me later what I didn't remember.

"You raced past, pale, eyes wild, muttering: 'I won't permit it. I won't.' We thought you'd gone screwy, received bad news, and freaked out."

That same day I filed a complaint with the head of the prison. In those days the position was held by a phlegmatic lieutenant colonel, a frontline officer, judging by his medals and ribbons for being wounded. Mishin had just one measly, dock-tailed row of two ribbons—obviously rear-guard awards.

The prison head called me in. "What are you inventing? What insults are there?"

And patiently hearing me out, he spoke calmly, in what seemed a sympathetic way to me: "Well, the lieutenant colonel perhaps said the wrong thing. Why push your principles right way, take offense? You're not on the same level. You take offense at your pals and friends. And you write that you want the lieutenant colonel to apologize. That doesn't happen. You don't want to talk to him? Not even get your letters? You know, that's not serious, it's childish. Maybe now you're insulted by me as well?"

"Soviet laws and the criminal code and the criminal procedure code clearly state that human dignity cannot be demeaned. Even the most evil criminals cannot be tortured or insulted. The lieutenant colonel broke the law. Until he apologizes to me, I will not talk to him, neither addressing him myself nor answering his questions."

"That means you want not to obey but to violate the rules, you want to resist authority. Don't you understand what that means?"

"I understand that I didn't break anything and don't intend to. I obey the rules, I work conscientiously. But I will not talk to a boss who insulted me crudely until he apologizes."

"That means you won't pick up your mail, you won't send letters. We won't make exceptions for you. Well, that means you're punishing yourself. And your family. They'll worry about you."

For over two months I didn't go for my mail or write letters. A friend of Gumer's called my family, told them I was fine, but that I wouldn't be corresponding for the time being. However, they could bring packages. (The food packages were brought by the storeroom manager.)

Then Mishin went on vacation, and the director himself started handing out and collecting the mail. I immediately got a large stack of letters from Nadya, my parents, Inna Levidova, and several packages of books. They included a textbook on Chinese, brochures—Stalin's speeches translated into Chinese—and dictionaries, Turkish, Mongolian, and others.

The director asked how many characters there were, was it hard to learn them, which languages I knew. He asked questions and looked at me with curiosity, clearly well intentioned. The next time he asked me if I had learned many of the characters yet, and I drew a few of the easiest to explain.

He looked at me with something like respect.

And the third time I went into his office, I saw Mishin sitting next to him, tanned, in a new field jacket with pilot's shoulder boards.

"And there he is, the huffy one. He almost challenged me to a duel. A real von-Baron. Well, are you still huffy?"

"Citizen Director," I said, looking between them. "I can't add anything to what I've already said. The citizen lieutenant colonel insulted my family, and until he apologizes—"

"All right, all right. Well, I admit that I expressed myself incorrectly, that I was upset. My nerves aren't steel, either. Well, I admit it in front of the director. Well, shall we consider the issue closed now? Agreed?"

"In that case—yes."

And since then and until the end, Mishin was always polite to me, even amiable. He didn't try to recruit me anymore, but as he handed my letters to me, he sometimes spoke: "How are things there now, are they tightening the discipline? The television sets are finished. Well, we'll try to get the movies back twice a month. Will you tell me why Jews are so against Soviet rule? Who gave them their rights, after all? Who put them in high places? And, they say that instead, you're friends with the Germans. And they killed Jews, they're fascists, after all. I have information, they still support Hitler. Do you know Korean? Is it like Chinese? I wonder how they come to terms there at the front, the Chinese and Koreans? If they have translators, they're probably Russians. Are you satisfied with the food? How about the warehouse? If you have any comments, don't be shy with them. Our goal is for everything to be in order."

I countered his determinedly folksy conversations and broad smiles with standing at attention. And if he offered me a seat, I sat the way German POWs used to sit in front of me: at attention—knees together, back straight, both hands on the knees. And I replied politely, but briefly, clearly, and vaguely: "Yes, it's in order," "The same, as before," "I don't remember, don't know," "I never noticed anything like that . . . Every nation has various kinds of people, more of some, less of others. I don't know which there are more of—and I never heard of anyone counting them," "Completely satisfied," "No comment," "I don't know about the others."

He would frown, the smile extinguished, and nod—"You may leave"—but he never insulted me again.

Sergei and I, sealing the letters addressed to the Central Committee, went to see Mishin together. It was dangerous to talk to him about these letters alone.

He looked at us warily. "Why are you together? Come in one at a time."

"Citizen Lieutenant Colonel, we have one issue."

"What is this, a collective? Not allowed! Collectives are severely punished."

"No, sir, Citizen Lieutenant Colonel. Each of us has a separate letter. But they're addressed to the same place—the Central Committee. And the subject is the same—of state importance. We're asking you to send them via special secret mail. There."

"Why is the envelope sealed? It's not allowed."

"You may send sealed envelopes to higher government and Party organs. There's a paragraph about that in the rules."

"And where are the copies?"

"No copies, no rough drafts left. The letters are absolutely secret. Of special state importance."

"Are you complaining about the new administration?"

"We would never call personal complaints secret state affairs. You've known us long enough."

"Yes, I certainly do know you. And why aren't you sending them through the administration of the sharashka? Through Major Shikin, as is required by regulations?"

"Because of state considerations, not personal ones. It's simpler to say that we trust you more. But we do not have the right to reveal the contents of the letters even to you."

He looked at the envelopes, frowning, turned them around. "All right!"

Not even two weeks passed before Sergei and I were called one at a time to see Major Shikin.

A young man, in civilian clothes, but with military bearing, sat in his office. "I'm an instructor from the Central Committee. Did you write this letter?"

He asked questions to the point, with interest, with sense. He recorded all the answers. When we started talking about the phonoscopy experiments, I said that I couldn't give him concrete details, since I had signed a very strict release form. But the MGB, of course, still had the materials of the two phonoscopic expert evidence that I gave, one of which was indubitably successful, and the other elicited grave doubts, but even now I was still convinced that phonoscopy was a fully realistic affair of state importance, and the results of months of serious research had been destroyed here. This was a heavy loss and had to be remedied as soon as possible.

Shikin was not present at our conversations, but he stopped Sergei in the hall and said: "Complaining? Did he put you up to this? What do you mean 'your own idea'? That means you're the instigator? Why didn't you come to me, the way you're supposed to? Well, we'll find out now why you're the only two trying to undermine the authority of the administration."

He called me in the next day and told me the same thing, and then said that the request for my next visit could not be granted. "Since you have committed another violation— Maybe *you* don't see it that way, but I say it's a violation . . . Things are getting lax here. You've started thinking too highly of yourself. You forget who you are and where you are. But we'll clear this up. We'll clear it up very thoroughly."

A nauseating chill traveled along my ribs. Why the hell did I start with that letter? Now they'll send me to Vorkuta or Magadan. And I had almost three years to go. I wouldn't make it in a mine or in the forests. And the old fart of a clerk from the Central Committee wouldn't help.

Sergei acted cheerful, but he was uncomfortable too. "Yep, brother, I think we soaped our own rope. A muzhik complained to the tsar about a military leader. The leader still doesn't know what will happen to him, but the muzhik's been hanged."

Anton Mikhailovich came in and spoke with reserve, but he didn't seem angry. He talked to the captain a long time, with Gumer, then came over to the stands. Sergei was reading the newspaper aloud from the booth, wearing earphones. The specialists were changing the panels.

Then he called me over. "They say you have initiated a correspondence with the government. You didn't follow my advice. I'm very sorry about that. You obviously overestimate your abilities. And overestimate my good feelings for you. I confess that I am tired of defending, saving, fighting, arguing that your scientific and technical merits balance out all your flaws and sins. I'm sick of it. And I'm simply tired. Understand? I wish you the best."

I don't remember how long my anxious waiting lasted. Each day was longer than a week. And suddenly—joy. First Gumer, and then Evgeniia Vasilievna, told me that Major Shikin, from whom all the threats emanated, was no longer dangerous.

Both the willful lord Anton Mikhailovich and the dispassionate executive Konstantin Fedorovich and all the other engineer lieutenant colonels, majors, and captains knew well enough how we worked; they knew how to turn our talents to profit the work and themselves. The new chief, Naumov, squeezed us stupidly and indifferently, without distinguishing among individuals. To him, all of us—the notorious special contingent—

were a faceless crowd of low beasts who had to be used.

And Shikin must have believed that all of us or most of us were enemies and that he could expect low deeds and nastiness from any of us. He must have envisioned himself as a trainer of wild animals, using whip and bribe to make the dangerous beasts serve the state.

He was the compleat Cheka operative of the thirties and forties—ignorant,* suspicious (out of "revolutionary vigilance"), cruel, and certain that no one could be trusted. And it was better to overpunish ten times than not to punish even once. He kept exposing somebody's intrigues, who was planning or had already committed a crime.

Several zeks and free employees were moving an old turner's lathe from the top floor to the basement. They were having trouble on the narrow stairs. They tripped twice. Then someone discovered a crack in the lathe. Shikin started a case of sabotage. The investigation dragged on for about three months. Anton Mikhailovich managed to save two participants in the move—excellent engineers. Thanks to him there was no trial. The other movers "got off" with many days in the cooler and a transfer to a strictly run camp. One of the free employees was fired.

Among the Germans working in the sharashka was an elderly professor of chemistry. He had been born in St. Petersburg, studied in the Russian Gymnasium, and left for Germany in the early 1920s. He attracted Shikin's hunter's instinct by speaking fluent Russian. He stayed in the lab less frequently in the evenings than the others. Weakened by hunger and illness that he suffered in prison, he complained of sharply deteriorating eyesight, and asked to have his glasses changed, because it was particularly hard for him to work at night. The prison medical office couldn't get an eye specialist. Shikin started a case of sabotage against him. He questioned all his fellow countrymen. Some of them told us that Shikin was trying to prove that the professor was "agitating for sabotage" and was conducting "fascist propaganda."

The order promulgated after the close of the investigation said: so-and-so "embarked on the path of sabotaging his own creative initiative," for which he was being punished with twenty days in the cooler and being sent to a strictly run camp. Many memorized that marvelous formulation: "sabotaging his own . . . initiative."

A former inmate, chemistry professor S., a seventy-year-old man, morbidly puffy, humble, and kind, friendly to everyone and unconstrained in his conversations even with prisoner colleagues, worked in the chemistry

---

*Once he called me in the lab: "Which foreign languages do you know? Do you speak Austrian, too?" Almost snorting in reply, I answered honestly that I understood a few Austrian dialects, for instance, Viennese, Styrian. "Well, then, come to my office—there's an Austrian here who specifically requested that you translate."

lab. Sometimes they asked him to mail letters addressed to their relatives. One such "writer" didn't stand up to Shikin's questioning and confessed, and the kind old man was rearrested.

Probably Shikin knew simple human attachments, too—to his parents, a woman, his children. Maybe in his free time he fished or played dominoes. But his ruling passions were surveillance, accusation, exposure, punishment.

And it was these very passions, so natural in his calling and seemingly meritorious in that line of work, that brought on his downfall.

Dmitri Sh., a radio engineer who worked until 1945 in Berlin at the Telefunken Laboratories, was sentenced to ten years under Article 58-4 (collaboration with the international bourgeoisie). A skinny, swarthy, clumsy, and shy man, he spoke both Russian and German with difficulty and a strange "mixed" accent, with a predominance of Polish and Romance-language intonations. He was born in Brazil, his father was the son of a Pole and a Russian woman, his mother the daughter of a German and a Brazilian woman, and his great-grandparents included a Ukrainian, a Spaniard, an Argentine, an Englishwoman, and a Jewess. He naturally did not reveal the last when in 1938 he came to his German grandfather to enter the Berlin radiotechnical institute. He graduated during the war. But he didn't get around to leaving for Brazil since he married a German woman and was supposed to become his father-in-law's heir to a small, profitable business.

"I don't understand, I can't understand, why this was my fate. When I was arrested in Berlin, I was enervated absolutely—*ganz kaputt mit Nerven.* Understood nothing. The first investigator captain, such a fine young man, said: 'You have a cocktail of different bloods, different nations. You have Russian blood, Polish blood, but you worked for the Hitlerite Germans and therefore you are a traitor to your homeland.' He laughed; I cried. The second investigator major, so rough, shouted: 'You are an agent of the Gestapo, an American spy.' Threatened: 'If you don't confess, we'll shoot you, hang you, send you to Siberia to work in the mines for twenty years.' But I confessed everything, I told only the truth. I told them everything, how I lived, worked, did, I swore, gave my *sventa*—my holy vow: as God is my witness, I am no traitor, no agent. Then they brought me to Moscow, to Lubyanka. There the investigator, a senior lieutenant, so correct, proper, intelligent, he didn't laugh, didn't shout, wrote down everything as I said it. He promised, there will be a trial, just, legal, objective. Then I went to Butyrki, I thought for the trial. No. A lieutenant colonel came, showed me a paper—a special commission *in absentia* gave me ten years. For what? Why? I don't understand. I don't."

He worked in the radio laboratory from morning till midnight, rarely went out for walks. Usually right after lunch and dinner he went straight to his panels. He had no friends or pals. He didn't play chess or dominoes.

It was hard for him to talk. He couldn't follow fast spoken Russian. Our Germans didn't keep company with him either. Kurt used to say: "He spent almost ten years in Germany. Studied. Married a rich young woman. He worked and made a good salary. But he didn't like it there, you see. He missed his Rio de Janiero. Basically he's either an idiot or a schizophrenic. Don't you understand why he was sent up? Very simple: he's a living refutation of your propaganda. You maintain that all the Jews and all the crazy people were killed in Germany. And here's a crazy half-Jew who was flourishing, working for a famous company. Look at his eyes, his nose— a typical Eastern Jew. In Poland all converted Jews called themselves Poles. And besides—he's a living illustration of the racial theory: here's what happens from miscegenation. Sort of a psychopath or a cretin. No, it's not an accident. It wasn't the Germans who invented the study of race. In America the great majority of criminals and madmen are mestizos, mulattoes, and quadroons. And here's a perfect example to contradict your propaganda. Naturally your commissars couldn't leave him at liberty. He was lucky they didn't liquidate him."

At dinner they said that Dmitri had been called from the laboratory and taken away without his gear. The next day the order was made known: he was sent to the cooler for twenty days for "criminal relations with a free employee." At first no one could believe it. They said: Shikin's really crazy, making up absurd, delirious charges. But that same day on our walk the details of the unbelievable event were under discussion.

Auntie Katya, a cleaning woman, wide-hipped, round-faced, pale—she could have been forty, she could have been sixty—in a shapeless black coat, a dirty white scarf, was almost indistinguishable from her co-workers in the same coats and scarves. They came an hour and a half before the beginning of our workday to wash the floors in the laboratories and offices.

How Dmitri and she found each other no one knew. Neither he nor she told anyone the story of their love, or perhaps, it was only a friendship. But someone noticed their assignations in the early-morning hours—Dmitri rushed to the lab, barely finishing his breakfast, before opening hour— and during the lunch break, in corners of the cellar. And someone else saw her coming out after him from a bathroom that had been closed until then.

And the all-knowing camp janitors knew that Shikin had exposed the ill-fated pair with the help of herring.

Our dining room had two inevitable, constant dishes: wheat cereal and large herring. For breakfast and dinner, and frequently for lunch as well, we were given large, glistening, pinkish-greenish pieces of fatty and very salty herring. You were tormented by thirst after eating it. And many of us didn't eat it at all or left part of it. The new arrivals marveled: how could prisoners be so choosy! Those who liked it gathered the leftovers, soaked them, and then marinated them in old eggplant-caviar or jam jars, which we could obtain in the warehouse.

And Dmitri gave his girl friend gifts of these jars of herring.

Shikin found out about it and personally searched Auntie Katya at the guardhouse when she was leaving after work. He found empty jars in her bag and pieces of herring wrapped in newspaper and rags in her pockets and inside her dress—the standard pieces from the prison dining room.

In the throes of righteous wrath and caught up in the hunting spirit, he detained the deathly frightened "criminal," called two supervisors from Mishin's group, went to her apartment, and searched the place. They found numerous jars of marinated herring and some semiliterate notes that were allegedly Dmitri's love letters.

Shikin compiled a protocol and sent the weeping Auntie Katya with a supervisor to the regional division of the militia. But unexpectedly they had problems there. The militia did not deem it necessary to make an arrest on the basis of a note from an unknown major and a verbal report of a supervisor. They got Auntie Katya to sign a form and let her go. The head of the division was doubtful also about the legality of a search made without a warrant.

A few days later—either through the efforts of Mishin, who was settling an old score with Shikin, or because the militia or some of the sharashka officers "signaled"—the Directorate ordered Shikin removed from duty for "violation of the law." Evgeniia Vasilievna said that he had been removed from the security organs completely.

After the cooler, Dmitri was sent to a camp. Auntie Katya was fired, but she was not prosecuted.

Gumer told me that Shikin had been planning to take care of us for "snitching" to the Central Committee; he had already called in several zeks and free employees, started gathering a *kompromat*, a compromising affidavit. But Naumov wouldn't do that kind of thing. He wanted to get rid of all the prisoners at the sharashka. And at the last meeting he announced that all the officers, particularly the ones "attached," had to study urgently, learning everything possible from us, so that in a year's time the special contingent could be totally replaced.

"That new pug-nosed Lieutenant Vanya is going to replace Sergei, and the big-boobed Valya is going to pump you for all your acoustics and linguistics and all your foreign languages."

In the winter of 1951–1952 I began studying Chinese. At first I was interested in the characters as an aid to my basic work.

On the spectrograms (sound pictures) of speech the outlines of separate sounds changed depending on the voice, intonation, and speed of pronunciation. Written letters also change depending on the handwriting and effort of the writer. But the shape of a letter is relatively simple and more stable than the drawing of a sound spectrum. There are incomparably more characters than letters. Even the most barely literate Chinese must memorize no fewer than 2,000. The differences among them must be recognizable independent of handwriting, style, and speed of writing, and yet in terms of drawing they are more complex than sound pictures. Therefore I wanted to train myself as I studied the characters to better memorize and read sound pictures.

And for my studies in "hand" etymology I found the characters that retained the rudiments of depiction, symbolic signs for the hand, the most interesting.

And prison fate unexpectedly presented me with a teacher.

A few Russian engineers and technicians from China were brought in. Vladimir Petrovich V., a young engineer from Harbin, had studied Chinese in Gymnasium, and remembered at least 1,000 characters and had a tolerable mastery of the literary (Northern, or Mandarin) dialect. At first we studied with Zhen-Zhen, but, distracted by other worries, he quickly tired of it.

The further I went, the more it was to my taste. And I already had hopes of reading ancient Chinese philosophers in the original, whom I knew only in Russian and English translation. And I dreamed of future trips to China.

In 1948–1949, I kept a newspaper map in my desk to follow the movements of the people's armies.

I did not believe what they wrote about the ties between Tito and the Bulgarian and Hungarian Communists on the one hand, and the Gestapo and Anglo-American intelligence, on the other—just as earlier I had not believed in the capitalism-restoration intentions and espionage activities of Bukharin and Trotsky. But in those days any opposition could weaken the garrison of the besieged fortress, damage the crew of the storming warship. And that's why particularly dangerous oppositionists had to be defamed mortally.

But now socialism had won in several countries, and Stalin said that national democracies had to follow their own paths. Then why couldn't we permit free discussions and comradely disagreements? Why deal so harshly with opposition?

Well, maybe, all this was necessary because in Poland, Czechoslovakia, Hungary, the GDR, and Bulgaria, Communists coexisted with bourgeois parties and therefore harsh discipline was still called for. And we were threatened from without also—the atom bomb, West German revanchists, everyone who was frightened by our victories. And did that mean that we had to tighten the screws again?

I couldn't find a real, certain answer to these questions, but I found happiness thinking that enormous China would not be subordinated the way Eastern Europe was, and that the Chinese Party would not be publicly dishonored like the Yugoslav.

I considered Stalin's strategy ultimately correct. And I was at least convinced that it could not be altered and that criticizing it would be extremely harmful. However, I understood then, too, that our society certainly was not socialist and calling it one was merely passing off a wish for reality—because we had entered into the earliest "slaveholding period of primary socialist accumulation." (I came up with that "theorem" back in my early arguments with Solzhenitsyn.) And that meant that "barbarian means of overcoming barbarism" were unavoidable. I was convinced of this by everything I had seen and experienced at the front, in prison, in camp.

For a while I hoped that the victories and conquests would weaken the fear of any disagreement, which bred state terror. I had hoped that our comrades in the West, nearby in the people's democracies, and in distant places where Communists were becoming members of the government would be a good influence on us, help us overcome barbaric traditions and manners. And then finally, all the civil rights that they had to rescind in 1918 would become real again—Lenin had said that this was a temporary repeal, brought about by the intervention and the Civil War. The "Stalin Constitution" of 1936 reaffirmed and even expanded these civil liberties. But they remained frozen because fascism was attacking, World War II was about to start.

The first rumors of disagreements with Tito seemed good harbingers of a new democratic development in the Cominform.* But soon came the vicious damnations of "the fascist clique," the trials in Sofia and Budapest, and some officers at the sharashka said out loud: "We'll soon be doing a little shooting in the Balkans. Give Tito's gang what for. Clear the air."

In China the Red Armies moved swiftly. They fought infrequent but always victorious battles and even more frequently won bloodless victories; the garrisons of large cities, divisions, and corps of the enemy capitulated before them.

Zhen-Zhen and I discussed for hours the possibilities of return communications: Moscow—Peking—Moscow. We knew about China from the books of Tretiakov, Pearl Buck, Malraux, Agnes Smedley, and Anna Louise Strong, and I also had read the reports of German antifascists and American magazines that appeared in the sharashka. The stories of our "Russian-Chinese" colleague confirmed much of what we had read about the extreme stability and healthy national morality—conscientiousness, scrupulous honesty, extraordinary industriousness, natural discipline, moderation, politeness, and other qualities characteristic since time immemorial of the Chinese of various classes. Even the bourgeois authors admitted that the Chinese communists, in contrast with the "Westernizing" Kuomintang, cultivated these national virtues in their armies and in those regions that they already ruled. And I wanted to hope that we would be able "to borrow" from the Chinese not the "wisest ignorance of the foreigners" (Griboedov), but those good qualities that were necessary for all peoples and the work of socialism.

Vladimir Petrovich, the only son of an engineer who worked on the

---

*Cominform (Communist Information Bureau), an international organization founded in 1947 to spread communism. (Translator's note.)

Chinese-Oriental Railroad [which went through Manchuria but belonged to Russia], graduated from the Gymnasium in Harbin and the radio division of the Manchurian Polytechnical Institute; he had worked as an engineer in a private Japanese-Manchurian company manufacturing radio equipment. He married a woman from his institute classes. She was due to give birth in the fall of 1945.

Soviet troops entered Harbin in August. The numerous Russian inhabitants greeted them shyly at first but warmly. The conquerors of Hitler's empire easily got their revenge for Port Arthur and Tsushima [Russian defeats in 1904]; columns of Japanese POWs wandered grimly through the city. They were taken away echelon by echelon to the west, to Siberia.

The new Russian newspapers and radio spoke eloquently about the victories, successes, and achievements of all the republics of the Soviet Union, and most of all of the great Russian people—the elder brother of all the other nationalities—about the genius and kindness of Stalin, about the marvelous and happy life of the Soviet people.

It was clear that much of this was propaganda, exaggeration, overembellishment. But the military victories were indisputable. Russian soldiers and officers looked hearty, were much better armed than the Japanese, and behaved generally with dignity. There were a few robberies and rapes, but in wartime in any army such incidents are not unknown. Vladimir Petrovich and his family and friends were becoming more and more trusting and friendly toward the victors, the Soviet authorities.

One day on the street Vladimir Petrovich was detained by a patrol. They invited him politely to the commandant's headquarters, to check his documents. There they filled out a form and took him to a cell with about twenty people in it—mostly Russian Harbiners, several Japanese and Chinese. They were promised: we'll check quickly and let you go, there's no need to inform your families; everyone in the city knows that people are to have their papers checked.

Several days passed. He again requested permission to inform his family, for his parents and his pregnant wife would be worried about him.

He was taken to prison and there an investigator, a proper senior lieutenant, said: "As soon as we clear things up, you will go home yourself."

"What else still needs clearing up?"

"Well, you have to help us with that. If you are a truly loyal Russian man . . . tell me, why did you become a citizen of Manchukuo*—a puppet of Japanese imperialism, the fiercest enemy of Russia?"

"But I was born here, in Harbin. And the government of Manchukuo formed while I was still in nursery school. I had no choice about becoming or not becoming a citizen. And my parents have lived here since the turn

*A Japanese puppet state (1932–1945) in China. (Translator's note.)

of the century. Our grandfathers moved here when the railroad was being built."

"You studied at the Polytechnical Institute, and it was under Japanese command, and that means, Japanese intelligence. What intelligence orders did you carry out? A frank confession and conscious assistance in the investigation will guarantee the speediest release for you. If not, you have only yourself to blame."

They didn't beat him or torture him. They interrogated him only three or four times. And then he and a few hundred like him were sent to Western Siberia to the camps. Another investigator there—a captain, tired, distracted, not very educated—saw him. He spoke unconvincingly about the decisions of some extraordinary Far Eastern military tribunals, coordinated with the decisions of some international courts. For some reason it was supposed to follow that the Harbin Institute and the company for which Vladimir Petrovich had worked were military criminal organizations. The captain didn't shout, or curse, or threaten, but said in a business-like and almost indifferent manner that Vladimir had to "confess frankly" to the crimes that he himself had participated in and also to name his accomplices and all other criminals that he could remember. That was the only way to mitigate his sentence. And even earn his freedom. But if he continued to cover up, "pull rubber," "pretend to be a virgin," and "complicate the investigation" (Vladimir was hearing these Russian expressions for the first time), he could be asking for the *vyshka*.

"You don't know what *vyshka* means? Fine education the Japanese gave you. *Vyshka* is nine grams of lead in the back of your head and into the ground without a coffin. Understand? Of course, nowadays, they might hang you, too: a rope around your neck and a sign on your chest: 'Spy.' So people will have something to look at. So, decide for yourself."

By that time Vladimir was extremely emaciated, worn out by disease and hunger. He had been arrested in a summer shirt and light slacks. In the fall, during the Siberian frosts, they gave him old, torn underwear and a worn cotton padded jacket. They huddled two or three to a scrawny straw mat in the chilled barracks. A lame wit kept repeating: "Skeleton to skeleton, rubbing warms the bones." They put sacks and rags on top of their thin blankets. His consciousness was fogged by unending depression and despair.

The threats did not frighten him. Death meant an end to unbearable horror. The investigator pushed a sheaf of papers toward him. "Write everything that you know and remember: names, addresses, nicknames, codes, concrete assignments. Everything!"

It took him two pages to write the story of his short life, his family's address, and added: "Please inform my family of my death."

The investigator rubbed his eyes, read it, looked at him with the same distraction, without irritation. "Well, whatever you want. But you're not allowed to write abroad."

Another few months passed. He suffered from scurvy, pellagra, pneumonia, had a vague idea of time passing. He was called in again, this time to a different officer, who handed him a thin sheet of paper. It carried a hard-to-read typed text. Inked in were his name, date of birth, address, and numbers at the end. A special commission of the NKVD of the USSR sentenced him to twenty-five years of deprivation of freedom without confiscation of his property. His term began on the date of his arrest and ended in August 1970. He would be over fifty by then. And his wife, too. His son—or daughter—would be twenty-five. And his parents were unlikely to live that long.

He worked in the camp shop as a technician. He was given treatment, grew healthier and stronger. He was paid in kind—bread, canned foods, grains—for repairing radio sets for the bosses and the free employees. When he was brought to the sharashka, it seemed like heaven to him. Real engineering work demanded both knowledge and imagination. He was surrounded by well-wishing comrades, and the authorities were polite and understanding. And life was calm and ordered.

Tall, thin, with a broad brow and large glasses, always reserved, serious, he seemed glum, alienated; he rarely smiled and spoke little. Some of the noisy "good ol' boys," who were informal with colleagues young and old, considered him a supercilious pedant, who thought too much of himself. But he was merely incurably well bred. His rather dry politeness hid a sedate kindness and a whole, unflawed moral consciousness. He didn't know how to pretend, lie, intrigue. His glumness came from his ceaseless depression, which he didn't want to, and probably couldn't, verbalize. He couldn't stand sentimentality or pathos in literature or films.

We studied together, at first daily after dinner or right before lights out. He wrote out the characters in calligraphy. He patiently taught Zhen-Zhen and me. "You have to precisely retain consistency and direction in every stroke, every line. Now look—you always begin this way. And then you write like this—from the right, to the left, down. It would be best, naturally, to have a brush and ink. You have to hold the brush completely vertically."

He said that an individual's personality is revealed by the way the characters are drawn. Old Chinese are certain that a bad person cannot be a good calligrapher.

Later my family sent me a textbook, dictionary, and books. Our lessons became more infrequent. He gave us "homework." The first, and only, Chinese book that I read with the help of Vladimir Petrovich and the dictionary was a translation of Stalin's speech at a rally of combine operators.

Unsettling rumors sprang up in the fall. The free employees told us that the majority of bosses in the new management "were not used" to dealing with prisoners and were demanding that we be removed from the institute that was directly subordinate to the Central Committee of the Party. Anton Mikhailovich and the senior sharashka officers were trying to convince them otherwise, insisting that they wouldn't be able to manage without special contingents. And there were a few old-hand Chekists in the Directorate who knew our worth. However, Naumov was also insisting on "purging" the institute.

In the yurts, in the dining room, the only talk and arguments were about the new rumors.

"Before the end of the year we'll be taken to a special camp somewhere in the northeast."

"No, we'll be sent to another sharashka near Moscow, in Kazan, or on the other side of the Urals. Everyone will be taken to the distant camps without the right to correspond. We know secrets, after all. That means we'll never see liberty. Now we'll spend the rest of our lives finishing our sentences."

"We'll be lucky if they don't finish us off right away"; "They'll send most of us away, but about fifty of the most indispensable ones will stay here"; "No, only twenty, no more"; "Not even twenty. Just a few specialists, whom they can't do without, will be settled at Lubyanka or Lefortovo, and they'll be brought here by a Black Maria twice a day."

"Who gets to determine who's indispensable? Anton, for instance, needs you with your articulations and other shit. But stupid Naumov doesn't give a damn about anyone. He doesn't understand a thing about anything. And so he considers it all bullshit, and maybe even sabotage."

"We'll be lucky if they just send us somewhere far away to hack out coal, chop trees, build socialism in some separate zone, for they could set us up in a way that will make us think of Lefortovo as a sanatorium."

I wanted to believe the best rumors, or at least, not the very worst.

Sergei, Valentin, and Semyon definitely belonged to the top ten "indispensable specialists." But they, just like me, either consoled themselves with hopeful rumors, or grew depressed from rumors that promised inevitable calamity.

One of the few who remained calm was Viktor Andreevich Kemnits, a Moscow engineer, sentenced under "the case of the writer Andreyev."

Daniil Leonidovich Andreyev, the son of the famous writer,* was arrested in 1949; he had written a novel that the MGB found to be anti-Soviet and even terroristic. Following his arrest, several dozen of his friends and acquaintances were arrested, too. Viktor Andreevich had been to the author's house only once or twice at readings from the novel, since he worked hard and was often away on business. His wife, Anna Vladimirovna, had been there more frequently and had heard the reading of the chapter in which one of the characters either expressed the desire that the great leader

---

*Leonid Nikolaevich Andreyev (1871–1919), best known for his play *He Who Gets Slapped* (1914). (Translator's note.)

die or thought aloud about what might happen after his death.

Therefore, Viktor Andreevich was sentenced to ten years under Articles 58-10 and 58-11, and his wife, like the author himself, also under 58-8 (terrorism). Tall, broad-shouldered, with a large head and a steep broad forehead, bearing a slight resemblance to Eisenstein, he moved smoothly and easily. His protuberant light eyes had a trusting gaze. The son of Russified Germans, he spoke German slowly, carefully, with the wooden stilted vocabulary of our school textbooks, but he remembered prayers he had memorized in childhood. Specialists said he was an experienced and gifted designer. But his main passions in life were music and flowers. He always knew what music broadcasts were scheduled. During those evenings when the easygoing officers were on duty, he would come to the acoustics lab to listen to tapes of symphonies and concerts and to reminisce about the prewar conservatory. He told me how he had first heard Scriabin's music.

"It was staggering. No, I can't explain or describe it. Suddenly a new world opened, unknown—just a second before unknown to me and even unimaginable. But it was mine—my personal world. For the first time I heard music that was completely mine, about me. Mozart, Beethoven, Tchaikovsky, Chopin are wonderful, marvelous. They always astound me. Excite me. Make me happy. Please me. But they are always writing about something wonderful—earthly or heavenly. But it's all out there somewhere. And Scriabin is here, around me and in me. He expressed everything that I could never have expressed—my hopes, joys, pain, fears."

And he spoke with almost the same enthusiasm about flowers, how he managed to grow them in the most difficult city soil, in rocks and rubbish. Together with another passionate gardener, a former tank colonel, he headed a volunteer gardening brigade. They took me in, too. Right after reveille, before breakfast, and in the evening before and after dinner, tearing an hour or so away from superurgent work, we dug, planted, weeded, and watered. In the garden in front of the sharashka building and in the camp between the rows of yurts we made flower beds, and there and along the paths we grew pansies, nasturtiums, daisies, marigolds, nicotianas, carnations, narcissus, asters, gladioli.

When the talk turned to books or poetry, Viktor Andreevich sighed sadly.

"You should talk to my Anna Vladimirovna: she's read so much more than I, she understands literature better and poetry, too. She was very sick before the war—a flu that caused complications with her heart. She had to leave the stage. And she was such a marvelous dancer! It was hard for her to quit. She became a choreographer, director. During the evacuation she worked in clubs, gave artistic readings, too. She declaimed Pushkin, Lermontov, Nekrasov, Akhmatova, and Pasternak so beautifully: she knew dozens, hundreds of poems by heart."

Viktor Andreevich could not stand talk about the rumors.

"It's absolutely pointless. We can't check any of it. And we can't affect the future in any way. It doesn't depend on us. Then why upset ourselves and waste our breath? Why don't we listen to Beethoven's Third Piano Concerto one more time instead."

The laboratory was still headed by Captain Vasilii Nikolaevich, coldly polite. And his direct assistant was Senior Technician Lieutenant Anna Vasilievna.

Little Anechka, thin, with grayish reddish brown hair, long face, pale, and a thin nose dotted with blackheads, was a shy and homely girl, but when she smiled she sometimes looked pretty. She came to the sharashka in 1949 right after graduating from the institute of communications. After the first few weeks, she gradually grew used to us, and when she had evening duty, she joined the conversation. She got the very books Solzhenitsyn and I asked her to get from the central libraries on the outside, and together we thought up explanations in case someone in authority asked why she needed the works of the Prague linguistics circle, the old books on philosophy, history, linguistics, psychology, and literature that we requested as material necessary for solving the problems of secret telephony.

For some time she worked as Solzhenitsyn's assistant—foreman of the articulation team and announcer. And naturally, she fell in love with him. When he was taken away, she grieved for a long time. During those evenings she was on duty, she would sit next to me, ask about him, and complain, almost weeping. "Ah, he's so stubborn, so stubborn. How many times did I warn him that Anton Mikhailovich would be displeased, very displeased."

A year later she grew ill, had an operation, and then recuperated for a long time. She returned only after several months, tanned, plump, and more austere. She barely nodded in response to our joyous welcome; she answered questions about her health curtly, monosyllabically, almost roughly. "It has no bearing on our work."

Soon we began to notice that every time she was on duty, Captain Vasilii Nikolaevich stayed, too; they would sit in his corner, whispering, sometimes disappearing for long periods. They were both short, quiet, gray— at first they seemed a very touching pair to me. But Anechka was becoming more and more severe, strict, and even bitchily irritable.

The free employees explained that Vasilii Nikolaevich was married and had children. His wife was incurably ill. As a member of the Party and an "officer of the security organs" he couldn't break up his family. And the Komsomol organization had already chastised Anya "for amoralism," and that's why she was going crazy and biting everyone's head off.

I felt sorry for her. But her constant angry picking on me, her incongruous and crude remarks elicited more and more irritation. I said that I refused to work with her. She got angry, but grew flustered and quieted down. Vasilii Nikolaevich called me over.

"You had an unpleasant talk with Anna Vasilievna. No, no, I don't want any explanations. I admit that she was overly harsh. You know she's been very ill. Complications. Nerves. But you could control your temper, too. You've had a bitter experience already. But now, the most important thing is our work. We have very serious new tasks before us."

He spoke more gently and more volubly than usual. "Let's plan to avoid conflicts like this in the future. Anna Vasilievna will no longer deal with articulation. There are other female announcers. And in the future, you will work on articulation and phonetics only with Valentina Ivanovna, and on analysis of spectra, with Ivan Yakovlevich. In case of any problems or whatever—come to me directly."

Valentina Ivanovna at first reminded me every day that according to the plan of the institute and the orders of Lieutenant Colonel Naumov, she had to get her candidate of sciences degree no later than the following year. "Which sciences? Well, that's where you can help me. Anton Mikhailovich thinks that I won't be able to do it in 'technical sciences.' I need more production-practical work. And then you're not a specialist in technology, are you? You're a candidate of philological sciences, right? I find that more to my liking, too. I love the poetry of Simonov, Surkov, Gusev, Shchipachev.* But most of all, I love music. I play the piano, the bayan, the guitar, and all the stringed instruments. I even compose. I've already composed one waltz and two polkas. But none of that is needed here. If I were married and my husband were a good man, a real man, then I would study only music. I'd go to the opera, the operetta, to concerts. And I'd read a lot of good fiction. They say you've studied foreign literature. Please make up a list of, well, everything I should read in world literature. I studied Russian literature back in grammar school. You know, I prefer Lermontov to Pushkin. Pushkin is too flippant, even a libertine. And I love Turgenev and Tolstoy. He's the greatest writer in the world, isn't he? No, I don't like Dostoevsky. Of course, I've read him. But it's all so decadent and hysterical. And I don't like Chekhov. He's a pessimist, everything is so gray. Well, Gorky, of course, very much! I'll tell you—but this is a big secret—I want to set his 'Song of the Stormy Petrel' and 'Song of the Falcon' to music. Yes, yes, the most important thing for me is music. I think that music is most important for culture. It uplifts people morally. We don't appreciate it yet here. On radio and in our clubs, it's not appreciated enough. And do you know why? Please don't be insulted by this, but it's because the Jews are running our music. Yes, everyone knows that. Wherever you look, there's some Oistrakh or Gilels. And whose music is performed the most? It's always Blanter, Pokrass, or Shostakovich. Oh, no. You're wrong there. Shostakovich is certainly Jewish. Shostakovich— Rabinovich. Well, maybe, he's one of the converted ones. But his music is absolutely not Russian. It's cosmopolitan. Everyone knows that. Comrade Zhdanov said so, and there have been Party resolutions about it. Of

*Minor sentimental poets. (Translator's note.)

course, he hasn't squeezed out contemporary Russian composers completely—Soloviev-Sedoi and Khrennikov can hold their own. But it's even hard for them. In the conservatory, on the radio, at the Bolshoi—Jews are in charge everywhere. For some reason the feeling is that they're all born musicians and the Vanyas and Manyas should stick to fooling around with accordions and balalaikas. Yes, yes, I know that for a fact. I understand that it's not pleasant for you to hear this, but you're not a musician yourself, that's why you don't know about it.

"All right, let's get back to work. Please, come up with a topic for my dissertation. Anton Mikhailovich said that if you really wanted to, you could help me write a dissertation in your field . . . well, about telephone intelligibility and those visible sounds. But so that it would be for a candidate of sciences degree. And also, speaking of foreign languages, I studied German at school and at the institute, and now they tell me that English is more important. So please help me with that, too. Vasilii Nikolaevich said that we could study right after work and even sometimes during working hours if there are no urgent projects."

I came up with a topic for Valentina Ivanovna: "The Physical Parameters of the Intelligibility of Russian Speech." For that work we had to complete and systematize the data we already had on articulation tests of various telephone channels—varying in frequency response, conditions of interference, and so on—and the related research on the analysis of the spectrum of speech through sound pictures. I was planning to support all this with references to books and journals and references to language history, speech physiology, and phonetics, and naturally, to compare our data with those published by foreign telephone specialists, electroacousticians, and linguists.

The topic and outline of the dissertation of the junior technician lieutenant were approved. And I decided that my work in the acoustics lab had taken on a new lively meaning.

The usual articulation tests and sound-picture study of telephone channels had become a daily grind. From time to time some daring technical idea might captivate me. And I was beginning to come up with new improved ways of testing that very system. But in all those cases I was always an assistant or controller, but never the author, the independent scientific worker.

But in the dissertation that Valentina would defend I could make true discoveries. In that work I wanted to present my concepts of speech signs, of the three-dimensional structure of the sound flow of speech, my ideas about the actual role of its formants, about their "superphysical" polysemantic content, when, by slightly changing the distribution of energy in a frequency, the speaker asks or orders, verbalizes thoughts, gives shades of mood, expresses tenderness or wrath.

I included a chapter on the physical bases of the individual characteristics of a voice in the outline of the dissertation.

Valentina Ivanovna was pleased. She had a general understanding of what I was talking about. And I tried to explain as simply as possible the essence of each of the proposed sections. "Yes, yes, I understand that. But I'm not sure that I could explain it in a way that others might understand. I don't have any experience . . . in scientific work. You know how they taught at the institute—you cram and you pass. And once you pass, you forget it. And then I studied with big breaks. I began before the war. Then I was evacuated. Then I was mobilized into the security organs as a telephone operator. I graduated in Moscow through the evening courses —it was so hard, so hard. And it was hard for me financially. A girl has to dress, you know. They say beauty is better than all dresses. But those are words. At the institute and at work all the men thought I was pretty. It's nice to hear compliments, of course. But I'm not a fool. I know that if I had come in a padded jacket, shabby dress, any old hat, thick stockings, and worn shoes, not caring how my hair looks, no one would have even looked at me, and if he did, it would be to think: 'What a mess, scarecrow, dummy.' I could only take the evening classes or correspondence courses —I had to work.

"My mother helped me out sometimes, of course. She's a doctor, and she was at the front in the war. But then she married a Jew, also a doctor. And he cares only about his own children. He has two grown daughters and a son. They're all in medicine. The Jews have taken over music and medicine, the two best-paying professions. Mother's husband has pull everywhere, connections. When Mother pushed him, he helped me at the institute, too. But basically, Mother's marriage is unhappy. He's such an egoist—only for himself and his own. And he's capricious to the point of obnoxiousness. Either he doesn't like the food, or the apartment's not clean enough, or why did I buy a piano and why do I spend so much on clothes. And why did I go to Sochi when they had a dacha in Malakhovka. Why would I want to sit around their old dacha. One of my friends, a very cultured man with an important position in the organs, says that there are more Jews in Malakhovka than in Jerusalem; they have two synagogues there. No, that's not anti-Semitic. Nothing of the kind. The anti-Semites want to kill all Jews, the way the Germans did. Anti-Semitism is a fascist trait, and I'm a member of the Party. And this friend of mine graduated from the Marxist University. That's just your Jewish blood speaking, even though you don't look like a Jew at all.

"No, no, and no! I don't want to kill anyone, and I'm not against all Jews. I know that Karl Marx was a Jew. And Lazar Moiseevich Kaganovich is a respected comrade. And there are good musicians and doctors. But every nationality has its flaws. We Russians have drunkenness, messiness, we're devil-may-care and uncultured. We don't know how to get ahead, we can't protect anything, we trust everyone. And the Jews are sneaky, mean, and stingy. But they have their virtues, too—they know how to get ahead, they stick together a lot better than the Russians. You call me an anti-Semite, but three years ago I almost married a Jew. He was graduating from our communications institute, from the day division. But he was sent to the Far East, and what was there for me to see? Mother's husband promised to help, to have him sent to Moscow or somewhere closer, but he couldn't, or rather, he didn't want to. My fiancé used to write so tenderly, so passionately at first, and then he stopped. They told me that he got married there, even had a kid. But I'm not sorry—to each his own. Jewish husbands are good when they have Jewish wives. But my mother has had such a hard time, that now all she dreams of is a divorce. Well, enough chatter, let's work. You explain clearly to me what I'm supposed to do; better yet, write it all down. I forget. Girlish memory!"

She understood a lot when we spoke about the physical nature of speech, about how in the living resonators—the larynx, nasopharynx, and mouth —flows of meaningful sounds, speech signs, are formed, mixed, and modulated. Looking at sound pictures, oscillograms, drawn diagrams, she quickly learned what was what. But she seemed to forget as quickly things I thought she knew solidly, and she was quickly sidetracked from any task —from checking the articulation tables and from memorizing English verbs, from decoding sound pictures and from the new section of the dissertation, which she was supposed to not only read but understand in connection with the preceding sections and the outline of the ones to follow.

"Interesting? Of course, it's very interesting. I'll read it a little more and think about it later. So, you're completely convinced that these second formants, the hubs, are the central things for intelligibility? Did you think of that yourself? Aha, that means the Americans were first after all. But maybe there were some Russian scientists even earlier? It would be good to prove that. You know, I love the opera more than anything. And I dream of composing an opera. Now you can help me, write a good libretto. To make a contemporary heroic and lyric opera. With heroic deeds and love. One friend suggested I base it on the novel *The Young Guards*, about young partisans in the Ukraine, but I don't want to. Everything there ends sadly, tragically. I'm pessimistic about life sometimes: I'm so unlucky, I have so many problems. But in music, in art, I'm for optimism, for joy of life— Yes, yes, of course, I checked all the tables, and the average is fifty-four or fifty-six percent intelligibility; I'll write the conclusion in a minute. Now, why are you double-checking? But why is that a mistake? You said yourself that *zh* and *sh*, *d* and *t*, *g* and *k* can be interchanged. Why only at the end? You mean, if it's *pas* instead of *paz* and vice versa—that's not a mistake. But if it's *zap* instead of *sap*, then it's a mistake? I don't remember your saying that. Well, then, I forgot. Girlish memory, you know. And what do you come up with? Really? Less than fifty percent? And I already told them fifty-six. The captain from the laboratory was so happy. And now we'll have to disappoint him. Maybe we shouldn't bother? I think it's better if people feel good. What difference will five or six percent make?

All right, all right, I know: honesty, accuracy, conscientiousness. I had that back in grammar school. We'll do it your way."

December. Monday. A dark morning. The first ones out for morning exercise in the cold came back upset—there were three big Black Marias by the watchtower, and the zone was filled with screws.

At the morning roll call the duty officer announced: "After breakfast everyone is to remain in the yurts. Don't go anywhere without special permission. What do you mean 'have to work'? You were told not to go out without express permission. I can't explain anything, when the time comes, you'll be told."

In the dining room, over breakfast, we learned that many men were already packing their things. And the duty officer was walking around with a big list.

So, everyone was being sent away! At least, the majority.

Anxious trepidation made me shiver.

At the exit from our yurts, screws stood around and paraded up and down. They watched to make sure no one went any farther than the toilet. They didn't even let us go to the medical office. "If you're very sick, we'll report it to the duty officer—he'll send the medical assistant."

Our window was right opposite the gates to the sharashka zone—we could see people going in one and two at a time. We could tell that they were going in to fill out their special forms, and to hand in their equipment and instruments.

A few clever men managed to drop in on us on the way.

"I lent (or borrowed) a book, a towel here." They said good-bye, they had time to say: "There's a whole column of Black Marias. And the duty officer has a thick file of lists. So long, men! Maybe we'll meet in Butyrki or in transport."

We watch to see whom they're taking. We try to figure out if there's a system to it. At first it seemed that they were taking only workers from the shops and technicians from the laboratories. But then they led past an engineer. And another one. And two Germans—chemists.

Lunch. The empty places of the first shift in the dining room were filled by people from the other shifts (we ate in three shifts). We questioned our new neighbors.

We learned that the Germans hadn't been sent away. Evgeniia Vasilievna had insisted that they be brought to the laboratory for an hour to finish work on the ceramic parts.

Catching the duty officer at the door, I started telling him that I had a very important analysis going on unfinished in the lab, and that if I didn't drop in at least for a half hour, there might be a serious accident. But he was unmoved. "If it's necessary, your chiefs will tell us. Otherwise there's nothing I can do. No, I won't even report it. You see for yourself what's going on here."

After lunch several people from our yurts were called in—the first category ones.

In the laboratory, in my desk drawers were notebooks; memo books; files of manuscripts—outlines of books and articles, my unfinished work on "hand" word roots that link various languages; an article attempting to understand the nature and source of national hostility, nationalism, and chauvinism; poetry, remarks, plans. And part of Solzhenitsyn's notebooks, which Gumer hadn't had time to get out (he took out my "packages" in small sections, so that his pockets wouldn't bulge). And Valentina's dissertation wasn't even half done and the materials were piled up and she would never figure them out herself. All that—my seekings, doubts, discoveries, sorrows, and joys of the last three years—yes, there had been joys! And what was awaiting me there, where they would take me—in the cell, in the camp barracks? What joys? An extra bowl of gruel, an extra hour of shirking.

With heartbreaking effort I tried to convince myself as I had more than once in the past (and I had managed in the most damned times): Don't dare give up! Don't regret a thing. Don't whine.

The best way of cheering up oneself is to cheer up others. If you want to get rid of fear, of the vile fear of impending disaster, then laugh and joke —even stupidly, even crudely, vulgarly—laugh and joke.

I saw that Sergei was doing the same thing. There were anxious sparks in his eyes, and his cheek was on the verge of twitching. But with merry maliciousness he kept up a four-letter commentary on the proceedings, instructing Semyon and the others who came to the sharashka straight from Lubyanka or Lefortovo. He taught them how to handle criminal prisoners. He picked on me as well.

"Well, and how are we to understand all this from the point of view of historical inevitability and dialectical materialism?"

I picked up on it and started recalling the awesome events of the past: St. Bartholomew's Night, the Sicilian Vespers, Peter the Great's punishment of the *Streltsy*.* And I quickly put together something that rhymed, entitled "The Morning of the Streltsy Execution."

At dinner there were even more empty seats.

Finally—lights out! That night many suffered from insomnia. Some cried out in their sleep.

The next day they also let us out of the yurts only to go to the dining room and to the toilet. A few more of our people were called in. Men from other yurts were brought in to take their places.

*The *Streltsy* were Russia's first professional soldiers. This elite corps first supported the reign of Sophia, Peter the Great's half-sister, and eventually revolted against Peter, prompted in part by his cruelly implemented reforms. They were executed in 1698. (Translator's note.)

On the third morning during prisoner count the duty officer said: "After breakfast, you go to work. As usual."

Of the 400 zeks who were working in the sharashka at the beginning of December (there had been over 500 in the spring), approximately 70 were left. And three janitors for the camp. But the acoustics lab did not lose a single prisoner.

We understood—Anton had stood up for us.

Valentina was glowing with smiles, her eyes moist. "I had worried so, I was so anxious—I thought I'd never see you again."

I was touched, even though I guessed that her anxiety and joy related primarily to Sergei. From the first she had gazed lovingly at him from afar, blushing when he came near, adoring his jokes. He noticed, of course, and showed off, giving her soulful looks and speaking either with a languorous overtone or a majestic roar. But he didn't want to get too close to her. His brief stormy affair with Evgeniia Vasilievna had only recently ended.

"There was more fear than pleasure in it. You had a lucky break—hours alone with your girl, and in a secret place; the regulations required that you be locked in from the inside. And what about me? Grabbing stolen moments in a dark corner. Scared by every noise. You can turn impotent like that."

Sergei's "attached" free employee Ivan Yakovlevich, or Vanya, unlocked the safe, getting out our notes, blueprints, and workbooks. The young technician lieutenant was a student in his last year of the evening division of the communications institute. Of medium height, scrawny, but agile and trim, he looked at everyone with his big boyish eyes filled with greedy curiosity. Sergei quickly tamed him. Later he even sent letters to his family through him. Vanya belonged to the Komsomol and had an unshakable faith in the rightness of the Party line and the genius of the great Stalin. Not very bright or overly educated, he was a kindly person, incapable of hatred and suspicion. Even though he tried to display vigilance, he became attached to Sergei and me with a childlike trust. In the evenings he came by to talk about international politics, history, war. My views were closer and more comprehensible to him than Sergei's irony and direct mockery, but what he found temptingly attractive about us both was our critical attitude, totally new to his experience, toward the newspapers and official propaganda, our independence of thought, and freedom of speech, which did not resemble the officialese to which he was accustomed. Sometimes he did muster his courage to "fight back." When in a conversation about the famous proletarian poet Demyan Bedny I noted that he had been a heavy drinker even before the war, Vanya howled: "That's impossible! One of the oldest members of the Party. A personal comrade of Lenin and Stalin! That's a real enemy lie! I'll never believe it!"

For a time after that he was huffy. But then, once again, as though nothing had happened, after talking shop—he had become the foreman of the articulation team—he began asking: "Had you heard before that the Germans almost had the atom bomb? And what do you think, are the Americans seriously preparing for biological warfare? First they released all those Colorado beetles, and now there is information that they are preparing rats infected with the plague. Well, how do you think we should respond to that? And what do you think, if there's a war, will the East Germans stab us in the back?"

After our two-day separation he greeted us triumphantly, almost hugging Sergei and me. His happiness was so sincere and selfless. He wasn't thinking of dissertations yet. Sergei was teaching him, yes, but he didn't need me for anything.

Anton Mikhailovich greeted us more warmly than he had lately. "Well, the ranks have thinned, but the advance continues! Fewer in number, but better in quality. We didn't lose anyone from our laboratory. Now you can work quietly and productively. Well, we can merely guess about the deadlines. Do you drink tea? In cases like this, the most appropriate thing is tea leaves. You can obtain more accurate information from that than from any rumor. But today you can work calmly. As for what will come in the unseen future, we will find out when the time comes, at the right time. The outline for Valentina Ivanovna's dissertation has been approved. Well, it's a very interesting plan. As far as I can tell, Valentina Ivanovna is intending to create with your help something like an acoustic-phonetic encyclopedia for all times and nations. The basic method is 'haul out onto the table whatever's cooking in the oven.' In any other case I would have objected, insisting on limits, on more concreteness. But since this is the first work of its kind, I find it possible to give my 'all right.' One chef used to say: 'Out of ten pounds of meat it's very easy to prepare two servings of a pound, a pound and a half each; but from two pounds of meat it's very hard to create ten portions of even a half pound each.' Well, let's have your ten pounds, but it had better be good-quality dissertation meat. You may be able to carve out a final portion from it. I hope that the respected Valentina Ivanovna will present an excellent dissertation. I ask only that you remember that it needs to be not only written but also defended. Yes, *nota bene*, defended from certain learned opponents in front of a scholarly court. I don't want to frighten you, Valentina Ivanovna; naturally, this won't be a duel to the death, but fencing with rapiers with buttons on the tips. But a certain dueling ritual must be followed—that is, the order of scholarly discussion. Your opponents may express doubts and arguments. When do you plan to finish? No, I'm not rushing you. Speed is of the essence only in catching fleas. But slowness is also punishable. And your deadline, Lev Zinovievich, expires rather soon? Two and a half . . . Not too long. You've acquired knowledge and experience here that could serve in other places for the good of the homeland and as a support for you. Naturally, with good behavior, as I've told you more than once. Common sense and decorum are useful for everyone and everything. But for you they are vital. Isn't that so, Valentina Ivanovna?"

And things went on in the old way in the laboratory. But the scare of those two days prompted me to put my archives in order. I kept them in the laboratory desk because I was less worried about a search there. And then the unusualness of the texts in several languages could be explained by the unusualness of my work. And it was simpler to hide poetry and notes on history, philosophy, and literature among my many scientific and scholarly notes. In the yurts our things were searched, as a rule without us, on the eve of all holidays and whenever the authorities deemed it necessary. If anything "not permitted" was found—instruments, drawings, or notes that the screws could think came from the work area—the "criminals" were called in to see the prison and sharashka security officers, interrogated, forced to write explanations. That's why in my nightstand and the plywood chest under my bed I kept only books I got from home, a few dictionaries, and outlines of works on linguistics.

I numbered and titled all the notebooks, pads, and files left in my desk. I compiled a detailed list of my "personal scientific archives" and typed it in several copies. The pads and notebooks with poetry were called "Translations from English, German, Chinese, and Other Languages" and "Materials for the Study of Foreign Languages." Letters and photos of relatives, certain newspaper clippings, drawings, friendly put-ons, pads with poetry by Russian and foreign poets, prose quotations, and precisely marked references I collected into a separate file, frankly marked "Personal Family Archives," and also gave it descriptive headings.

The only thing I could count on was my hope that "Saint-Bureaucratious" would for once be efficient. And my hopes were eventually justified.

We greeted 1953 without joy. Of the fourteen residential yurts, recently filled to capacity, only four held inhabitants. The duty officer on New Year's Eve was a muddle-headed and picky captain, whom we called Pythagoras, or Lobachevsky, or Einstein—he was always getting mixed up during prisoner count, counting over and over.

That night he came by several times and demanded without anger but naggingly that everyone "lie in their sleeping places": "You're not supposed to sit up at night. I know, I know, it's New Year's. But you have to maintain order in all the years, old and new. Whoever wants to celebrate must celebrate without breaking the rules. Others, for instance, want to sleep. See, there are people lying down, the way they're supposed to— resting. And you're breaking the rules. I told you an hour ago, lights out, and you're sitting up again. I'm telling you for the last time, I'll start writing down names and reporting to the chief. You'll be punished. Who needs that? Come on, turn out the light. And whoever's on the entryway, finish up smoking."

At midnight in the dark yurt we congratulated one another. "Happy New Year! Let's hope it passes in the old place. And that there will be no new problems."

Someone started singing an old prison song of the thirties in a low voice:

> The New Year brings new orders
> But the barbed wire around our camp is old.
> Severe eyes stare from all sides
> And death threatens from all sides.

On the first workday of the new year both the prisoners and the free employees—officers and civilians—greeted one another just like all the people out there beyond the fence: "Happy New Year! New luck! The best of everything in the New Year!"

A few chocolates lay on my desk. Valentina smiled flirtatiously. "That's for you and Sergei Grigorievich from Grandfather Frost."

January 13, 1953—the news of the arrest of the Kremlin doctors, "murderers in white coats."*

On the radio and in the newspapers there were curses for the vile hirelings of international imperialism, agents of Joint,† insidious Zionists, enemies of the people.

Valentina, Ivan, Gumer, and Evgeniia Vasilievna told me: "Several pharmacies have been closed for urgent checking. There were rumors that Jewish pharmacists were selling poisoned cotton. In the polyclinics patients are refusing to be treated by doctors with Jewish names. In some schools Jewish boys were beaten up. An old man was shoved out of a commuter train when he argued with people who were denigrating the damned race. A first-aid physician said that there are Jewish suicides almost daily. An old woman doctor poisoned herself, a member of the Party, a war veteran. A doctor hanged himself after a patient died unexpectedly."

During those days Valentina moderated her exalted hatred of Jews. Once she even spoke with sympathy of her stepfather, who had been fired.

"Of course, he does have a terrible personality. He's an egoist, he thinks he's the center of the universe. But he's a knowledgeable, experienced doctor. He spent the entire war at the front; he was wounded, decorated. People have to understand that there are all kinds of Jews. Now they're

---

*In 1952 the Kremlin's leading physicians, most of whom were Jewish, were arrested on the trumped-up charge of plotting to kill Stalin. The "doctors' case" marked the beginning of a strong wave of anti-Semitism. (Translator's note.)

†The American Jewish Joint Distribution Committee (established 1914) sent American funds to aid Jews worldwide, including those in Russia and the Soviet Union. (Translator's note.)

firing everyone from the security organs, even those who have only a Jewish mother. I can understand that—it's necessary for vigilance in the security organs. But doctors can be of use."

The anxious tension seemed almost palpable. It was felt not so much in the words spoken—in brief, even more reserved conversation about news in the papers, about vicious rumors—as in the pauses, in the accidental glances, wary, suspicious, or sympathetic.

Nikolai Vladimirovich A., an old-timer of the sharashka, a not so young engineer from somewhere in the south, sometimes argued with me hostilely. He did not hide his feeling that the October Revolution was the greatest disaster of Russian history and Marxism-Leninism a pretentious pseudoscience. On one of those days he said grimly: "Do you know, I always had a certain antipathy for Jews—rather, a distrust. Many representatives of that race played, shall we say, a rather dubious role in our recent history. But now I am convinced that no decent Russian can permit himself to treat Jews badly. Now, when such open, obnoxious anti-Semitism has become the reigning spirit of the authorities, it is shameful to appear to be in solidarity with them in any way. Recently I talked with our Germans. Some are snickering maliciously. But two of them—intelligent, decent men—said the same thing happened in their country under Hitler, and they considered it a national shame, even though they are nationalists. And how can this exist here, in Russia, where Communist-internationalists rule? I could only tell them that I was a Russian nationalist and also considered all this our national shame and thought that Soviet internationalism did not differ too much from German national socialism."

Sergei and Semyon pestered me. Could I possibly justify this, too, with higher considerations—historical necessity, the interests of socialist states.

Sergei, as usual assertive and temperamental, either argued angrily, mocking me, or cajoled me earnestly. Semyon, with deliberate calm, harassed me skeptically and rationally with clever questions, catching me in actual and seeming contradictions.

Countering their arguments, I tried to explain to them and to myself: "The Zionists naturally have terrorist organizations, too. Five years ago they were active in the Palestine against the British, the Arabs; they exploded bombs, killed people. They killed a representative of the UN, the Swede Bernadotte, they killed the Jordanian king, and someone else. The Soviet Union has begun helping the Arab countries now; that must be why the Zionist terrorists are trying to function here as well. They probably recruited one of the Kremlin doctors. But it's impossible for all the people named in the news reports to be conspirators. I don't believe that Mikhoels* was a spy. And it's crazy, bizarre to suspect and blame an entire race. Of all the people in the world, certainly we old prisoners know how

*Solomon Mikhailovich Mikhoels (1890–1948), Jewish actor and director, at one time chairman of the Jewish Antifascist League. He was killed on Stalin's orders. (Translator's note.)

these cases are built up. One son of a bitch—a spy or an anti-Soviet conspirator—cracks and to save his own skin names not only his co-conspirators but also all his acquaintances and even mere strangers, even on purpose; to cover up and protect the real criminals, he blames as many innocent people as possible. And the organs like noisy cases, with lots of people involved, a broad scale."

In January and February 1953 the disgust and horror were even more tormenting and hopeless than in 1949, when they were persecuting cosmopolites and the pamphlets were riddled with parentheses: Yakovlev (Holtzman), Kholodov (Meyerovich) . . . And more vicious and persistent than that, a vile thought pursued me—it's a good thing I'm in prison, that I have no choice, I don't have to appear publicly and no one will demand that in the name of my duty to the Party I denounce Veselovsky and Shamil, Yuzovsky and Shostakovich, that I lie about priorities, about Russia's agelong originality and cultural independence.

I realized then that the MGB and the Procurator's Office, the courts, and a significant portion of the Party and state apparatus were filled predominantly with immoral, cynically conscienceless careerists or conscientious but ignorant, stupid order-followers. Both types were corrupted by privileges, bribes, the tinsel of awards, medals, and uniforms. They needed hostility toward Yugoslavia, persecution and execution of Bulgarian and Hungarian oppositionists, war in Korea, and within the country, the affair of the Kremlin doctors, a pogromlike persecution.

But perhaps this was another clever maneuver of Stalin's goal-oriented tactics and strategy? A purge of the rear guard before the inevitable war with the Anglo-Americans? And he was trying to win Arab support. In the East our allies were China, Korea, and the Vietnamese insurgents. Whom did we have in the West? Only unarmed Communists who were being squeezed more and more in France and Italy.

But Stalin was no longer General Secretary. Instead of the Politburo, the Twentieth Congress of the autumn of 1952 gave us the multimembered Presidium. And it was all run by Malenkov—he had given the most important speech at that Congress—he was the youngest, and they said "he hates all Jews."

And we learned that Molotov's wife, who was Jewish, had been arrested and so had Kaganovich's brothers; someone said of the Jewish minister Mekhlis, who died suddenly, that "he shot himself in time."

Evgeniia Vasilievna told me: "Now it is known for certain that Abakumov had been arrested and sentenced because he had missed the doctors' conspiracy and even Lavrentii Pavlovich himself was given a talking to for that."

Perhaps there was a movement of some new dark powers that were pushing out Stalin? Weren't his latest articles about the economics of socialism aimed at them? He wrote then, without naming names, of people "who did not understand that in our country, too, the objective laws of value operate." That affirmation was in contradiction to everything that had been affirmed by our propaganda before.

I tried to understand the causes and meaning of the new events.

I could easily imagine what was happening in the prisons—Lubyanka, Lefortovo, Sukhanovka—how the tired, embittered investigators were exhorting, squeezing, and beating out confessions and information. And the suspects—recently well-off, high-ranking doctors—were losing their minds from lack of sleep, freezing in the cooler, weakened by hunger, deafened by curses, threats, exhausted by beatings. I imagined it all so clearly that it terrified me, caused me pain.

But what was happening there, in Moscow, in other cities? What were my family, friends, former comrades, and acquaintances experiencing? The horror of not knowing, not understanding crowded me even more, suffocating me with despair.

But work went on as usual. We checked the intelligibility of new channels. Articulation tests went on. I added up the errors in the tables. Examined, measured sound pictures, calculated, figured. Listened to the chatter of Valentina. Replied to the questions of the bosses, Ivan, my comrades. After work I taught the officers German and English. Wrote and rewrote pages of the future dissertation for someone else. And every morning before prisoner count, overcoming my fear, I turned on the radio in the entryways between the yurts and listened to the news, articles, resolutions of meetings, letters from workers and schoolchildren, scientists, and artists praising the heroic Dr. Lidia Timashuk,* demanding "merciless retribution." And then in the laboratory I listened to Gumer whisper and Ivan and Valentina talk in low tones: "Beaten up at school . . . Pushed from a bus . . . Beaten almost to death in a line . . . They say they gave shots in the hospital that infected people with syphilis . . . Hanged himself . . . Poisoned himself . . . Jumped from a fifth-story window . . . Fired . . . Thrown out of the institute . . . ."

Around me there were those who were sincerely incensed: "This is almost like Hitler." And there were those who rejoiced: "They tripped on what they had fought for." And over and over people asked, some sympathetically, others hostilely: "Why is it the Jews everywhere and always? In antiquity, in the Middle Ages, in modern times? Dreyfus in France, Beilis† in Russia, total extermination in Germany. And now in our country it's 'cosmopolites without kith or kin,' 'murderers in white coats.' Why is it this race elicits so much hatred, such persecution?"

*Lidia Timashuk was a physician at the Kremlin hospital. According to official reports (January 1953) she was allegedly the first to expose the doctors' conspiracy. Ecstatic articles and poems were written about her. In April 1953 the Presidium of the Supreme Soviet rescinded its ukase bestowing an order on Timashuk.

†Accused of ritual murder in 1911 in Kiev; acquitted in 1913 after a dramatic and controversial trial. (Translator's note.)

How could I answer those questions when I myself realized that all the explanations I knew—by Lessing, Marx, Vladimir Soloviev, Lenin, Gorky, Freud—were inadequate.

There is one regularity to history. Explosions of mass hostility to Jews occurred during or after mass disasters, social crises. In medieval Italy after an earthquake, Jews were buried alive; during the plague, they were burned. In Spain after the destruction of the Mauritanian states a harsh impoverishment began that was not alleviated by all the conquests and victories overseas. It was then that the Inquisition began persecuting heretics, Jews, and Marranos (Christianized Jews). After the heavy losses of the Spanish empire on the shores of England, in the Netherlands, and in Germany, they were almost totally killed off or exiled. This did not protect the most Christian kingdom from poverty or bloody internecine wars in the next three centuries. The first pogroms in Europe were the work of the Crusaders on their way to the Holy Land. In the Ukraine, Jews were attacked by the rebelling Haidamaks. In Poland, mass anti-Semitism spread after the partitions of the country; in Germany, after the Napoleonic Wars. In France the Dreyfus Affair was one of the consequences of the defeat of 1870. The Hitlerites gained many followers after the crisis of 1929–1932.

"And so what? That just proves that Judaism has some secret evil powers —catalysts, yeast, that bring on fermentation in society, microbes that bring on mass psychoses."

"Mystical blather! When the Armenians were massacred in Turkey, or Negroes lynched in America, or all white men killed in China in 1900— what were the ferments or microbes then? No, it's just that both here and there people are savages, barbarians. Just the way they were under Genghis Khan, Tamerlane, under all the ancient and semiancient conquerors who wiped out entire nations."

"Well, antiquity has nothing to do with it. Man always was, is, and always will be an animal. It's only in zoos and the circus that they sometimes manage to train predators so that, as in the Scriptures, the lion lies with the lamb. I saw this once: rabbits lived in a small pen—cowardly vegetarian rabbits. A hare was put among them. But just in case, in a separate cage. During the night they chewed through the wooden slats and tore out the hare's belly in chunks. And most frequently the people taking part in a pogrom are frenzied rabbits. In ordinary circumstances they are peaceful ordinary people. But as soon as there's something the least bit unusual—famine, war, plague, revolution—they tear apart anyone usually considered foreign. In Turkey it's the Armenians; in Germany and Russia, the Jews; in America, the Negroes; in Africa, the whites. Catholics kill Huguenots, Muslims kill Christians—"

"You mean it's all nature? And therefore incurable?"

"I don't know, I don't know. Maybe someday. But not in our lifetime."

These arguments outraged my Marxist reason and cruelly wounded my world perception, developed by humanitarians from the Evangelists down to Korolenko. I could not and would not believe in the innate bestiality of man.

Hitler wrote in *Mein Kampf* that racism was a law of nature. "The wolf does not crossbreed with the bear, the dog with the cat, the goldfinch with the eagle, since this is a distinction of races prescribed by Providence." But the differences between human races and peoples cannot be compared with the different species of animals.

"And why not? Even Marx and Engels called man 'the animal that manufactures tools.' I studied that myself when I took dialectical materialism."

"You were a lousy student. You deserve a D! It was some Englishman who came up with the term before them—'tool-making animal.' Marx and Engels merely quoted him, though sympathetically, but not at all as a precise definition. However, even if you do compare people with animals, the differences between human races are not the differences between wolf and bear, dog and cat, but between different breeds of wolves, dogs, or cats. A German shepherd and a poodle differ more than a Swede and a Bushman or a Negro and a Chinese. But even among animals different breeds of one species coexist and crossbreed. And the males of one herd fight over the females and food, and they fight just as viciously as they do with strangers. And man, no matter how you twist things—believing Freud, or Pavlov, or even any racist theory—is still not an animal. 'The voice of the blood' is an old wives' tale. But even if you allow a certain reality to the 'voice of the blood,' then surely it can't be stronger in man than the voice of reason? And anyway, there are no 'purebred' races. Just in the last two millennia in Europe the Celts, Romans, Greeks, Scythians, Saxons, Slavs, Finns, and Mongols mixed and intermarried. And European Jews have the same genetic cocktail. There are no mysterious ferments or microbes. There are merely various forms of a lie, many centuries old and brand new, and the same old irrational but incontrovertible prejudices: if Ivan steals, they say Ivan stole it, but if Abram steals, they say a Jew stole it."

For me the historical necessity and fecundity of assimilation was self-evident. It was proved by the German poetry of Heine, the first German peasant writer Berthold Auerbach, the Polish poet Julian Tuwim, the Russian music of Rubinstein and the Soviet composers with Jewish names, the Russian art of the sculptor Antokolsky and the painter Levitan, and such Russian writers and poets as Pasternak, Selvinsky, Bagritsky, Svetlov, Ilf, and Vasilii Grossman.

"They're Russian only in language. That way any German or French writer becomes Russian in translation. I don't know music or art, but you compare Pasternak with Yesenin, Bagritsky with Tvardovsky, Grossman with Sholokhov . . . You can tell right away who's Russian and who's sort of."

"Why don't you compare Yesenin with Mayakovsky, and Tvardovsky with Aseev or Khlebnikov; they're all Russian by blood, but the differences between them are as great."

"Oh no, you can't prove anything to me that way. You have to feel it, with your guts, your blood."

"Well, and what difference do your guts feel between Ioffe and Popov, or between Kapitsa and Landau? Between physicists and mathematicians of different blood?"

"Come on, don't get mad, you're a good man. I respect and love you. But your guts aren't Russian. And I don't consider that a failing. On the contrary, I value you as a friend and comrade more than all my Russian friends. And basically I'm a confirmed internationalist, believe me—no less than you. But I can see and feel: race is a fact. Now you and Semyon— even though he has a Russian mother—both of you are feeling this more or not more but certainly differently than I, Sergei, Nikolai, and Vadim. Even though you try to explain it all away, and I'm just nauseated by all this baloney about the doctors and Stalin's stinking anti-Semitism. Yes, yes, I do mean Stalin's. You're wrong to console yourself and try to convince yourself. He's the one, the father and friend of all peoples, who came up with it. Just as it was before with the kulaks and subkulaks, and then with saboteurs and enemies of the people; now it's Tito's clique and Jewish conspiracies . . . 'I recognize the whore by her walk . . .' He's such a clever beast! Maybe he is a genius, but what an evil one. He always knows whom to blame for his sins and vile deeds. And he always finds assistants, and toadies, and squealers. He incited all the village lowlifes, the ne'er-do-wells, drunks, and thieves envious of other people's wealth against the better farmers, who were branded kulaks. And he got the masses going against the saboteurs and enemies of the people, everyone who was sick of the five-year plans, the lines, the hungers, the failures, the absence of this, the lack of that. There are the guilty ones! Sic 'em! Beat them mercilessly! Back then, Party heads fell all over the country, and some of our brethren, too —engineers and other clever intellectuals—so that they wouldn't think and discuss and by accident expose him, and spill the truth.

"And now somebody has to answer for all the mistakes. He took aim right after victory. Remember his toast to the great Russian people, for their humility, patience, and trust. He wasn't hinting, he said it outright: any other people would have kicked a government like this in the ass, but our people put up with it. It was supposed to be a toast to our health, but actually he spat in everyone's face. Nevertheless, here everyone went off 'in stormy, never-ending applause' and so on. Our father praised us. And now these long-suffering people need some new fodder or they'll kick up their heels. There are no new kulaks; the enemies of the people business was all fucked up—they killed off all the marshals, generals, the best military men and they ran off along the Volga, to his native Georgia, wiped out Leningrad. So now he's come up with a new one: 'Beat the Jews!' An old tested trick, used by Tsar Nicholas and Deputy Purishkevich. In 1905 it helped a bit: the ones attacking the Jews didn't attack the state. But it didn't work in 1917. I don't know what he's counting on now. Well, so he'll have a hundred or two hundred doctors and nondoctors shot and hanged; and several thousand or a hundred thousand sent up, to Vorkuta and Kolyma. What will he do with the rest? Yesterday our gentlemen officers were saying that all the Jews will be sent to Birobidzhan, that they were rushing construction on barracks and shipping wheat there for gruel. Is the wisest of the wise really hoping that after that the Americans will start running from Korea or that Adenauer and Ulbricht will become buddies and ask for Soviet citizenship? I think this is just as much a trick of genius as the time Stalin embraced Ribbentrop, swearing eternal friendship with Hitler. Confess, back then all you clever enthusiasts sang a refrain: 'Oh, what a genius, what a strategist! Now we'll haul in all the imperialists!' And you hauled. Of course, think: the entire Baltic area, a good piece of Poland, Bessarabia. You got burned by the Finns, of course, but you still got a piece there. And then what happened? What did those genius tricks bring us? The official count is seven million dead. That means, figure three times as many. And how many crippled? How many orphans and widows? How much was destroyed, ruined? Where is he headed now? He managed to fight off the German cannons, tanks, and planes because the long-suffering people fought as hard as they could. And the Anglo-American imperialists helped. With cannon, and canned meat, and Studebakers. And they fought, too: half of Germany was blown into bits and smoke. But now, what will help against the atom bomb? Jewish pogroms?"

No, I didn't want to agree with him. I didn't want to believe that it all came from Stalin.

At our sharashka we observed the monstrously senseless, chaotic tossing away of equipment and apparatus and of priceless scientific and technical documents. New zeks who came from recent arrests, as well as some officers, told us that the same thing was happening in other places. And the German plants and laboratories were being taken apart in barbaric, marauding, and predatory disorder. All this wasn't according to Stalin's will, it was against it.

One evening in the laboratory, turning on the radio, I heard the news of Stalin's illness.

That evening and the following days both the free employees and the prisoners at the sharashka talked about it, very little and cautiously. Some walked away from the conversation. But in the yurts, in our own circle, I don't think we could have talked of anything else.

"Well, if it's been announced, that means it's the end!"

"But maybe they'll cure him?"

"If they had hopes of curing him, they wouldn't have announced it."

"Our Germans are scared—when he kicks off, a real mess will start, and we'll be the first ones they get rid of."

"They may wait with us, but the pogroms will be horrible. They'll say the Jews bumped him off."

"But maybe it'll be just the opposite? Some relief might come. The new bosses will have to be more careful, try harder, so that they have trust here and abroad."

"And who are the new bosses? Do you think they know any other way of bossing? For all of them the only possible authority is based on fear. That means: suppress, send up, shoot! Beat your own people so that strangers will be afraid."

"That may be, but you have to take the international situation into account. Help from the Chinese will be zero and a fucking tenth. They're fighting in Korea a hundred to one and still up to their ears in shit. And as for the love of the Poles, Germans, and Hungarians—the leaders know that without reading the papers. That means, they must understand what will happen if the Americans start up for real. I saw them deal with Germany. You couldn't begin to describe it. Hundreds and thousands flew in two or three formations. You shoot down one or two—but a hundred thousand go on. And they cover everything. It's called carpet bombing. There's no escape! And now they have the atom bomb, too. One lands, and it's as if Moscow never existed."

"Stalin was one who still took risks, intrigued, tried to outsmart. He's an old man of the 'pre-1917 mold.' He still counted on the masses, on the class struggle, on the Chinese cannon fodder. And he had the habits of a criminal, grabbing by the throat. And if that didn't work, he could lick ass, like that time with Ribbentrop. But the younger men understand that with the atom bomb, with computers everything is different now. For us to catch up with the Americans, we have to swim through shit for another hundred years. That means we have to sit down, think, scratch behind the ear, call a conference: 'Come on, Uncle Sam, let's be honest! Let's not compare cocks, let's become honest pals. You help me, I'll help you.' And that's when liberty will smile on us. 'And I'll return when the snow melts.' "

"Sentimental pap! Even though you're speaking thieves' slang, you're still thinking like an overeducated dreamer. They probably won't fight, but what can we expect from them, from Lavrentii Pavlovich and Georgii Maximilianovich [Malenkov]? Do you have any idea how many of us there are in the prisons, the camps, the sharashkas? Well, how many millions? Ask him. Last year he and I and some mathematicians made scientifically precise calculations. We took the election data for one year and then another and compared them with the population tables in the encyclopedia —in the first edition. In the second they don't give population—it's a state secret! And according to all the laws of statistics and the theory of probability we got an average of fifteen million! With a possible deviation of plus or minus two or three million. And think how many officers, screws, and various free employees are fed by the camps and prisons? And how many stool pigeons, security officers, investigators, procurators, judges, convoy soldiers? More than the population of some middle European country! So how can Beria or Malenkov ease up on us? It would be doomsday for them: millions of former zeks and hundreds of thousands of unemployed screws are scarier for them than the atom bomb. No, we can't expect anything good."

"Everything is so fucking lousy now, it can't get any worse. It's like the Ukrainians say: 'Khai girshe, aby inshe [Let it be worse, as long as it's different].'

"Well, that's exactly what it will be—girshe."

It would be worse. That's what I thought most often, too. My importunate thoughts were like splinters. Stalin was incurably ill, of course. (In the camps I had learned enough about medicine to understand the meaning of the bulletins.) Even if by some miracle they extended his life, it would be the existence of a speechless paralytic. But most likely, there would be death, and very swift. Was this why the whole affair with the physicians was started? And what had they wanted from it? To blame them for the inevitable death, in order to later destroy thousands and hundreds of thousands in a barbaric revenge ceremony in memory of the dead? Or had they wanted to get rid of the honest doctors loyal to him and invented this conspiracy, knowing how suspicious and doubting he was? He believed them and thus cleared the way for the real killers. One theory didn't preclude the other. The doctors had been done away with both in order to kill him and to have "concrete suspects"—to begin enormous pogroms and to finally cast off the rudimentary vestiges of Bolshevism-Leninism.

I spoke about this in front of Valentina, when she began talking like this: that the same doctors had killed Stalin.

She batted her eyelashes in fright and waved her short manicured fingers. "Oh, what are you saying?! What are you saying?! If they hear you, then both you and I—"

Sergei interrupted her quietly but masterfully. "What's the matter with you, Valentina Ivanovna? He didn't say anything out of the way. I was standing right here, I heard everything. He's suffering for the health of Comrade Stalin and keeps saying all the time that he hopes that the best physicians in the Soviet Union are taking care of him and that they will cure him to the joy of the country and the fright of our enemies. I've heard him say just that more than once. And I can't imagine what you had misconstrued. It's just your nerves. These days are very nerve wracking."

Then he cursed me out. "If you don't care about your life, then you could at least think of others, you humanist. You know that in these cases they don't take just one person. Especially now. We have to outlive him. Outlive him, not stick our necks in a noose."

March 6. He died yesterday! It had been expected for several days. And still, it was such an explosion. And as if in the aftermath of an explosion

I'm deafened, shell-shocked. I see and hear as if through a heavy rain: there's light, but everything is blurred, loud but indistinct.

The radios play funereal music: Mozart, Beethoven, Chopin, Tchaikovsky, Brahms.

Valentina Ivanovna's eyes are red. "I wept all night. Mother is simply hysterical. There was a meeting here this morning. Konstantin Fedorovich spoke. Even he, such a dry old stick, barely controlled his tears. One woman draftsman fainted. I keep worrying I'll black out, too. And do you know what I can tell you? I saw how the simple folk are suffering. The soldier in the hall was crying like a baby, and all the cleaning women. While some of the comrade officers, members of the Party, right after the memorial meeting—I heard them myself—talked about soccer. One—I don't want to say who, I'm not a squealer—was talking with a smile. Now I can see that you're suffering. I know about people, I can always tell who's sincere, and who's pretending. And Sergei Grigorievich—even though he's always against everything, but I can see he's suffering. While others are just the reverse. And it's so painful to see certain members of the Party and Komsomol walking around as though nothing has happened."

Anton Mikhailovich did not come by during those days. Vasilii Nikolaevich told someone on the phone that he had had a heart attack, a nervous collapse.

In the yurts the tension had dropped. Even though no one gloated openly. And the supervision, on the contrary, had increased noticeably. The number of screws on each shift had doubled or tripled. They constantly patrolled along our main road, which cut across the courtyard, and peeked into the yurts.

Among my comrades I sometimes caught glances glistening merrily, and in others, maliciously curious—how do you feel now? But most behaved as though nothing important had happened. During those two December days when so many of us were taken away, everyone had been much more anxious and sorrowful.

And I compressed myself, squeezed myself tight, like an empty fist. I didn't want anyone to look inside me to guess what I was thinking. I didn't want the bosses and screws to think that I was pretending to be sad, and I didn't want my fellow prisoners to imagine or understand how bad I felt, what memories were flooding me.

That July morning of '41 a pale-faced Nadya awakened me. The black paper-plate face of the speaker reproduced the familiar, accented voice— "Brothers and sisters, I am appealing to you, my friends!" And then the bitter words, bitter, but they seemed extremely sincere and courageous. And the light ring of glass, the gurgle of water. That homey sound created a sudden sensation of closeness. Nadya's eyes glistened, tears about to burst out. And my throat constricted.

A November evening that same year in a trench. Darkness. Frost. Snow falling slowly, heavily. Cannons rumbling occasionally in the distance. Frequent rocket flares on the other side, one after the other. A flickering pale multicolored light. The radio operator ran out of the mud hut, shouting: "Stalin's talking! The broadcast is on! Stalin's talking from Moscow!"

And his voice again, his accent, his unhurried speech. It seemed that he spoke calmly, confidently. A soft, almost intentionally clumsy joke: he compared Hitler to Napoleon—a kitten to a lion.

The next morning in Valdai, in a little old house. An aerial attack. The roar of explosions. The house trembles, jumping away from its foundations. And we're lying on the floor, huddled up to the cold stove by the radio receiver. There's a parade on Red Square. And he's talking again. From the Mausoleum. The same voice, the same intonations, but new, unusual, unexpected words. He promises victory "in half a year, a short year . . . You will be blessed by the great sign."

Moscow. January 1944. Father visited me in the hospital after meeting a comrade of Sanya's. (My younger brother, Aleksandr Kopelev, had been a sergeant of the artillery.) The friend told my father that he saw Sanya in September 1941 in a forest near Borispol. They were breaking out of an encirclement.

That night at a halting place Sanya read his poetry about the future victory. He had already been wounded in the shoulder. In the morning they broke across the road. Sanya ran with his pistol, shouting: "For the homeland, for Stalin!" No one ever saw him again.

February 1945. Street fighting in Graudenz. The last battles in which I participated. A happy, intoxicating excitement—we're advancing. Our communications helped the artillery. I gave the commands directly into the loudspeakers to fire. We all knew victory was near. The city was surrounded. And the main, general victory was near, too. Choking with joy, I shouted: "For our children, our loved ones, our homeland, for Stalin— fire!"

They had turned one of the empty yurts into a storeroom: they piled stools, tables, mattresses, all kinds of rubbish in there. They didn't lock the door —who'd bother to steal from there. That's where I went when I couldn't stand it. I remembered and wept. The cold, the semidarkness, the dust, and the sour musty smells soothed me.

And in all this time there wasn't another word in the newspapers about the killer doctors.

Why wasn't there any propaganda now? Maybe they were merely putting it off? When the funeral pomp in which foreign guests participated was over, the bloody wake for domestic consumption would begin.

· · ·

March 9. The day of the funeral. At roll call the duty officer said: "Today no one will go to work. After breakfast everyone back in the yurts. And no movement on the grounds."

Again, as on the morning of the "great departure," several supervisors at a time stood on guard by our door. They were grim-looking. "Heightened vigilance."

And it was quieter in the yurts than during shirking hours. Some slept, some read. The players softly rattled their dominoes, swearing in low tones. It was only in the entryway that there was a greater crowd than usual, smoking, listening to the radio. Beethoven, Chopin, Tchaikovsky. Tragic, tense voices of the announcers: the report from the Hall of Columns, where the coffin stood; telegrams of condolence from grieving, shocked people. I listened constantly. I tried to hear something beyond the words, in what was left unsaid—the old habit of reading between the lines. Malenkov spoke. A confident voice, the intonations and pronunciation of an educated man. I noted his indifference. All the turns of phrase were correct—majestic bereavement. But he could have spoken that way at the funeral of any minister or marshal. Not for an instant, not in a single word was there the feeling of immeasurable, bottomless grief—of a great, irreplaceable loss. Nor was there any human warmth. Or measured sorrow.

Beria spoke with Stalin's accent, but much faster. He said the official, indifferent phrases about the deceased "great leader" almost in a patter. But he clearly stressed the lively intonations, his confidence in the future. And there were words of peace and words once again about peace. And a respectful gasp when he spoke of Malenkov: "the student of Lenin and comrade-in-arms of Stalin."

Aha, he was already simply "a comrade-in-arms." "The king is dead, long live the king!" Someone whispered behind me: "Hear? Student of some, comrade-in-arms of others."

Molotov mumbled tensely, stuttering, and suddenly his voice broke and he sobbed. The only sound of unfeigned grief.

The radio blared the funeral salutes, the sirens roared. Opening the door, I peeked outside.

The screws shouted in anger and fright: "Shut it! You can't go out!"

The sirens and roars were barely audible in the courtyard.

"I'm not going out. I'm just listening. Why don't you be quiet."

They stopped short. They grumbled under their breaths, and behind me Sergei joked: "Why are you sticking your nose out to them, and shoving your ass out at us? Why don't you stand at attention and salute while you're at it."

In the next few days we heard about the mortal crush on Trubnaya and Dimitrovka Streets. Hundreds killed, suffocated. No, thousands! Vanya gave us a description of how he made his way to the House of Unions, ducking under trucks, how his pass really helped "after all, it's stamped in large letters—CC CPSU." He spoke enthusiastically, bragging, mentioning the crushed people in passing, the "whole columns of ambulances." He forgot that he was supposed to be grieving. There was a horrible credibility to his childish chatter. And I thought: Nicholas began his reign with Khodynka, and Stalin ended his with one.*

However, the tension soon eased. A day or two passed, and it seemed as though everyone had forgotten everything. People worked as usual and talked about the usual things. There were still official announcements, telegrams of condolence from foreigners and fellow countrymen, quotations from articles and letters in the newspapers.

And there was still nothing about the killer doctors.

Sergei Prokofiev died. The same day as Stalin.

Five years before, he had been berated by Zhdanov, naturally with Stalin's knowledge; for Stalin had said earlier of Shostakovich: "Muddle instead of music."

Viktor Andreevich said that Prokofiev was a great composer. Semyon agreed with him, and he knew more about music than I did. There were brief memorial announcements about Prokofiev, short reserved notices, barely noticeable in the newspapers framed in black.

But his music will live on and on. And when did Zhdanov die? He was forgotten very quickly.

And even in the first days after the speeches, salutes, and sirens the memory of the very greatest faded perceptibly.

*Khodynka Field in Moscow was the site of the tragic death through crowding and stampeding of over a thousand people during the celebration of the coronation of Nicholas II. (Translator's note.)

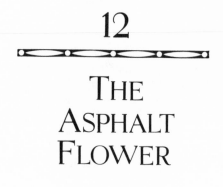

12

THE ASPHALT FLOWER

Of the bunch of newly arrived prisoners I noticed the youngest one—pale, thin, with big eyes, and wearing an old Red Army overcoat slung over a worn, chewed-up, but neat and obviously foreign-made, jacket. He stared beseechingly at the old residents of the sharashka who passed by, smoking their cigarettes. "Please, a smoke. Please, a little bit smoke."

He inhaled greedily and seemed to turn even paler.

Hearing German, his eyes flashed and his whole body moved, as though dancing a jig. "Oh, my God! You speak German?! My name is Kurt A. Please, explain to me, what is this place? Where are we?"

The first lunch—after the gruel at Butyrki—he called a luxurious feast. He was issued bed linens at the supply room and made his cot. "My God, I haven't slept on a sheet and a pillow with a pillowcase in four years."

Blissfully puffing on a cigarette, he told me his story, stressing his bookish turns of phrase. "Well, I guess I can do my twenty-five years here. Even though I got them for nothing, no reason. No, I'm not a Nazi and I never was one. I'm a hereditary proletarian. Berlin asphalt flower. My father was a master craftsman at Siemens, and I worked for various companies—first at a lathe, then as an electrician, and then as a molder. I became a foreman and then a master craftsman myself. I didn't spend a single day either in the barracks or at the front. Weak lungs. Flat feet. But most important—I had protection. They kept masters like myself out of the army. They sent me to other plants as well—to branches to set up the work, to train others. I spent a lot of years in Vienna. Marvelous city. Friendly people. At first my colleagues gave me dirty looks: a Prussian—'Piffke.' But then we got on excellently. Many said that in personality I was a real Viennese—I live and let live. After the war the Soviet bosses appreciated me. The understanding Russian engineers in shoulder boards knew what a high-class precision mechanic was worth. But suddenly I was called in by an officer of counterintelligence: 'Why are you, a Berliner, working in Vienna? How long have you been in the Nazi Party? What were your orders for sabotage?'

"I tried to convince them that I had never joined the party; my father was a Social Democrat, my mother's brother even a Communist, and my cousin a Young Communist. He used to bring leaflets over even after 1933. And I, like all the workers, belonged only to the *Arbeitsfront*. Well, and also to the Strength Through Joy Association—I went to concerts, took seaside vacations. However, I didn't spend a single day in the party or with the storm troopers. I told them about myself in detail, the pure truth and only the truth. No, they didn't torture me. They hit me a few times. I kept telling them my words were easy enough to check, they can check the office records in Berlin, the papers were all there. But they said: 'Your Berlin doesn't exist anymore; it's *kaputt!* Who are we going to ask there? And which papers?'

"They sent me to Butyrki. In one year I was interrogated only three times. Politely. Properly. They wrote down what I said. Then they let me look at the whole file. A translator sat next to me, explained things. There were very brazen denunciations in it. Two Austrians and one Pole, supposedly working in my crew, wrote that I was a Nazi, a fanatic, cursed the Soviet Army, agitated for sabotage. I tried to explain that it was all lies. 'I didn't know those people. They worked somewhere nearby. They couldn't have known me either. Ask the people who had worked with me.'

"But the investigator shrugged it off. 'It's time to close the case. It's been dragging on too long as it is. You can tell your side at the trial. You are accused under Article 1 of the International Law passed at Nuremberg.' Yes, yes, the very law under which they tried Göring, Hess, Ribbentrop, and Streicher. But they were all big shots, leaders of the party and the Reich. I was just a nonparty proletarian. He just laughed: 'Fine, tell that to the judges.'

"But there was no trial. I was simply called in by the prison duty officer and told the decision of the Special Commission—twenty-five years."

Kurt was sociable, talkative, liked to show off his education. He remembered many excerpts from the monologues in *Faust* and used any excuse to recite, carefully maintaining the literary "stage" pronunciation. He often sang songs from *The Threepenny Opera*—"*Ja, der Haifisch der hat Zähne*"—and also knew by heart many surrealist poems by Morgenstern.

He maintained that he was a confirmed antifascist, democrat, but he always avoided politics, preferring sports, chess, women, and good wines; but he had always loved to read and therefore understood a few things in other topics as well.

"Not all the Nazis were alike. Himmler was a horrible person, a ruthless *Reichheine*, Ley was a drunkard and tongue wagger. But you have to give Hitler his due—he was a marvelous orator who hypnotized his audience. Even his most ardent enemies admit that he was a great state administrator. What he managed to do with impoverished Germany, squashed by Versailles and the crisis! In 1932 we had eight million unemployed. The economy was dying. Decay everywhere. On the brink of civil war. And in five years he created a powerful country; and then in one more year he conquered all of Europe. And in another two years he had conquered the area from the Pyrenees to the Caucasus, from the Sahara to the North Pole. Of course, he made a cruel mistake. He strained the springs too far. He overestimated his allies and underestimated his enemies. The Germans fought European-style, according to the old traditions: the army fights, the people work. But the Russians carried on total war, sparing nothing. And when we realized it, it was too late.

"In Butyrki I spent a whole year in the same cell with generals and officers of our General Staff. Churchill himself called the General Staff of the Wehrmacht the best in world history. So I learned everything that went on. Stalingrad was the Führer's miscalculation. The Italians and Rumanians opened our flanks and rear. The Hungarians also fought a lot worse than they had assumed. A hopeless cauldron formed. And it was only then that we declared total war. We still might have won if we had used the V-3. Even the V-1 and V-2 had demoralized the British. The V-3 would have brought them and the Yankees to their knees. But Roosevelt and Churchill let the Führer know that in that case they would begin total gas war against German cities. And by then even the soldiers had forgotten about gas masks. Tens of millions of people would have died. And the Führer gave the order not to use the new weapon. Yes, yes, of course, he was wrong. He trusted his subordinates too much. Göring assured him that the Luftwaffe would always overcome all enemies. And the Führer held up the development of the V rockets, refused the atom bomb. But the Yankees produced flying fortresses from their carriers, put drunken Negroes on them, and launched terrorist carpet bombing of all the cities. They ran at the front. In December 1944 in the Ardennes our Christmas attack almost threw them back into the sea. But they turned Berlin, Hamburg, Cologne, and Frankfurt into ruins, and Dresden—an open city—a city of hospitals and art—they destroyed in two days. The war became suicidal for Germany. Of course, Hitler was at fault in many ways. But we'll see what judgment history brings.

"Linge, Hitler's valet, was my neighbor in Butyrki. He told me that the Führer was pleasant in a human way, polite, modest, moderate in his eating habits. Didn't drink at all. Now that doesn't suit me at all. I'm afraid of teetotallers. Most of them are cold, cruel pragmatists. Hitler's ascetic habits turned me off. And of course, he did lack education. A man of the people. A self-taught genius. He understood art, architecture, and sculpture very well. And he drew and did watercolors himself. My cousin is a doctor of philosophy, a specialist in the arts, and certainly no Nazi—his brother was married to a Jew—and he said that the Führer could have become a great artist if he had given up politics.

"Linge told me in detail in the cell how in 1940, when our troops took Holland, some officers and soldiers went to visit Kaiser Wilhelm at his farm. He received them very ceremoniously—only standing on the garden terrace. They clicked their heels: *'Majestät . . . Majestät.'*

"And he nodded patronizingly. 'I congratulate you on your victory, my brave men!' And immediately sent a telegram to Hitler: 'My Führer, I congratulate you and hope that under your marvelous leadership the German monarchy will be restored completely.' Understand? 'Monarchy restored.' The Führer both laughed and was angry. He repeated it several times. 'Believe me, Linge, we have to get down on our knees to thank the Social Democrats for getting rid of that conceited fool. You see, he's still hoping that the German people will restore his throne and I'll serve him instead of Bismarck, whom he himself fired to Germany's woe. What an idiot!'

"Yes, the war in the East was a fatal mistake—a chain of fatal mistakes. Goebbels admitted that right after Stalingrad. Do you remember his speech in the Sports Hall in February? Now there was an orator no worse than Hitler, I'd say—*eine Rednerkanone!* Smashingly eloquent. Before '33 both the *Sots* and the *Kots* [the socialists and the communists] feared his speeches more than all the revolvers, billy clubs, and brass knuckles. After Stalingrad he was the first to say: 'We miscalculated.' And he explained how and why.

"Everyone who saw your Red Army when you helped us wipe *Polackenland* off the map was astounded: the soldiers were pathetically dressed, their rifles were old-fashioned, no automatic guns at all, the artillery was on horses, like under the tsars and kings. Your tanks were fast, but the Poles set fire to them with their guns. Of course, the old generals, the ones who traditionally loved Russia, warned them: 'Appearances are deceiving. Ivan is dirty and unkempt, but he sees clearly and hears acutely. His trousers are rough cloth, but his fists are steel.' But when Stalin tried to conquer Finland, it turned out that your steel wasn't strong either. The Finns were beating your hundred-times bigger army. The Germans who moved back from the Baltic states spoke very condescendingly of Soviet soldiers.

"Even if our reports in the first months of the war lied, exaggerated even by three hundred percent—even so, we had millions of prisoners. And our soldiers who reached the Volga, the Caucasus, saw along the way how your people lived, how much poverty there was, filth, disorder. There wasn't a village or city that could compare with ours or with any European country's. Only a few of our military men could read your books or judge the theater or music! The majority of the soldiers were workers, peasants, little people. They recognize the tangible, real values. They saw your roads, your housing, your goods. Of course, your tanks, your cannons, and your guns and planes were also completely real. Some of our people realized that early on. But there weren't many of them. Hitler's major mistake was in the East. The enemy turned out to be much worse than even the most cautious had imagined. Your generals in Finland and Poland herded your men to slaughter so as to convince us of your false weakness. And then they fought the same way with us for the first year—senseless mass attacks, right into machine guns—'Hurrah!' And our generals realized too late that these were trick maneuvers, that all those bloody losses and defeats were clever traps. And that's how your strategy beat the

Wehrmacht. Eastern perfidy overcame German straightforwardness.

"No, no, that's no fantasy. I'm free of nationalism. And I love you and admire your nation and your culture. Tolstoy and Dostoevsky are geniuses. I read *War and Peace, The Brothers Karamazov,* and *Crime and Punishment.* I esteem Russian music, Tchaikovsky—I'm ready to listen to the *Nutcracker Suite* every day. But I love my country and know its history. Its enemies always calumnied the Germans. People envy us because we live better, richer, cleaner. And in the first war the French and British falsely accused our soldiers of atrocities and rape. They destroyed Belgian churches and blamed the Germans. The British were the first to use gas. No, no, I know that for a fact. That's the way you were taught, too. Of course, you know our language and culture better than the others, but you were taught tendentiously, too. I know for sure that poison gas and air bombardment were used first by our enemy. Well, in Russia it may have seemed otherwise, but on the Eastern Front the initiative always belonged to the Germans.

"What do you mean Guernica, Coventry, Rotterdam? Those are all fairy tales of your propaganda. In Spain our pilots simply participated in battles and in transporting troops. I know two pilots very well—they were in the Condor legion—extremely honest guys. They told me about everything in detail—they never bombed a peaceful settlement. And in this war the British started bombing our cities first. Our aviation had to respond. In Holland, Belgium, Denmark, and Norway, the British and French were preparing surprise attacks. Our side beat them to it. But the planes of the Luftwaffe bombed only enemy troops, fortifications, and transport. And in Poland our men started the war in a chivalrous way. But the Poles first threw themselves on tanks with sabers and spears like suicidal madmen— and then after their defeat behaved like bandits, attacking from behind corners. In cases like that, international law permits harsh repressions.

"Yes, I know about the concentration camps. Your propaganda has drilled them through my eardrums. But that was the SS, and the black SS at that—the civilian guard units, and not the SS troops, which is something your people always confuse. The SS troops were simply the select units. The guards, of course, had their share of crude bastards, including those who guarded the concentration camps. They were capable of any cruelty, any vile act. But every nation has its degenerates. And what happened when your armies tore into Germany? They raped girls and old women. And how many innocent people did they kill for nothing. Just like that: 'German, Fritz, *kaputt!*' But I understand, they were degenerates, made even worse by vodka. And you want all Germans to be responsible for the degenerate SS, for the death camps? And you're exaggerating again. Your propaganda maintains that in Katyn the Germans shot Polish officers. In 1943 there was an international commission there, and it was proved definitely: it was your revolvers and rifles at work there."

Telling about himself, Kurt most often recalled his amorous adventures with various "fiancées"—young girls and ladies from good families—and with pretty prostitutes. Some of his stories sounded like the plots of adventure novels. A beauty would lure him to a mysterious dive, he would notice that they were slipping something into his wine or switching glasses, and he would cleverly pour the poison into his pocket. The beauty, after passionate embraces, thinking him asleep, would disappear, and he would escape through a window or door, making his way along dark corridors, hiding in niches behind drapes to avoid the mysterious types who had been planning to rob or kill him.

He picked up Russian quickly. He made friends among the free employee workers and technicians. In the evenings he made rings, manicure sets, and cigarette cases out of stainless steel and sold them to the free employees. They paid him in kind: sausage, canned goods, candy, and sometimes even vodka.

Twice a month they showed movies to the prisoners. They set up a screen in the large cell. They showed Soviet movies and even a few foreign films. The Germans sat in a group around me, and I translated. Kurt sometimes argued heatedly with those fellow countrymen of his who snorted disdainfully, "Propaganda."

"No, no, I don't agree. This is real art."

He liked a few old, prewar films, but films about the war angered him.

"Tendentious hackwork—Kitsch! No better than what the Nazis did. It's been five years since the war ended, but for you the Germans are still either idiots or animals. Even though you always shout about your internationalism."

He berated the Italian neorealist films. "It's all lies! Talentless, lying films. They were made only because there were Communists in the Italian government. What stupid nonsense! The Mafia existed a hundred years ago. Only your people could believe that it's possible in contemporary Italy. There is poverty, however. It's the edge of Europe, after all. Perhaps there are people who steal bicycles. But to make a movie out of it, to turn it into a tearjerker, ah, the poor boy! Now that's real degeneration of art . . . decadence. The Italian Communists make movies like that on your orders. And they show them here to convince you how bad life is under capitalism.

"I always loved the poetry of Heine, the music of Mendelssohn. In school I had two friends who were Jewish. One was a doctor's son, and the other the son of a hotel owner. His father fought near Verdun, had been decorated with the Iron Cross of both classes, belonged to the Stahlhelm, the Steel Helmet. There were decent people, real patriots among the German Jews. But during World War I, tens of thousands of Eastern Jews from Poland and Russia fled to Germany. In the years of inflation it was they who took over trade, industry, publishing houses, theaters, motion pictures. In Berlin all the best houses belonged to the Jews; they were in charge of retail trade, in the majority of banks, and naturally in politics.

No, no, the Nazis didn't only lie, they exaggerated a lot, of course. But Jewish politicians and Jewish writers set the tone for both the Communists and Social Democrats. Even in the National Party, among the monarchists, in the Steel Helmet, the Jewish influence was felt.

"The Eastern Jews with earlocks arrived in their caftans; but they quickly learned how to assimilate. They have a special talent for mimicry and an amazing racial solidarity. In Berlin the first Spartacists-Communists were led by Polish Jews—Rosa Luxemburg and Karl Radek—and by German Jews—Liebknecht and Pieck. Who told you they were pure Germans? Are you certain? Well, then they were married to Jews, "*jüdisch versippt.*" And were connected with the Jewish milieu. In Bavaria in 1919 the Russian Jews—Levine and Levin—and German Jews—Toller and Mühsam—created a Soviet revolution. And all the Social Democratic governments of all parts of Germany had Jewish ministers—Eisner, Rathenau . . . And they're the highest masters of advertising. The best example of that is Einstein; he was an ordinary, average mathematician who came up with some fantastic, dubious theories, but after the war, when the Jewish influence was strengthened, he was declared a world genius.

"No, I'm sorry, you can't know that. You're not a mathematician or a physicist. You have a Marxist world view and Einstein as a Marxist is dear to you. But he calls himself a Marxist. Well, if not a Marxist, then close to it. Let's not argue about particulars. The whole picture is what's important. Jews predominated in the German Communist Party. Of course, for window dressing, on the tribunals they put out people like Teddy Thälmann—a Hamburg bully and a drunk. Or Toller—an intellectual miffed by fate. But the leading power was Neumann and his commissar. This isn't Nazi propaganda, these are facts!

"Well, and how are things here? Many prisoners and some free employees told me that the Russians and Ukrainians don't like Jews either, because they grab the best jobs, the best apartments. Yes, yes, I don't argue with you there, there are many Jewish prisoners here. But they tell me that it's only recently that the pressure has been put on them—after the war. Because while Russian soldiers were dying at the front, the Jews were finding themselves cushy spots in the rear, getting rich and buying meals. Naturally, I don't believe in that too much. But all that is being said here, in the worker-peasant socialist heaven. That means not only Nazis are against the Jews!

"Yes, yes, I know it's many centuries of prejudice! Yes, yes, I know that Germans elicit hostility in many foreigners. Both before and now. The Germans are envied. But Germans moving from Germany melt into other nationalities and selflessly serve other countries. When the United States was being founded, hundreds of thousands of Germans lived there. And the first Congress discussed the question of which language to consider the state one—German or English. English won by one vote—which was cast by a German. Well, naturally you would consider that a fairy tale. Because the textbooks you used were written either by American nationalists or by Marxists."

It was impossible to make him change his mind about anything he once considered the truth. Any disagreement he discounted as "distortions of propaganda."

Between 1950 and 1953 there were fourteen or fifteen Germans and Austrians working at the sharashka, and he somehow became their leader, even though many of them were older and better educated than Kurt.

He tried to develop our respect for his protégés. "Horst R. is a very serious practician and a diplomaed engineer. But Dr. Fritz B. is already a *Doktor-Ing* [a doctor-engineer]. And that means that he is a scholar-engineer of the highest class. I don't pay special attention to academic degrees. We have a tradition in Germany of bourgeois respect: ah, doctor, ah, professor. But I know quite a few who put in their time for the dissertation —read, crammed, copied, and there you are—doctor of philosophy. But doctor-engineer is something quite different. You have to prove your scholarship in practice for that title."

Our foreigners didn't have money for a long time. All the other prisoners after two or three months of work at the sharashka began receiving a salary ranging from 50 to 150 rubles a quarter, depending on their category. That money and the money from our relatives we received in the form of coupons that could be used with requests to the supply shop. Every month supplies were brought in based on requests. You could order butter, sausage, soap, canned food, condensed milk, tooth powder, tobacco, socks, razor blades, and so on.

Every time the requests were made up, Kurt came to those of us he considered his friends and pals. "It would be nice to get a half kilo of butter for Tony K. He's the youngest of our group and he's such an emaciated Berlin kid. Could you order some cigars for Dr. B.? It's his birthday soon. How about some candy or marmalade for Engineer F.! He's missed sweets for so long. And for engineers L. and M., please, they really need toothbrushes and toothpaste. It's so disgusting to clean your teeth with a soapy finger, and the soap we're issued stinks of offal."

I can't remember him ever asking for something for himself.

Naturally, we ordered soap, sweets, and butter for him as well. He thanked us exquisitely and rushed to "respond." He brought me a manicure set delicately made of stainless steel and a ring with a seal. And several times he got a pint of vodka or a flask of spirits through his free colleagues.

My good relations with Kurt withstood quite a few disagreements, but were undermined by the military events in Korea. He took such pleasure in the advance of the Americans, was so angered by the intervention of the Chinese and their successes, that we argued more and more angrily. For a time we barely spoke.

Soon after Stalin's death the new head of the prison changed the supply chief and the dining room chief. It turned out that we had been robbed for a long time. Most of us were supposed to have had food and smokes of the highest category long ago.

Kurt learned the pleasant news first. He had customers among the screws. He hurried to tell me the news that we would be getting twice as much meat, butter, and sugar as before and that it turned out we were supposed to have two eggs, not one, the way we had been served up to now. And much more pork and red caviar every other day, when before it was served only occasionally on holidays and in tiny portions.

"I heard you all talking about the Jewish doctors being released. And I had doubts. You always hope for the best, you're a Marxist optimist. But now I see the silver lining on the horizon, too. Maybe it's really the dawn at last?"

In May 1953 some of the officer engineers and even some of the prison workers told us that soon all the Germans would be sent back to Germany.

Kurt reestablished our friendship. We spent long hours chatting and arguing peaceably. There were talks going on in Korea. A lead article in *Pravda* discussed portentously and vaguely criticized "the cult of personality, alien to Marxism." After the amnesty for criminals and repeaters, the free employees kept bringing new rumors that soon there will be a political amnesty, too, told us about the staff reductions in the MGB, reduced from a ministry to a "committee."

All the Germans were called to be shipped out at the same time in the middle of a workday. Kurt and his best friends—engineer Horst L., engineer Horst R., and technician Hans N.—came to say good-bye to us in the acoustics lab.

Kurt had written down my family's address on a cigarette box and memorized it long before. Saying farewell, he repeated it several times.

"I'll write to you. Probably from some place in Siberia. But maybe, now they'll let us correspond."

Convulsively mobile, like the first day at the sharashka, he smiled and joked, but alarm glimmered in his feverishly shining eyes.

Two years later in Moscow—already freed but not yet rehabilitated—I received a card from Italy: a lacquer-shiny photo of the city-republic of San Marino—"Greetings from vacation, Kurt A., Horst L., Hans N." That's how they signed themselves, and that's how I have called them here.

13

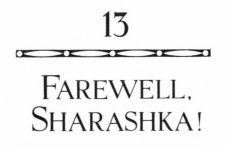

FAREWELL, SHARASHKA!

The achievement of understanding that every person
is another I, equal in some sense, is what creates the
moral bases of human society.

— VYACHESLAV VS. IVANOV, "Odd and Even"

April 4. Early in the morning, on my way from the yurt to do my exercises,
I turned on the radio in the porch. Quietly—most were still asleep. And
I heard: ". . . illegal methods of investigation . . ." And then the names of
the doctors who were freed and found innocent. And in conclusion: "We
were broadcasting the lead article from the newspaper *Pravda.*"

The joy was stunning, deafening; I ran into the neighboring yurt instead
of my own. Probably simply because I was standing closer to that door.

"The doctors have been freed! They're innocent! The lead article in
Pravda spoke of illegal methods of investigation. All the doctors have been
freed!"

Heads lifted from pillows. Someone sat up on his cot. "What are these
stupid jokes. Are you fucking crazy? Did you forget April Fool's is over?
Give him some water and take him into the air, so that he can come to his
senses. People get punched in the face for jokes like that."

"But it's true, it's true! They just announced it. They'll repeat it soon."

Even the angriest curses did not upset me. Joy flooded me, was bursting
inside me, making me dizzy.

That whole day and for many days after, that's all people talked about.
Not much arguing. Mostly quiet discussions, friendly, sharing the informa-
tion received from their free employee friends. Comparing. Assuming.
Doubting. But mostly hoping.

In the new Council of Ministers Malenkov became chairman; Beria, Molotov, Bulganin, and Kaganovich, deputies. The number of ministries was
reduced—they were combined, done away with—staffs were cut back.

"Aha, that means they're squeezing the bureaucrats!"

And something that affected us directly: the MGB was no more. Instead
there was the modest Committee of State Security (KGB) under the Council of Ministers. In the newspapers and on the radio there were persistent

phrases about legality, humanitarianism, about the politics of peaceful co-existence.

We learned that Abakumov was released and named to the new committee. We remembered only bad things about him: a cruel boor, a tall stout man with the face of a brutish butcher. But he had spent two years in prison, maybe he had grown wiser.

Voroshilov was named chairman of the Supreme Soviet. The out-of-favor Marshal Zhukov became deputy to Defense Minister Bulganin.

We discussed every appointment thoroughly. I remembered Bulganin from the Northwestern Front as an obstinate fool. Everyone knew about Zhukov: harsh, severe, ruthless, cruel, but a talented strategist; weaned on the battlefield, not afraid of the rulers. That's why Stalin didn't like him; they even said that he feared him and was jealous of him.

We were pleased by the announcement that Khrushchev became a leading secretary of the Presidium of the Central Committee. I had heard of him before; one of Nadya's relatives, who taught his wife and daughters English and had lived in their house for long periods of time, had told us that he was crude, not well educated, but smart, clever, kindly, and a "Party member of the old school," that is, he couldn't stand high living, luxury, acquisitiveness, toadying, and he didn't boast. His wife darned his socks and his grandchildren's socks; she lived on a modest household budget, and the maid and the chauffeur ate with the rest of the family.

At the sharashka good rumors beat newspaper reports or added to them, giving us even more hope. The security organs were cutting back more than half their personnel. All Chekists were stripped of the officers' ranks obtained in recent years in the MGB. The only ranks that counted were the ones received in actual army service. Many colonels turned back into captains overnight. Some of our people saw prison officers, yesterday's captains and senior lieutenants, in sergeants' stripes.

Evgenii S., despite his youth, was an experienced radio technician and an old zek. He got in before the war; he received a new sentence in the camp. The best mounter in the acoustics lab, he was a virtuoso swearer in both four-letter words and criminal argot but used a refined, worldly tone; a grand master of dominoes, he also read avidly. We first became friends as neighbors in the lab—his desk was closest to mine. Then I began giving him German lessons. His term ended in the summer of 1953. He was or tried to be a notorious pessimist. "Only jerks can hope for freedom. They'll shove a cock in our faces, not freedom. We won't even be trustees. The only way we'll get outside the zone is in a wooden jacket with a tag on your toe. And that's after they stick an awl through your belly at the guard booth."

At night he screamed horribly, sometimes roundly cursing some criminals, or bitches, or vipers with easy jobs. During the day he worked selflessly, until he was ready to drop. He improved other people's models, and he invented his own. Exacting Sergei used to say that he would give half a dozen inexperienced engineers for one such experienced technician.

In the middle of a workday Evgenii suddenly appeared in my corner, happy and mysterious; impatiently he nodded at Sergei to come over.

"Well, citizen comrades, old chaps, and learned gentlemen, now I think I'll begin to believe the most comforting of rumors. I just heard this in the can. I swear, I never thought I'd live to see the day. I was sitting in the stall, thinking. That's the only place where you can really feel alone. I heard two men come in. They were talking. One sounded familiar, like the major from the office, a fat-faced guy—he's sort of the personnel prick. I didn't recognize the other one. They started to piss and continued their conversation; which one of their men lost his shoulder boards, which was fucked over completely. And I heard this major say, and with such bitterness: 'They think they can manage without us. They'll fire us all and then they'll come crying.' Do you understand who *they* are? The leaders, the government is *they* as far as our citizen bosses are concerned. We've lived to see it, pals!"

Evgeniia Vasilievna began inviting me more frequently to her office. The experiments with the wire were over, but I continued to help her translate articles from British and American journals.

"Rumin has been shot! Now there's someone I would never have suspected! He headed our Party enlightenment section once. He gave lectures himself. Such an educated, cultured, well-bred man. And everyone knew how much Lavrentii Pavlovich valued him. When Abakumov was sent up, they said that it was Rumin who had exposed him. And now this! It's even strange. Well, you know, how things happen: if there's a campaign, one answers for many. Of course, there were excesses in the organs. Things like that happened under Yezhov. And now the business with the doctors. Recently I thought of what you had said then—maybe the whole business was arranged by those who wanted the death of Comrade Stalin. That's even terrible to contemplate. Now they've started purging the organs—going over each person one by one. It looks as though they'll open up something."

The prison administration was changed. The chief was once again Lieutenant Colonel Grigoriev—the "fair-minded front liner," who had been in charge at the very start of the sharashka—and Solzhenitsyn had taught me how to deal with him. He toured the yurts, greeted us dryly but amiably, recognizing old acquaintances. And right after his return our nourishment changed sharply. All the years before we had been gypped. The foreigners, who were kept in the third category the longest, were stunned by the innovations. A young engineer, an Austrian, told me in complete seriousness that after this experience, he would probably join the Communist Party when he got home.

"Before, I supported the Socialists. But then I became convinced that they were weak, losers. They were defeated by the Black Front in Austria, and Hitler squashed their colleagues even earlier in Germany. I used to think that Communists were senseless dreamers, and that if they tried to realize their utopias, it could lead only to famine and terror. And I was convinced that the Communists could find a following only among the primitive, Asiatic peoples—the ones who were accustomed to deprivation, humility, to a mass herd existence. But today I can say that my world view is changing. Five years in a Soviet prison, in our *'so genannt* sharashka' and these marvelous reforms—such speedy progress—have convinced me. And not only me. The majority of our Austrians and Germans just recently were absolute pessimists; they had no hope at all. But now even our old Nazi and capitalist Bayer says that he hopes for a better fate. And some of them are all ready to shout: *'Heil Genosse Malenkov!'* or *'Heil Genosse Beria!'* "

Valentin Sergeevich—the ever-hopeful Valentulia—hurried in on the double one morning from exercises and called Sergei and me. "Listen, listen, listen! I just met the chief. He started talking to me himself: 'It's good that you exercise. We'll get a volleyball net. We'll arrange matches.' So I told him right off about the TVs. How they took them away last year. He didn't even stop to think. 'Well, if you can construct something again, I'll give you a yurt—it will be a clubhouse for cultural relaxation.' And he asked: 'Who can be in charge of that?' I remembered that both of you had gone to see Naumov. I didn't mention the vacuum guys, just in case. I mentioned only you. He said let them come, even now, if they can make it before work."

The preliminary meeting with the main specialists lasted several minutes. We knew that some parts of the dismantled television sets were hidden in the zone.

I reported to the chief just as I had that first time, "military-style," that everything could be done in one day, if he would only give permission. He spoke to us politely, a straitlaced businesslike official, knowing neither passion nor prejudice. Sergei started a trusting explanation about the fact that the parts of the sets, even though merely rejects and parts of parts, strewn about all over the place, could be quickly turned into a primitive homemade but still usable set.

The janitors started cleaning up the yurt that was assigned to be our clubhouse that very morning. During lunch the rush brigade built a plank platform and was knocking together benches for the audience from stools and planks and a pedestal for the television from old nightstands. An hour after the workday ended it was installed.

The chief came in as we were enjoying a travelogue. Everyone jumped up. He waved for us to sit down. "Before the deadline, then? Overfulfilled the plan! I see you really are masters and specialists."

All the foreigners were taken away.

The spring ukase on amnesty pertained only to short-term criminals and nonpolitical prisoners. It obviously didn't refer to us. Only one of the janitors "fell under it."

However, in those same days, first in a front-page article in *Pravda* and then peppering the longer articles throughout, came the phrases "personality cult, alien to Marxism-Leninism," "the restoration of Leninist principles and the Lenin style of intra-Party democracy." Newspaper articles, radio and television news warmed up our hopes.

Gumer, Ivan Emelianovich, and some free employees heartened us with rumors of secret ukases that would free "without special noise" political prisoners, and some people said that they were already starting "to free the fifty-eighters."

But soon after the amnesty order, unpleasant rumors began circulating about increased brazen thefts, muggings, rapes, and murders in Moscow and other cities. The concept "amnestied" became a curse word, a bogey equivalent to "bandit." Gumer told us that in Kazan, where his relatives lived, workers in some districts were forming their own vigilante groups since the militia was incapable of dealing with crime. These units, armed with steel rods, brass knuckles, and knives, set up ambushes; when they caught a thief or mugger, they killed him on the spot. In a few cases they made him first show them the hideout, and then killed everyone there. In that way they cleared up the town in a week and not one of the proletarian lynch mob was called in by the militia.

Pessimists began saying that the amnesty had been invented just for that —to frighten the people, to build up mistrust of zeks, and in general to bolster the feeling that an iron hand of the "organs" and enormous camps were necessary to maintain law and order. After the first stormy infusion of joyous hopes, dark, evil doubts returned.

The newspapers carried an official announcement of the premiere of the opera *The Decembrists*, attended by the members of the Presidium of the Central Committee and the ministers. This was the first time I ever read anything like it. Everyone was named in strict alphabetical order. In Stalin's day the order of the members of the Politburo was no less important than the placement long ago of the boyars: Stalin, Molotov, Voroshilov, Kaganovich, Zhdanov. Then Voroshilov fell back to fifth place, and Zhdanov moved up to third, and even to second place, but before his death rolled back again.

I asked Ivan and Valentina: "Why isn't Beria on the list? Is he on vacation now? Has something happened to him?"

Ivan grew angry. "That really shows your ideology. You're always suspecting something or other."

After the official announcement of Beria's arrest and his connections with British intelligence, Ivan was thoroughly imbued with extreme, respectful trust for me.

· · ·

In the summer of 1957 he came to my house and told me what he knew for a fact: "Vyacheslav Mikhailovich [Molotov] is displeased with Khrushchev. He's overdoing it, he keeps blaming Stalin for everything, but he's heading for another cult, his own." He learned this from some relatives who worked for the Ministry of Foreign Affairs. But he must have been bothered by the fact that my distrust and dislike of Molotov was stronger than all the doubts elicited by Khrushchev then—after the invasion of Hungary—and that I was thinking differently about Stalin now than I had in the spring and summer of 1953, when I found unfair the intentional, demonstrative forgetfulness, underscored by vague hints of a dangerous cult of the personality.

First from Valentina and then from Vanya and Evgeniia Vasilievna we heard extremely important news: Malenkov, it turns out, was Lenin's nephew. The son of his sister . . . no, of his cousin. Apparently not a blood relative, but he had been brought up from childhood personally by Lenin and Krupskaya. This was kept secret, to protect his life. He was the one who traveled to factories and communal farms.

The ukase lowering prices was issued. The most significant drops were in the price of bread, potatoes, and other food products.

The kolkhozes were excused from back taxes.

On June 17 in Berlin and other cities of the GDR, workers went on strike. There were fights in the streets with the national police. But everything passed. The newspapers wrote about "the facts of just discontent" of the workers, reports of "a new style of administration in the GDR." (Not a single word about Soviet tanks firing on German workers appeared in the Soviet press.)

Personnel cutbacks everywhere and a ban on overtime. At our sharashka, too. This created unusually long leisure hours. After five I could select from (or mix): walks with friends to discuss political or sharashka news, the study of Chinese, watching TV, working on the flower beds . . .

In the clubhouse yurt a string orchestra sprang up; our director got us mandolins, balalaikas, and domras. We started a choir, and I was in the basses. We sang old folk songs.

We had to work that much harder during the day. I had to speed up the work on the dissertation. I didn't want to condense anything. I couldn't shirk—even if I wanted to: I was too caught up in the work, which seemed important and necessary. Valentina would start studying, outlining, cramming zealously for a while and then cool off, repeating irritably or sadly that nothing would come of it anyway, it was all a waste, and she should be defending something technical. "You were talking about a spectrum analyzer built by Sergei Grigorievich and someone who was taken away; you said it was a marvelous piece of work, much better than anything the

Americans have. Why can't I do my dissertation on that? Ivan isn't planning to defend it, he's not even thinking of it, and I could master that much better than all your philosophy."

Controlling my irritation, I cajoled, convinced, flattered shamelessly. There was very little time left.

And what if they let me out in the summer or the fall? But I probably wouldn't be allowed to remain in Moscow.

Trying to imagine myself in the shoes of Malenkov or Khrushchev, I thought that after the bitter experience of the first amnesty, the newly released people would be settled in distant regions, put under surveillance, and then gradually, each case would be examined and permitted to move to capital cities. And who would do the examining? The apparatus was still the same. They executed Rumin, Beria, some of them were purged, fired, sent up. But Rudenko was still Procurator General. And most of the procurators and judges were the same ones who had accused, sentenced, and refused appeals.

I had to hurry before Valentina gave up on the dissertation. I wouldn't find another "author" quickly. And without one my anonymous work would stay in the archives, without bearing fruit. In the sharashka we were still officially nonexistent. We still couldn't even go near the safes, signed nothing with our names, and were not listed as authors or inventors of anything. Naumov hadn't changed at all.

In May I applied for a visit. In June someone heard that the head of the prison was permitting all close relatives, without limiting the number. And that the visits would no longer take place in the prison but under certain "more pleasant conditions."

I asked Gumer to tell my family to bring my daughters. The Sunday morning of the meeting, I tripped and twisted my ankle. Terrible pain. My ankle turned blue and swelled up. But worse than the pain was the fear that they wouldn't let me go. And that Nadya and my mother, who would come for nothing, would be frightened.

A nurse—one of the few who remained from the former prison staff— had always been rather kind to us, gentle, even though she put on an act of severity. She hurried to the yurt, since she lived nearby, examined my foot, squeezed hard, and bandaged it very tightly, putting in splints.

"Bear it, bear it, if you want to go. There's nothing broken. A severe sprain, a small torn tendon. Bear up."

We trusted her, we knew she had been at the front. She gave me several pills: "Take one at a time, chew it up, if the pain is very bad." She brought me two crutches.

My comrades were touchingly concerned: they held me up, helped me into the car.

A joyous surprise—they didn't take us in Black Marias, as they had on all the previous occasions, but in an ordinary bus.

. . .

A sunny day. The streets were crowded. The joy of recognition—the square behind the Agricultural Exhibit. There was an incalculable multitude of *free* people, in their Sunday, summery best. It seemed that they were all merry. And most important—so many children! Long-unseen children, tiny ones in carriages and parents' arms. Amusing toddlers with toys, with ice cream. Schoolchildren—boys and girls—alone, with grown-ups, in noisy herds. Here they were right by the bus, so close I could reach out and touch them. I don't hear what is being said next to me. But I can sense that everyone, almost everyone, is also astonished. Someone asks me about something. I don't hear him. I can't, I won't respond. I'm afraid to turn around: it's hot under my eyelids. I have to keep from sobbing.

We drove out of town. Fields. A forest. More happy people in the villages, more children. We drove into a compound. A high wooden fence. We saw a large garden. Several buildings. The duty officer explained: "This is Bolshevo. It used to be a special camp, too, now it's being taken down. Go to your right."

Far off to the left, we saw groups of free people. Our relatives.

"And you [this was for me], wait a bit. And whoever is going to help you, he should wait, too. You'll go through after all the relatives have been brought in. Or your people will see that you're on crutches, and they'll worry."

I limped off, and I didn't seem to feel the pain anymore, just heaviness. And I was touched by the unusual sensitivity of the screw. There was a large gazebo in the garden, an overhang rather, glassed in, covered with ivy and creepers. There were several tables inside, long ones and square ones. I was seated at a separate small one in the corner. The duty officer wanted to make sure they didn't notice the crutches first thing.

And there was Mother, Nadya, Father. And a dark-skinned, black-eyed young woman. Sort of familiar, resembling the pictures I have. A small, or rather, a stocky young woman—no longer a girl. It's Maya. They didn't bring Lena. Mama and Nadya explain, someone called, an unfamiliar woman's voice—"bring your daughters." They didn't believe it—after all, the notice only mentioned parents and wife. Then Inna Levidova called; she was also asked to let them know by phone that they could bring the girls. (Good old Gumer—he realized they would have doubts.) And still, they decided to bring only Maya—she was older.

The supervisors were off to the side somewhere. No one stood between us. We sat at our own table, just like a family. Maya on my left, close up, tender, a quick-eyed fast talker. Her finger was bandaged. She had sprained it playing volleyball. She told me about her school. She was graduating next year; definitely going to a polytechnical institute. She used to dream about studying geography, but that was childish. Being a mechanical engineer—that was the present. She spoke about books, poetry, her girl friends, her teachers. I listened and barely heard her. How she looked like Ronya

—my father's sister. She, too, had been dark-eyed, with dark curly hair and prominent cheekbones. And she used to get excited this way, talking, arguing . . .

In 1919, when Ronya was a Gymnasium student and the contact for the Kiev underground revolutionary committee, she was arrested and cruelly beaten by counterintelligence. Many years later my mother told the story in whispers to her girl friends: "They raped her, infected her." They left her unconscious in the investigator's office. She came to in the middle of the night. She staggered out. In the other rooms officers were partying with prostitutes. As she left the building the guards laughed: "The floozie's drunk." She made it to her comrades. They got her through the front lines. She was sick a long time and spent almost a year in a psychiatric hospital.

This was also considered a terrible secret in the family. But her emotional illness disappeared when she contracted typhoid fever.

She had a powerful, yet gentle contralto. I loved to listen to her sing when I was a child Ukrainian songs, Gypsy romances. In the early 1920s she married Mark Klubman, who was also in the revolutionary committee. He waited for her to be cured and married her knowing that she could not have children. They both studied. He was in law school, worked as a procurator for a while and as a judge somewhere on the Volga, and by the late twenties became a dean, and then prorector of the Saratov Juridical Institute. Ronya wanted to become a biologist, but her illness, I think, kept her from graduating. She worked in libraries, then as a lab assistant in agrolaboratories. Every summer they came to Kiev and then to Kharkov to visit us and the grandparents. In 1933 Mark was appointed head of the political section of MTS in Kharkov Oblast, two years later he became an instructor of the Central Committee of the Communist Party (Bolshevik) of the Ukraine, and in 1937 he was arrested and given ten years. Ronya wrote appeals, protests, sent letters and telegrams to Yezhov, Vyshinsky, Stalin, asking to see them. She came from Kiev to Moscow, lived with us. In late 1937 both of us went to the conservatory. We heard Tchaikovsky's Sixth Symphony. She wept silently.

That was the last time I saw her. Soon after she was arrested. But in a little more than a year, in 1940, when she was still under investigation, she was released.* And she wrote and telegraphed again, fighting for Mark's release. She lived in Kiev with her parents. When the German troops were approaching Kiev, her younger brother Misha was already hospitalized with a serious spine wound. He and my brother, Sanya, an artillery sergeant, whose battery stood in a suburb, believed that our great counterattack would begin any moment. And Ronya believed it, too, and so did my grandfather and grandmother, and they couldn't leave Misha. The

*After Yezhov was exposed in 1938–1939, the new security commissar, Beria, released several thousand prisoners. (Translator's note.)

hospital was evacuated; Misha died somewhere en route. They didn't have time . . .

In April 1944 I was passing through Kiev from one front to another. The woman janitor told me: "They were taken away over there—to Babi Yar —on the second day. That's how long the line was. Many of them knew by then that they were being killed there. Your grandfather was very sick, his legs didn't work. Your grandmother and Ronya pushed him in a wheelchair. Your grandmother was still strong. She was over eighty and had lost a lot of weight—all dried up—but she walked straight as a stick. And Ronya had grown gray and very thin, too, and she had lost all her teeth. But her eyes were still the same, like coals. That day she told me: 'I know they're going to kill us, but it doesn't matter, the victory will come. And when our people return, tell them to avenge us.' "

Mark lived to be released and rehabilitated. He died in Saratov in 1957, a pensioner.

I was seeing Maya for the first time after that March evening in 1947, when I was arrested the second time. They were taking me out of the house, and she—sick with an ear infection, a fever of 104—embraced me with her hot arms, asking: "Will you be back soon?"

This new meeting six years later had both joy and the bitterness of inevitable memories. (My Kiev grandmother used to cook radishes in honey—an incomparable taste of bitter sweetness.)

I kept staring and staring at my grown-up daughter, grown up, happy. And without understanding why, I felt a sharp anxious pity. Later I thought that it was because of my memories of Ronya, of the thoughts about how Maya would live after school—after all, she would have to mention me on all her applications.

Mother and Father, interrupting each other, assured me that the lawyers and some very well-informed friends knew for sure that very soon all the cases under Article 58 would be reviewed and I would naturally be acquitted.

Nadya looked calmer and healthier than at our last meeting, smiled more naturally, joked, told me about our daughter's merry pranks. But that was also the time I learned about the punishment of my friends. The ones who had written to Stalin on my behalf.

Back in 1950, Abram Mendelevich mentioned the Mytishchi Laboratories. It turned out that he knew Lieutenant Colonels Levin and Arshansky and had heard that they no longer worked there, because they had defended some Trotskyite. At the next meeting I asked Nadya what had happened to Valya and Misha, why they didn't work at Mytishchi anymore. She looked at my mother. "We hadn't wanted to tell you, to depress you: they had problems along Party lines. Misha is now living in Leningrad, he's married and very happy. Musya and Valya moved to Novosi-

birsk—they're very happy; Ivan Rozhansky is at the Academy of Sciences; Yura Maslov has been demobilized and is now in Leningrad, teaching at the university. Galina Khromushina is still at TASS, Boba Belkin is in Moscow at the university. We don't see any of them or write to them— after all, they had problems because of you; we don't want to get them into any further trouble."

And now, on a sunny day in 1953, after the hope-inspiring and bracing news, I heard that Musya, Valya, Misha, Galina, and Mikhail Aleksandrovich Kruchinsky had been thrown out of the Party back in 1948. Valya and Misha were soon demobilized. Ivan was transferred to candidate member of the Party. Yura Maslov, Boris Izakov, my attorney, and even the judges—the lieutenant colonel who acquitted me in 1946, the colonel who gave me only three years in 1947, and Ulrich himself, chairman of the military collegium, and his deputies, Orlov and Karavaikov, who in November 1947 reduced my ten-year sentence to six—were all strongly reprimanded. The attorney said that all this happened because some high-ranking person from the Main Political Administration reported personally to Stalin, who said: "They must be punished."* But now total legality had been restored, and the same attorney was now certain that the reprimand would soon be removed from his record and even though Ulrich had retired he was still vigorous, and that he and all the other punished judges were very interested in a review of my case and would fight for it.

On the way back I barely noticed the fields and forests and Sunday crowds. My thoughts were hemmed in by an impenetrable mush of old hurts, doubts, hopes, and a new tormenting realization: there had been so much sorrow because of me, much more than I had imagined. Mother was falling apart. Nadya hid the misfortunes of our friends—what was she hiding of her own problems? And meanwhile I had been looking for "hand roots," inventing phonoscopy, studying Chinese.

But now, now everything would change. But what could change? No change could bring back the wasted years to my mother, or Nadya, or our friends, or me. And there was no way to quench or cure the sorrow—all the grief I had caused—and there was no way to redeem it.

Valentina had been on vacation in Sochi. She returned tanned and prettier. She complained about the frivolous resort males and that the sanatoriums were filled with Jews. She had forgotten much of what she had learned. But she laughed it off: "We didn't study that yet." And so, as I was writing the concluding sections of the dissertation, I had to explain the basic themes, the meaning of the introduction and the early sections to its "author."

She listened distractedly.

*Then I didn't believe it, but having read Djilas's book *Conversations with Stalin*, I allow that it might have happened.

"Do you think you will be released? I wish that for you with all my heart. Now everyone is saying that by next year there will be no one left of the special contingent. I heard that you will be sent to another special site. Will you have time to write everything? Finish it? That's good. I just don't know if I'll have time to master it."

(The dissertation defense did not take place: she hadn't passed the candidatorial minimal requirements.)

Gumer, Ivan Emelianovich, and all our free employee pals said that we would be sent off before the year's end, but they consoled us—not to the camps, but to Kuchino. There was still a large sharashka operating there.

Evgenii S. was taken away in May. Gumer got a happy postcard from him from Ukhta—Evgenii had been released there and issued a passport; he was working in a radio shop and was living temporarily in a dormitory.

We had another visit in the fall. A bus stood at the guardhouse again, but this time with beige curtains on the windows. And inside there was an iron box with individual seating cells.

They brought us to Tushino, to the factory building of a former munitions sharashka. In the corridor all different-caliber and multicolored targets stood and lay scattered about—silhouettes and painted figures in helmets, full height, bent, running, solitary heads over parapets.

The relatives were placed on the other side of a narrow table. Nadya and Mama had brought both daughters. Lena turned out to be bigger, taller than her older sister. She had a dusky tan, was slightly Mongolian-looking, and had blue-black hair and dark eyes. Very beautiful. She smiled shyly, replied with monosyllables. Looking at my daughters, I felt both joy and an inexplicable fear—what were they like? Would we understand one another?

Nadya told me that Musya had died in Novosibirsk. Musya!

In Kharkov in 1929 she was our bosom friend and "matchmaker." She and Valya had registered their marriage a few months before us. And their Irishka was the same age as our Maya.

In the summer of 1929 Nadya went on vacation with her parents by the Azov Sea. Musya stayed in town for a while and I came to see her every day to tell her how lonely I was, how I counted the days. She read me excerpts from Valya's letters. He was older than we seventeen-year-olds, by almost three years. That was a significant difference at that age. His letters—frequent and long—combined stories about funny incidents, interesting people, poetic descriptions of scenery, quotes of poetry and prose, ruminations on love, literature, and theater. They seemed to have a grown-up significance, and I began unconsciously imitating him. And I wrote daily to Nadya, if not a letter, then a postcard. And also folded the envelopes in half—Musya and Valya had turned those narrow packages into our secret Masonic sign.

About all that, about my love—my first big real love—I told Musya. She said: "Let's daydream! You and Nadya and Lida and her husband—she's bound to have a wonderful husband—and Valya and I will live in the same city—in Kharkov or Odessa or maybe Moscow or Leningrad—but it has to be in the same city. And like now—not far from one another. [We studied at the same school, lived in the same neighborhood. Musya, Lida, and Nadya had been friends since first grade; in school the trio had been dubbed "lemonade"—"Li-Mu-Nad."] Nadya will be a chemical engineer, she'll head a laboratory in a major plant. And Lida will be a chemist, too, but a scientist or a teacher. Her husband will be a professor of some exact science. Valya will become, naturally, the chief director of a new theater —a marvelous one, no worse than Meyerhold's. And you'll be an editor of a newspaper or of a magazine, or also a professor, but of history. Or maybe you want to do Party work? But of course along cultural lines. I don't know where I'll work—in a laboratory or a scientific library. But the important thing is that I'll have a salon. Don't laugh, don't be stupid. You don't understand, but I'm completely serious. We'll have a large apartment, furnished simply, but with taste—a grand piano, good paintings, lots and lots of books. And in the evening our friends and acquaintances will gather there. Interesting people will come—actors, poets, artists, musicians. We'll have home recitals, readings, we'll talk, argue. And I'll wear a demure black dress and patent-leather shoes. Well, maybe a string of pearls, but nothing else. I'll feed you all deliciously, I'll introduce good people to one another, and everyone will want to come to our house. Of course, we'll have children. Do you want a son? I want a daughter. And maybe, your son will marry our daughter. And Lida will have children. I think we all should have two children. That way, we may all become relatives."

She looked up from beneath her brow with her large protruding light-gray eyes. Her small, receding chin almost ran into the hollow between her thin collarbones. Her dark-chestnut curly hair hung over her forehead. Sparks of laughter in her eyes were replaced instantly by moist shimmers, and still smiling, she would already be wiping away tears.

"If only I live that long. My heart is no good, you know. But medicine is making great strides. Maybe they'll find a cure for me."

I saw Musya the last time in the winter of 1947, during my "intermedia," between prisons, when I spent two months free. They lived in Mytishchi, 20 kilometers from Moscow, in a crowded two-room apartment. Valya and Misha were lieutenant colonels then, doing a lot of work at the same military radio institute that they had worked in before the war. Musya looked very tired, complained of her illnesses. When I reminded her of her long-ago dreams, she smiled sadly. She told me that she hadn't had news of Lida in a long time—she and her husband lived somewhere beyond Leningrad. (Lida's husband, Lev P., an engineer, was arrested in 1936 and released in the spring of '41. He passed through Moscow. We met. He had lost a lot of weight, and had a dark unhealthy northern tan. He had flown in from Norilsk, a new city that wasn't even on the maps yet. He spoke laconically.

"I saw all kinds of things. You just can't tell it all. If you haven't experienced it yourself, you can't imagine it. You won't understand even with a half liter of vodka in you. And you certainly won't believe it.")

Nadya said that Musya had been ill for a long time, that Valya was working in a radio shop. They lived in a tiny apartment with her parents. The father was paralyzed. Then his legs were amputated. Even when he was healthy he had been intolerably cranky and demanding. What could it have been like for her now that he was sick?

But if six years ago Musya and Valya hadn't signed a letter to Stalin about me, their life might have been different.

I looked at my mother. She had been my attorney's main assistant: she found defense witnesses, insisted, begged, pleaded. She was saving her son. Even as a child I was irritated by her maternal egoism. And now she was interrupting Nadya, she didn't want her to talk about unpleasant things.

But I couldn't tell her that Musya's death, the travails of my friends were our fault—hers and mine. Her eyes with reddish veins had grown dull, her cheeks sagged, and her bluish pale lips were cracked.

No, I couldn't be angry with her and I tried to keep her from noticing, from guessing, what I had just been thinking. I felt suffocated by it—it was hard to talk.

Nadya understood everything. She started telling me about something else. Lida and her husband were living in Central Asia; he had been arrested again, then exiled, but now he was free, working as an engineer; they had a son and a daughter. Our neighbor's daughter, Nina, was getting married —he seemed like a very good fellow, a student. Lusya P. has a son, Vova, an incredibly bright, sweet kid. Maya had been in a Pioneer summer camp with Zhenya, the son of Inna Levidova. He is an amazingly educated, serious young man; he and Maya will prepare for the institute together; they had to apply next year.

And Mother hurried to tell me the newest and most reliable news about how my case would definitely be reviewed very soon. "You'll see, sonny, we'll spend New Year's Eve together. Now I know I'll live to see it."

But she spent New Year's without me. Mother died May 4, 1954, a week before our scheduled meeting.

A few days later I received a reply to my appeal, sent after Beria's arrest —a standard form from the Procurator's Office: "There is no basis for a review . . . Sentenced correctly."*

· · ·

*The last time I got a paper like that I was already freed, in May 1956 after the Twentieth Congress. Three months later, in September, I was reinstated in the Party, and in November the Military Collegium of the Supreme Court reversed my conviction as being unfounded.

On Evgeniia Vasilievna's desk lay a letter from the Central Committee on the Beria affair. She spoke, chain-smoking Kazbeks: "Just think! He was a British spy. And he was dealing with Tito and the Germans! Now it's clear, he's the one who came up with a provocative amnesty. It didn't cover people like you, but it let out all kinds of bandits. He was preparing an army for himself. And it was his agents who started that uprising in Berlin. And what bestial crimes he committed! I had heard a few things about him and his many women. Many people in the organs knew about it. But horrors like that! I would never have believed it before. But now you see how the Central Committee is exposing him—everything!"

I yes-ma'amed Evgeniia Vasilievna gladly. I wanted to learn as much as possible from her about what was going on, both in the "big world"— Moscow, the country—and in the "little one," where they ran our sharashka and our lives. The Central Committee letter pleased me at first: Beria's destruction was only to the benefit of us, his victims and slaves. But then doubts arose: I couldn't believe that he had been a spy, an agent of the intelligence service, a Musavatist.* Those accusations had the old bullshit ring to them, the same one from the years 1937–1938 and 1948. Weren't there enough of his real crimes, which we, the old zeks, knew all about? And what did the words "criminal ties with the Tito clique, with bourgeois nationalists" mean? In the same letter they mentioned unambiguously "the cult of personality."

I couldn't remember exactly the first time I heard the name Beria. But they began talking about him when his book appeared, *On a History of the Bolshevist Organizations in Transcaucasia*. He described how Stalin headed the Bolsheviks back at the turn of the century and how even in his youth he had been a wise, perspicacious, limitlessly brave leader of Georgia and Azerbaijan. He cited facts, earlier unknown or insufficiently researched, because Stalin, in his extraordinary modesty, tried to keep them from being known. This book was included in the curriculums of institutes, technicums, senior classes of school, and in all political enlightenment circles. Even before Beria's memoirs, *Pravda* published Karl Radek's article "Architect of a Socialist Society" (1934), a "futurological" ode in prose—"a lecture on Stalin in 1984." First one and then the other was chewed up by the machine they strove to perfect, just like Yagoda, Yezhov, Krylenko, and hundreds of totally unknown propagandists, Chekists, procurators, and judges.

In arguments with my friends in my last few years in the sharashka, explaining the nature of our problems, I came up with the metaphorical theory of the "Chekist leucocyte." The first socialist state in the world had to create extremely powerful and widely branched "organs of security," developing unique "leucocytes" for suppressing and destroying harmful

*The Musavat (Equality) was a national revolutionary party in Azerbaijan, founded in Baku in 1911. It was anti-Soviet. (Translator's note.)

microbes. In the thirties, in the difficult times of anticipating a war, during the war, and later because of new external threats, these organs grew disproportionately and the state got sick. Running out of control, the independent leucocytes attacked the healthy parts of the organism as well. But how do you cure the organism? Surgical intervention may be mortally dangerous—may cause loss of blood and inflammation. That meant that gradual, cautious, "therapeutic" reforms were needed.

However, the Beria affair was a surgical operation. Evgeniia Vasilievna said that the Beria guardsmen, disguised as athletes from the Tbilisi Dynamo soccer team, had filled several Moscow hotels, and that Marshal Zhukov commanded the troops that had arrested Beria. Tanks broke down the gates of his town house; before trial he was held not in Lubyanka or in prison, but somewhere in the cellar of the Moscow Military District Staff headquarters. And that's where he was shot.

Did that mean that the new administration recognized the danger of the "Chekist leucocyte"?

Another time Evgeniia Vasilievna showed me a secret letter from the Central Committee* on agriculture. A horrible truth: all the previous statistics—"indexes of successes and achievements"—had been blatant lies. I was tormentedly ashamed, but I felt a sense of trust for those who so willingly spoke of flaws, disasters, weaknesses.

In September and October even the newspapers published accounts about the Plenum of the Central Committee, acknowledging with a never-before frankness mistakes and miscalculations; they spoke directly of mismanagement.

The shooting was over in Korea. Peace talks were on. The radio and newspapers called ever more frequently and persistently for peaceful coexistence, for the restoration of "Leninist principles of intra-Party democracy." Every day one of the free employees—and no longer in whispers, but out loud—said that fundamental changes in all policies were imminent.

In the summer of 1953 many of the previously silent prisoners loosened their tongues.

Ernst K. had been a Party member from 1924. An early-orphaned son of a bookbinder—a German from Petrograd—the young worker became one of the first Petrograd Komsomol members. He studied at a workers' division and then in the Communist Institute of Journalism, worked in the editorial department of *Pravda* with Maria Ilyinichna Ulyanova.† In 1937 he was sent to the German Republic of the Volga region to head a publishing house, even though he barely knew German. In August 1941 he was exiled east under convoy with all the Volga Germans. And in the forest

*These special letters from the Central Committee were read in closed Party meetings open to members on all levels but not published in the press. (Translator's note.)
†V. I. Lenin's sister (1878–1937). (Translator's note.)

camp near Irkutsk he became the secretary of the Party organization.

"This was, you might say, a very original Party organization. Behind barbed wire! Only a few trustees were allowed to go beyond the zone—I as secretary, one engineer, one technician, two drivers. But everyone else, all the members of the Party Bureau and the old Communists—we even had participants of the Civil War there—went to work and back again in formation, with a convoy and guard dogs. Of course, we weren't called prisoners but special resettlers. But you still couldn't approach forbidden areas, and in the columns, if you took a step to the left or the right, the convoy guards would shoot without warning. Most worked in the felling of trees, and about a hundred and fifty in a woodworking factory, making boxes for rifles and furniture for hospitals. And some cleaned up in the zone. There were no women. They were kept in other regions. Only a few managed to correspond with their wives or sisters. Just in the last few years of the war people began finding each other.

"My Party organization had over three hundred members and candidates at first. And almost twice as many Komsomols. And there were only around three thousand men in the whole zone. So our proportion was quite high. We worked out of conscience. As everywhere—'everything for the front.' Many asked to join the active army. And I wrote request after request. I can say this: most sincerely wanted to fight against fascism, to prove that they were real Soviet patriots. But then the mood soured, of course. The food was bad. Scurvy began. And a new disease—dystrophy. There wasn't enough medicine. The task of the Party organization was to keep up morale, to explain, to help. I managed several times to get some help from the regional committee—medicine and forage. But right from the start, there were arrests. Even before the end of the war, over two thirds of the Communists and Komsomols had been taken. They took fewer of the non-Party people. The security officer demanded a report on each arrestee, of course. I wrote, as much as I could, with Party conscience, objectively. He complained to the regional committee. They got me for diminished vigilance; first I was simply reprimanded, then got penalty isolation with a notation on my record. After the war, in the winter, they arrested me and the whole Party bureau. They used Paragraphs 10, 11, and, of course, 1—since we were Germans, that naturally meant we were traitors; a few also got 7 and 9—wrecking and sabotage. And even 8—terrorist intentions. I got the whole bouquet. Because I wouldn't confess to anything. And even refused to give evidence. I was certain that the whole case was false and I wrote in my own hand—they gave me paper when I went on a hunger strike—that I was an honest Bolshevik, and Leninist-Stalinist, and that I had no intention of participating in a case like this. They threatened to shoot me. In one year I spent no less than two months in the cooler—five, ten, and fifteen days at a time. They didn't beat me especially, you might say—just when they were angered. They saw that it wouldn't work on me. And then the OSO gave me twenty-five years."

Ernst was a tall, thin, sinewy man. His dark, harsh-featured face resembled an American Indian's from the illustrations of Cooper's books: Sergei called him Chingachgook, the Last of the Mohicans.

He first talked to me in the corridor of the sharashka, near the stand where they posted the newspapers. We were reading a long speech by Mao Zedong that took up a whole page in *Pravda*. "Did you notice how he talks about internal contradictions in socialist society? Now that's a real, Bolshevist style of thought. Incontrovertible truth. No influence. Now that's a real Marxist-Leninist. What luck that there is a man like that!"

I missed Evgenii Timofeevich very much then, his opinions and thoughts, which seemed familiar to me. Sergei, Viktor Andreevich, and Semyon were close to me, but I thought differently from them: I labored to prove to them that they were substituting emotion for reason and couldn't see the "great socialist forest" for the KGB and GULag trees.

Ernst turned out to be a fellow thinker.

Fedor Nikolaevich B., a master molder, who worked in the machine shop, a dry old man of medium height, with a narrow whitish beard, used to shy away from everyone. As a young worker, he had participated in a Bolshevik circle in 1915, and in 1917 joined the Red Army, fought against the "white Czechs," against Kolchak. After demobilization, he worked in Moscow in a plant as a lathe operator and molder, but was drawn into union activity; he was elected to the plant committee and then to the regional committee and the Central Committee of the Union. In 1937 he was a member of the Presidium of the All-Union Central Soviet of Unions, one of Tomsky's assistants.

He didn't want to recall his arrest and investigation. "What is there to tell? I didn't remember what I signed. I'd forgotten by the next day. But I stayed alive. Healed my wounds. But I lost the hearing in my right ear."

He was sentenced to ten years. And in the camp they added a new term, which was to end in the fall of 1953. The head of the prison said that he wouldn't be exiled, as was customary before, but merely sent beyond the gates, and permitted him to let his relatives know.

"Maybe I'll find work in Moscow. Even though I'll be sixty soon. My wife died during the war. Heart attack . . . When we received news of our younger son's death. He had stayed with her. The older one had renounced us—he was a political director in the army. And now he's somewhere in staff headquarters. But my daughter and my younger sister and my sister-in-law keep writing me letters and sending parcels. And come to see me. This summer I saw my grandchildren for the first time. The youngest is called Fedya, like me; he's five, a bright kid—wants to become a general."

Ernst, Fedor Nikolaevich, and I constantly talked about when and why the distortions of Bolshevism began. Ernst spoke confidently: "Ilyich [Lenin] warned against it. You've heard of his will, haven't you? Ilyich wrote that Stalin had too much power in the apparatus, that he was crude and disloyal to his comrades. But Stalin promised the Party congress to keep Lenin's criticism in mind. And Zinoviev and Kamenev went around, begging their comrade delegates to believe the comrade General Secretary. Neither Trotsky, nor Rykov, nor Bukharin disagreed. Maria Ilyinichna told me all this. Of course, the Party had to fight the deviationists: both the Trotskyites and the right-wingers. Iron discipline is necessary. And centralization, too. The unfortunate part was that Stalin came out in charge. He subordinated the apparatus of the Central Committee and the provincial committees. And, of course, the GPU. While Felix Edmundovich [Dzerzhinsky] was alive, the GPU served the state. But Yagoda already served the General Secretary first. And as for Yezhov and Beria—well, they recognized only Stalin. He commanded them, but they influenced him, too—they frightened him, disinformed him, of course, in their own interests. After Kirov's murder, they scared him so much that he gave them full power—to send up or shoot anyone they wanted."

Fedor Nikolaevich disagreed softly, unhurriedly. "Well, that seems rather simplistic. A Marxist has to dig deeper. The main reasons lie in the fact that the proletarian revolution won in a backward peasant country. Our dictatorship of the proletariat was a minority power from the start. That has to be understood. We wanted to educate the masses. It's sometimes not easy to bring up a single teenaged boy. But you can't put millions of adult peasant men and women behind a school desk. They have to work, feed their families. And we started teaching them both the ABCs and the alphabet of communism. That's where the different opinions and directions came from in the Party. Before we used to have arguments about principles. In that document, which you call the will, Vladimir Ilyich also wrote that Trotsky and Piatakov were the most sensible leaders, but they like to administrate, to command. Trotsky was used to dealing with military specialists during the Civil War: 'Hep two three, forward, march! Get me Warsaw.' While the Democratic Centralists were just the opposite. They wanted total democracy—everyone to speak up on every issue, every trifle to get a discussion, a meeting. They all needed upbraiding. The Leningraders,* to tell the truth, were real Bolsheviks. So were the Muscovites who supported them—Nadezhda Konstantinovna [Krupskaya], Kamenev—Lenin's closest comrades. But they were all urban people—St. Petersburg proletarians or Moscow intellectuals. They didn't understand the muzhik, didn't sympathize with him, didn't trust him—just like Trotsky and Piatakov. That's why they maintained that it was impossible to build socialism in one country. In theory that may be true, but as a slogan it's harmful. It demobilizes the masses."

We walked along the camp street or sat on the benches behind the yurt near the flower beds—three zeks in blue prison coveralls who didn't have the right to get close to the barbed wire. Morning and night we were

---

*The delegates from Leningrad at the Fourteenth Party Congress (1925) were opposed to Stalin. (Translator's note.)

counted, like cattle. Without rights, and for many a year now, nameless slaves. But forgetting all that, we discussed enthusiastically and intensely the fates of the country and the Party, we recalled and argued as though at Party meetings of the twenties or with a group of friends, preparing for a discussion.

Fedor Nikolaevich, coughing and spitting, patiently heard out the fiery speeches of his opponents and replied, as though thinking aloud: "Trotsky, the Leningraders, and other left-wingers had well-organized factions. You can't fault them on that. Even though they conspired against the Central Committee, not one of them—Nikolai Ivanovich Bukharin, or Aleksei Ivanovich Rykov, or Mikhail Pavlovich Tomsky—or any of us—the so-called right wing—ever organized any factions. We argued openly and often had real fights. Once the comrades had occasion to argue even with Ilyich. And how! At the most difficult times, over the Brest peace, over NEP. But later we didn't take the new circumstances into account. The working class wasn't what it used to be. The majority of the best, conscious, active proletarians had left the plants. Some died in the Civil War, some went over to the opposition, some into the apparatus, like me. They stopped being proletarians; they grew fat, turned into bureaucrats, bourgeois.

"The ones who were still in the plants and factories were the tiniest minority there. And the millions of new workers were no proletarians at all. We still say 'class hegemony,' 'dictatorship of the proletariat.' But when you think about it seriously—the real power is in the apparatus. And Stalin realized that before the rest of us. The old men, Lenin's buddies, underestimated him. Not one of them ever thought for a second that he could replace Lenin. They elected him General Secretary—well, like a good militia commandant, or district policeman, in the old days—to maintain law and order, to discipline, to prevent fights for power. It was Zinoviev and Kamenev who pushed him. They were afraid of Trotsky, they were jealous of his relationship with Vladimir Ilyich, they spoke of Bonapartism. Later Bukharin and Rykov wanted his help to squeeze out all left-wingers and Trotskyites. And so his power grew—from opposition to opposition, from congress to congress. And still you can't overestimate the role of his personality. He didn't create the apparatus alone, and he wasn't the one who invented it. On the contrary, you might say he was promoted by the apparatus."

I tried to argue against that. And I explained—I didn't justify it, just explained—the perfidy of Stalin's cruelty in terms of historical traditions and contemporary conditions of society; I compared him to Ivan the Terrible, Peter the Great. Ernst was angry—how could I compare them. They were feudal lords, despots; they were supposed to behave that way, it was normal for their class, but Stalin betrayed the working class, perverted the principles of communism.

Fedor Nikolaevich did not get upset. "Historical comparisons are always undependable, even though they're sometimes handsome. The Mensheviks liked comparisons with the French Revolution: Lenin with Robespierre, Trotsky with Danton. But I don't think that's serious at all. Of course, Stalin himself alluded to both Ivan the Terrible and Peter. But the difference is that Tsar Ivan and Tsar Peter, however else you may judge them, really were revolutionaries—they broke down the past and began the new. But Stalin didn't come up with anything new himself. He just chopped other people's wood. Industrialization and collectivization like that were never dreamed of even by the wildest Trotskyites. If it weren't for all those 'achievements' of Stalin's, if not for the famine, and Yezhov's terror, we wouldn't have had to retreat to the Volga. Perhaps Hitler wouldn't have come to power."

But I sensed and was beginning to realize that it wasn't only a question of economic laws. Independent of "material factor," intra-Party discussion, leaders and apparatchiks, there were other powers that influenced people —spiritual and moral powers.

I had thought about that in East Prussia and in the early days of my arrest. I tried to clarify the nature of those powers for myself; I recalled the books of Tolstoy, Dostoevsky, and Korolenko and the people I had known before but had seen only as nice, good-hearted eccentrics, as the personification of "the exception to the rule."

In the summer of 1929 I was preparing for the entrance exams to the institute and was being tutored in mathematics by a distant relative, Matvei Meituv, or Motya, an assistant professor at the university. He was considered a mathematical genius. He was tall, very thin, stoop-shouldered, very swarthy, and thick-lipped. His tiny wife looked like a teenaged girl, with washed-out mousy-brown hair and high cheekbones. But at the same time they resembled each other in their kind looks and smiles. Their single narrow room was filled with bookshelves. A large engraved portrait of Leo Tolstoy hung on the wall. The New Testament lay on the nightstand.

We studied at the round dining table covered with a mangy plush cloth. He shoved algebra and trigonometry into three self-confident youths—two polyglot poets and myself, a "political activist," who recently "left the opposition." At times he even tried to explain the beauty and elegance of mathematical solutions. Eyes shining with inspiration and spittle flying, he would say: "How can you not understand? It's wrong if only because it's ugly. All this is dissonant. But if we do this . . . and then this. See? The simplest substitution. And now—everything is harmonious and beautiful!"

Once I tried to start a conversation about the compatibility of scientific and religious viewpoints; he declined briefly but decisively: "Don't, please, don't. This is the realm of faith, not knowledge. Feeling, not reason. I know, in this case I know for sure, that in these questions no one can ever convince anyone else. Nothing can be proved or disproved. You think one way, you believe in something else, and I can't argue with you. I can't and

I won't. I consider it pointless and fruitless. Now if you were to say that two times two is five or that the sum of the angles of a triangle is more than one hundred and eighty degrees, I would try to change your mind."

To me—a self-confident, seventeen-year-old Marxist—he seemed a rather stupid and naïve eccentric. He was very ill—tuberculosis of the lungs and bones. Faith brought him consolation and relief. This was enough—there was no point in arguing.

In 1931, at the university one of the students approached Meituv. "Is it true that you are a confirmed Tolstoyan and therefore you will not take up arms to defend the socialist homeland?"

Motya tried to avoid an interview and pointed to his right hand, racked with bone tuberculosis and trophic ulcers, twisted forever at the wrist.

"But if you were healthy? Then if there was a war would you join the Red Army?"

"I'd be in the medical corps."

"That means you refuse the honor of fighting in the ranks of the Red Army?! How can you explain that? Is it your religious beliefs? We want you to speak out at a meeting."

Motya said that he was a Christian and shared the views of the great Leo Tolstoy, but he did not want to participate in any disputes, he didn't want to explain anything. He wasn't a theoretician or a preacher; his calling was mathematics, and there was nothing in his lectures or seminars on math that could upset exacting atheists.

The next day the university newspaper, soon followed by the city paper, printed angry condemning lampoons about a "brazen double-dealer," who wormed his way into the university and who confessed cynically that he doesn't want to defend the socialist homeland.

He was fired immediately and about two weeks later, by the decision of the "troika" of the GPU, exiled for three years to Narym. His wife, seven months pregnant, followed him. "He can't even make himself a pot of tea. He needs help dressing and washing."

For a while his relatives got letters from them. They had a daughter. Motya taught at the school. They both wrote that they were very happy. Then he died, without finishing even half his term. She stopped writing. Simply disappeared.

I never forgot about Motya Meituv, about the wasted talent that could have been of such great benefit to the people, science, the country, about the extraordinary spiritual strength of the sickly, humble eccentric.

In 1937–1938 at the Institute of Foreign Languages, where I was studying, almost all the foreign professors and docents were arrested. That's when Fritz Platten was arrested and died. He was a Swiss socialist who had come to Russia in 1917 in the same car with Lenin and a year later saved his life. They were riding in a car when gunshots came out of the darkness. Platten lowered Lenin's head and shielded him with his own body. A bullet hit the hand that was covering Lenin's temple.

Platten conducted seminars in conversational language. He readily talked of his meetings with Lenin. He talked without bragging, without puffery, simply and ... extremely boringly; he recalled insignificant details, insignificant words. But we listened in awe. Once a quiet, shy girl kissed the scar on his hand. He was dumbfounded; he blushed and muttered: "What are you doing? Don't! No, no! We're not in church, after all. This is ridiculous."

Tall, gray-haired, but youthful and sturdy—he never wore a hat in winter and was a wonderful skier—he seemed a kindly old-world man, a naïve "revolutionary of the prerevolutionary type." When the secretary of the Party committee of the Institute, reporting on "increased vigilance" at a meeting, told us that Platten had been exposed as an enemy of the people and a Gestapo spy, I didn't believe it even then.

The arrests and killing of old Communists, the old friends and comrades of Lenin, creators of the Comintern, recent leaders of the Party, horrified me, but at the same time did not seem unnatural. Accustomed to thinking in historical comparison, I explained them away as the internal regularity of any postrevolutionary development: Cromwell had the Levellers shot, the Jacobins guillotined the Girondists, Danton, and the radicals, the "madmen." And the Bolsheviks first destroyed the Socialist Revolutionaries and the Mensheviks, then the Zinovievists hit the Trotskyites, the Bukharinites attacked both, and then finally came Stalin, who "squashed all."

But even before the war I began thinking about what I later came to call the contradictions between historical necessity and moral necessity. I began to have doubts—did Stalin's strategy really correspond with the demand of historical necessity? In 1941 and 1942 at the front I told a few friends that the first major defeats inflicted on us by Hitler came in 1937–1938. No one argued. (And after my arrest these words were not brought up in the investigation, that is, no one ever told about it.) We all knew that the commander of the Novgorod Army Group, Brigade Commander Korovnikov, who back in August 1941 was practically the first to stop the German offensive on the banks of the Volkhov and the Maly Volkhovets Rivers, retained the old-fashioned rank of brigade commander, and not major general, until that winter (he wore the old insignias, rhomboids, and not stars in his buttonholes), because he had been arrested before the new ranks were established (1939–1940) and had come to the front straight from a camp. Just like Rokossovskii and the commander of the Moscow proletarian division, Dmitri Petrovskii—the son of Grigorii Petrovskii, an old Bolshevik, leader of the Party in the Ukraine, and the brother of an executed journalist. Korovnikov was one of the few division commanders who advanced in July 1941, and he even won back the city of Rogachev from the Germans. When he was wounded and his division surrounded, he shot himself. An old Partisan near Pskov, a former kulak who had returned from Narym just before the war, told me: "Soviet power hurt me badly, took away everything I ever had. But there's no other government in Russia. And Hitler is a mortal enemy of our people, and that means of me. And the war is for all of Russia. There's nothing to choose."

After the war, I was convinced that the punishments meted out in the prisons and camps by the NKVD, MGB, and OSO were unfair, cruel, and simply senseless. Most often they harmed the real interests of the state and Party. The immorality of these punishments could not be explained by historical necessity, the way we explained the terror of the Revolution and the Civil War. Yezhovism, Beriaism—and ten years later, they'll be talking of Stalinism—were obviously in contradiction to historical necessity.

The more clearly I realized that I could not resolve these contradictions with the familiar methods of dialectical materialism and historical materialism, the more closely I listened to people who thought differently and tried to understand positions opposed to my own.

In my early Komsomol years I simply would not have heard even a very wise person if I knew that he was religious or a liberal or a Menshevik and so on. "Can any good thing come out of Nazareth?"

Later, on the contrary, I tried to learn how and what my ideological adversaries thought. That's why before the war and even more so at the front I carefully read Nazi books, journals, and newspapers, read and listened on the radio to the speeches of Hitler, Goebbels, Göring, and others, and not so much interrogated prisoners of war as asked them questions, trying to elicit frank, unconstrained conversations. Just as attentively I familiarized myself with the propaganda of the Vlasovites, the Benderovites (United Ukrainian Nationalists), and Polish nationalists. This was the study of the enemy, "ideological scouting," focused, motivated by curious hostility.

I never was a "militant atheist." Therefore even in my most quarrelsome youthful years I considered it shameful to insult someone else's faith and I did not want to disturb those who found solace and hope in religion. In prison I often envied the faithful: for them deprivation and suffering were infused with a higher meaning, and death did not frighten them. I could no longer return to the kind God of my childhood, believe in the existence of an eternal higher power that created our world. First of all, I couldn't believe that mortals could understand such a power and interpret its will, proclaim in its name laws, and then judge, punish, or pardon their like according to those laws.

However, I was always cheered by meetings with such believers, who resembled Motya Meituv in that religion for them was not a system of dogmas and rituals but the moral basis of man, the living source of kindness toward others.

In January 1944, after the hospital, in the days of my last stay in Moscow, a female friend brought me to the house of our former classmate. We drank plain tea with crusts of toasted bread and talked about how the war might end and what would happen afterward. We said that people had to become wiser now, kinder, more just. The war had revealed the true character of people, who was worth what, and after the war, naturally, there would be a flowering in economics, science, and technology. In the twenties, Europe and America had raced an entire era ahead of us. Aviation, automobiles, the movies, radio—all that was postwar progress. We had fallen behind the West because of our Civil War and the blockade. But now we would be the main victors. And social progress would not fall behind technological and scientific progress.

Our hostess, a young, serious woman who at first listened in silence to our talk, finally spoke softly, gently, and yet so that we dared not interrupt: "Progress. Before the war, at the institute—that was in the last era, seems like a century ago—I believed in progress then, in the radiant, wonderful future. Then we were evacuated. Mother and I nearly starved. I worked as a dishwasher, cleaning woman, seamstress—I sewed sacks and mittens. I worked a lot, but my head was unusually free. And I thought and thought. We had studied history—Egypt, Babylonia, Greece, Rome, the Middle Ages. Read books—ancient and new. And so what? People were starved, tortured, and killed then, and they are torturing, killing, and starving people now. In absolute numbers even more than ever before. More victims, more executioners . . . but there always had been happy people. There had always been the joy of love, motherhood, the joy of recovering from illness, being freed of danger or harm. And joy from music, poetry, a spring morning, of meetings with good, kind friends, of the sea, the forest. Just think, has the proportion of human happiness and unhappiness changed at all in hundreds, thousands of years? No, no— progress can't spare people from sorrow, from death. And it can't add any more happiness."

I recalled that conversation frequently. I tried to think as simply and fearlessly as she had. And I was no longer frightened when I read Berdiaev: "In history there is no straight line containing the progress of good . . . and there is no progress of human happiness—there is only the tragic discovery, even greater, of the most opposite sources . . . of good and of evil."

The necessity for immutable moral codes was perceived in antiquity by Hammurabi, Solon, Moses, Confucius, Lao-Tzu, Christ, Muhammad, Yaroslav the Wise. Many religious dogmas arose in order to suppress innate destructive instincts that are not subject to rational thought. I always perceived the New Testament as a poetic embodiment of the affirmation of the best and kindest spiritual strengths.

Thinking about what the socialist ethic would be, I believed that it would grow from the Judeo-Christian commandments, from the best traditions of Buddhism and Taoism. However, our morality, our categorical imperative had to be distinguished from all the moral codes of the past by an atheistic selflessness.

I saw it simply: religious teachings that arose in a commodity society concealed within them the principles of trade. In prescribing good and rejecting evil, they promise a payment for good behavior: if you are good in life, you will go to heaven after death, receive eternal bliss; if you sin, act evilly, you will end up in hell for eternal torment.

The possibility of repentance and forgiveness, the covering up of sin and the extreme development of such possibilities—indulgences, paid masses—reflected the most simple trade relations among people of the real world projected onto the relationship between man and God—superreal, otherworldly powers.

Humanity had not yet freed itself from the power of material forces that ruled in "the kingdom of necessity," from the power of the inscrutable element of the marketplace, from all the dangers brought on by the instinct of money-grubbing, predatory greed, envy, and rivalry of owners—therefore, religious laws were necessary and beneficial. I had always thought that way.

The new Stalinist Church policy, begun back in 1934,* and the ever-greater subordination of the Church to the government after the war proved that the wise leader had understood that. Without the participation of religious authorities it was impossible to establish and maintain human relations between people, between the individual citizen and society and state.

Stalin's "concordat" with Patriarch Sergei and the reestablishment of the Synod, seminaries, and several monasteries seemed to me a successful resolution of the problems that the "God seekers" Gorky and Lunacharsky had sought in vain to resolve. But the idealistic moral laws of socialism would be free of all illusions and all forms of "lies for salvation."

Marx, Engels, Lenin, and Stalin did not try to portray the future of humanity concretely, because they were primarily concerned with problems of history and contemporaneity, relations between classes and the state, the complicated intertwining of economics and politics. Social life and social consciousness were important to them. And that was why private life and private consciousness, the daily cares of "the little people," seemed insignificant to them.

Without doubting that the Marxist classics were right in dealing only with the laws of large numbers, I thought that their rightness was historically limited—actual only for their own time.

But Dostoevsky, in a single page of *A Raw Youth*, sang—sang like a poet, an artist—the future concord of people who were freed of religions, who

---

*In 1934 daily propaganda and grade-school and high-school textbooks began to stress "the historically progressive role of Orthodoxy in Russia"; the main Party poet, Demyan Bedny, was severely reprimanded for the crude atheism of his work.

did not believe in immortal souls. And that was precisely why they loved one another so tenderly, loved nature, loved their brief and all the more marvelous life. Dostoevsky, the author of *The Devils*, the enemy of the People's Will Party and friend of Pobedonostsev,* wrote about the people of a socialist godless society with extraordinary sympathy. And to me, a Komsomol, he was the proclaimer of a new absolute moral law for all time.

Even then I not only felt but understood the supremacy of Dostoevsky and Tolstoy, Goethe and Pushkin over my teachers. Marx and Engels had raved so about Dante, Shakespeare, Goethe, and Balzac, and Lenin had written about Tolstoy in a way that made it clear: "the classics of Marxism" looked up to the classics of world literature.

Ernst and Fedor Nikolaevich usually heard me out with a certain curiosity, condescendingly, my reasoning being to them the fantasies of a dreamer. But occasionally they were put off by my utopian blather.

But I was growing more convinced of the need to reassess other concepts of Marxist orthodoxy, to reassess them in the light of the same demands of moral law.

We were taught to respect the sanctity of large numbers. Mayakovsky praised "Hundredfiftymillion Ivan," maintaining that "the individual is zero, the individual is nonsense" and saw happiness in the fact that "you flow as a drop in the masses."

We considered individualism tantamount to egoism, self-love, "Meism," a trait suitable only to the bourgeoisie or the petite bourgeoisie.

But the Hitlerites also indoctrinated a fanatical anti-individualism in their kindergartens, schools, and barracks, teaching that "the general good is always higher than personal good."

I reminded them of this when we spoke about the premises and causes of the cult of personality. When the absolute superiority of some superpersonal power is maintained—of state, nation, class, or even of an enterprise or collective—when the interests and rights of the individual are subordinated to that power—man is the unknown soldier, a cog, an egg broken for an omelette—then inevitably the sovereignty of one power lover can arise: be it pharaoh, emperor, leader, führer. And the louder the greatness and holiness of the faceless majority is proclaimed, the more cruelly its priests—the praetorians, oprichniki, gendarmes, SS—repress the citizens without rights.

Ernst listened suspiciously, and suspecting me of attempting to justify individualism, tried to frighten me with comparisons to Bishop Berkeley, Schopenhauer, and even Nietzsche. "You're wrong. It's just the reverse. Every personality cult is the expression of individualism: Napoleon, Bismarck, Mussolini, Hitler—they are all typical representatives of their formations. Napoleon represents the early period of industrial capitalism, and

*Konstantin Petrovich Pobedonostsev (1827–1907), a conservative political philosopher and statesman, tutor and adviser to Tsars Alexander III and Nicholas II. (Translator's note.)

Bismarck, mature capitalism allied with landowners—Junkers; Mussolini and Hitler are the imperialist stage. In Russia, too, there were all kinds of cults. For instance, Kerensky. I saw the mass hysteria myself. And it wasn't only the Gymnasium students and the bourgeois intelligentsia who were going crazy. In the spring of 1917 there were still many workers, soldiers, and sailors who were enraptured by him: he was the people's tribune.

"And there was something like a cult shaping up around Trotsky, too. The Trotskyites, of course, exalted him. And as a counterbalance, the Stalin cult began: his toadies did their work. But every personality cult, of course, is in contradiction to proletarian ideology. You underestimate the role of the masses, the state, the Party. You can talk yourself into stating that there is no essential difference between us and the fascists. That's absurd. Napoleon and Hitler did not suppress individualism—on the contrary, they played on the personal interests of the 'little man.' For them cults are natural, historically regulated. But for us, a cult is unnatural, a crude perversion of Leninist traditions. Lenin would not have allowed such a thing."

Fedor Nikolaevich spoke softly, unhurriedly. "I wouldn't make that such a categorical pronouncement, if I were you. Ilyich, it's true, did not like celebratory feasts, flattery, toadying. But what he liked a lot less was being contradicted—*his* line being questioned, his orders not carried out correctly. He didn't care about external formal rites. But he held on to his authority hard. He used to laugh at Trotsky, Dybenko, Lunacharsky—they loved pomp and theatrical effects. He laughed, but he did admit that for the masses, for agitation it was necessary. And after his death a real cult of Lenin began. Yes, yes, a cult. I don't know how to formulate it in your philosophical terms: objectively, subjectivity, regular, irregular. But I do know what I saw and heard.

"When they came up with the idea for the mausoleum, some comrades spoke up: 'That's a cult! That's Church style, holy relics.' And Nadezhda Konstantinovna even cried at a session of the Politburo: 'It's an outrage! Ilyich would not have permitted it.' But Stalin, Zinoviev, and Kalinin maintained that it had an enormous propaganda significance and would influence the psychology of the masses. Rykov supported them. Bukharin and Kamenev vacillated, and Trotsky never even opened his mouth. He was already being reproached for his old disagreements with Lenin, so he kept quiet. So in our country the cult of personality began after Lenin's death with Lenin himself. I don't know what to consider it—natural, unnatural, or supernatural. Even then the leaders were losing touch with the masses. And the further they got, the louder they shouted, the more beautifully they wrote about the working class and the peasantry. And then back to the old mode—about the homeland and the people. And then they began treating Stalin like a saint, 'the father of the people,' the infallible pope. I don't know how all this works from the point of view of dialectical materialism and the harmfulness of individualism, but I think that from all points of view, we don't consider the personality of the worker, peasant, employee, or the personality, individuality of anyone, Party or non-Party, worth a cent.

"Now, for instance, our free employees are full-fledged citizens of a socialist state, even citizens of a higher sort—they work in a special place. But I heard some of them say straight out that their life is worse than ours. The work is the same, but they still have to worry about where they can buy wheat, how to feed and clothe their family, find a place to live. Remember there was a fellow called Petka in the machine shop? Remember? A fair-haired, pug-nosed kid—he was eighteen, but looked thirteen. He was brought straight from prison in a large transport to a construction site for a large factory. Then he worked for me, and he became a good turner. Well, for him, prison was like a sanatorium. He was the eldest son of a widowed kolkhoz worker—she had three very young children. She got sick, and he became the sole support of the family. He took a sack of cabbages and a sack of potatoes from the kolkhoz. The brigade leader had told him yes, but when the case started, backed down. Petka got the full ten years. And here he slept for the first time in his life in his own bed, with a sheet and a pillow with a pillowcase, and ate his fill—three times a day—for the first time in his life. And on separate plates. Even in Butyrki he was delighted by the gruel and straw mattresses. And here at the sharashka he thought he was in heaven. He worked well, learned enthusiastically. Tools were like precious toys to him. A sweet, quick, gentle, conscientious boy . . . It's terrible to think what it's like for him in the camps after our well-being. Well, who is he? A young worker from a socialist village. He is a personality, an individual. And there is an enormous number of personalities, of Petkas. I don't know what the theory is. Maybe you'll see this as individualism. I don't know what the fundamental differences are between the German cult and ours, I just don't know. But it seems to me they have a lot in common, too much."

On one of the first days of December, Vladimir Nikolaevich told Sergei and me: "Start finishing up your work. Do whatever needs less than two weeks. Everything else shape up as much as possible."

In the past, our people had always been taken away suddenly, without warning. This time we were given plenty of warning. And not only Gumer and Ivan Emelianovich, but Anton Mikhailovich himself told me that we were being sent to Kuchino.

"The living conditions and the work are basically similar to ours. Well, the character of the work perhaps will be less engrossing for you. But, why not hope—perhaps you'll manage to work on your phonoscopy. But I can cheer you up with something else: they say that over there they've already credited you with time that had not been accepted at our sharashka. So you'll be able to bring the awaited day closer."

Soon after that, the first group was sent off. From the acoustics lab,

Sergei and Valentin left, and from the mathematics group, my former assistant, Vasilii; a few days later Gumer told me that they were all in Kuchino.

There were only eighteen of us left in the sharashka, and another two zeks worked as janitors in the camp. In the evenings we strolled alone or in rare pairs along the snowy "prospect of trampled hopes," between the dark, boarded-up yurts, in the blinding pale violet light of the lamps.

I liked walking with Viktor Andreevich. He spoke softly of music, poetry, flowers. And he was the only one with whom I could walk in silence for long periods.

On one of those silent evenings he said: "You know, we're sad because we'll be leaving soon. I guess we're used to it. Or afraid of the unknown? I never would have thought that I'd be sad about leaving prison. But we're leaving a piece of our souls here."

I never did take up my phonoscopic research again. Some twenty years later I read that similar work was being done in Japan and West Germany; judging by published results, they haven't gotten too far past what we achieved in the sharashka.

The book on the physical nature of Russian spoken speech, which never did become a dissertation, was kept in the archives until quite recently. Probably, the results of our research and even some of our small discoveries —everything, that is, in it—have by now been studied much more precisely and thoroughly, and rediscovered.

The comparative tables of words from several languages in the roots of which one can presuppose the meaning of "hand" and the objects, actions, and concepts that are related to it are at home in dusty old folders, on the most distant shelves. More than a quarter of a century has passed; I never tried to return to them, to continue them. Realizing the unsoundness of my dilettantism, I knew that I could never catch up—I didn't have time. And now I think that if any of my linguistic suppositions and guesses are valid, then sooner or later real scholars will discover these truths and will study and expound them better. But I must do only that which no one can do in my place: tell the truth about the time that is reflected and embodied in my life.

In the history of the Marfino sharashka, born under the cupola of the defiled church "Ease My Sorrows," one can see the mold, the "working model" of several essential peculiarities of the entire life of our country then.

The sharashkas, compared to the camps, were "the first circle of hell" and a preserve sanctuary. Many of us hoped that in developing, inventing, and perfecting secret telephones, we would lighten our fate, and even if we couldn't earn a pardon or early release, we could at least obtain a good job after getting out. Others, who like Evgenii Timofeevich, Ernst, Fedor

Nikolaevich, and I, considered themselves Communists, were convinced that working for the benefit of the Soviet state had to be done under any circumstances with all our strength, without looking back.

Fundamentally different were the external general motivations, and endlessly varied were the personal fates and inner worlds—views, personalities ... But almost everyone worked not merely conscientiously, but enthusiastically, passionately, sometimes selflessly.

The engineer Georgii Dmitrievich I. was a confirmed monarchist. In a conversation once, Sergei called the last tsar "that imbecile Nikolashka." Georgii Dmitrievich blew up. "I'll ask you to refrain from such undignified talk in my presence. His Majesty the Tsar died a martyr's death. I hold his memory holy."

He judged literature very severely. "Leo Tolstoy, indubitably, was a great artist of the word: he was excellent at descriptions of nature, psychology, and so on. But he was a destroyer, an underminer, you might say, a perverter. It is Russia's great sorrow that highly gifted people destroyed and undermined the foundations of the state, of religion, and therefore, of morality: Gogol, and especially Herzen, and even Dostoevsky—even though he had repented, had become sincerely faithful, and wanted to serve the Church and dynasty, he still he couldn't control himself, he undermined—in *A Raw Youth*, in *The Brothers Karamazov*, in the *Diary of a Writer*. And Tolstoy was a brazen rabble-rouser and became a heretic. They didn't understand what a disaster they were setting up."

This intransigent foe of not only Soviet rule but even of the most moderate liberalism invented a system of "closed-circuit television" for congresses and conferences. His system let the speaker be seen and heard simultaneously on large screens in various parts of the room, in the lobby, and outside in the street.

Some colleagues teased the inventor—how could he, a tsarist loyalist— come up with something that would glorify Soviet rulers. He countered angrily: "Nonsense! This has nothing to do with politics. This is the fruit of engineering thought. A simple, but clever invention. And it's to everyone's benefit, it's good for theaters and concerts. It will serve more than just the political wastrels. I'm a Russian engineer and whatever I do I do conscientiously and the best that I can. I don't hide what I think of this regime, but technology is technology and science is science."

That was the thinking and behavior more or less of Sergei, Semyon, Valentin, and almost all the others who, like them, rejected the political structure, but worked enthusiastically and fervently.

In the late seventies I met a woman who had been a young free employee lab assistant at our sharashka. It turned out that she was still working there. She had recently defended a candidate's dissertation at the scientific-research institute we used to call the sharashka, and there were a few veterans from among the free employees there who had worked with us.

She recalled old times, asked questions, told me who had died, who had retired, who had risen to high positions.

"We were talking about you just recently. Someone had heard about you on the radio—the foreign radio. And we had talked of you before that, too, and about the others, about Solzhenitsyn, of course. At first no one wanted to believe that he was the same one who had done the articulation tests. I had participated in that, too. But when I saw his picture in a magazine, there was a story of his about that Ivan . . . yes, yes, Denisovich—I recognized him right away. And then I saw you on television—you were talking about some German writer . . . yes, Brecht. They were showing a movie that time, too, and then, I think it was Konstantin Fedorovich who recalled that we still had your work on acoustics, and he had somebody call you to come look it over and perhaps have it published in a scientific journal—you mean you were called then? So why didn't you get around to it? Well, now isn't the time for it. You've been expelled from the Party, haven't you? It was on the radio. A comrade told me recently—it doesn't matter who. You probably don't even remember him—he was younger than I. But he remembers you and had heard a lot about Solzhenitsyn and things. So he said: 'When they worked here there was some benefit from them, but now they only bring harm.' Don't be angry—he was talking in a political sense. We were just talking about why the institute wasn't working as well as it had. The old workers remembered you—no, not you personally, but the special contingent. How much you all invented, how many innovations and ideas. And this comrade said it was because there was iron rule then, in the whole country and in the institute. Everyone was afraid to goof off, or pretend, or work in a slipshod manner. The prisoners were afraid to land back in prison or somewhere up north, and the free employees saw their example and were also afraid. That's why there was no drinking; people thought more about their work, really cared about it. And now, they think about clothes, furniture, cars. And he remembered Solzhenitsyn and you, that before, you were valuable scientific cadres, and when Khrushchev rehabilitated everyone and started making noises about the cult, you started writing about it, making appearances. But then it turned out that the cult was just an excuse, and that actually you were against the Party and against Soviet rule. Don't be hurt, please—I personally don't think so, it's what he said. You see, he's the son of an old official of the security organs; he suffers over Stalin a lot and over work and labor discipline. He's a good worker himself and a modest, decent man."

She didn't remember if anyone had disagreed with that modest sufferer for Stalin. At any rate, she hadn't. After all, it was true that people had worked much better before.

I started to tell her that if the engineers and technicians who had been so valuable as a special contingent had been left on the outside, if their inventions hadn't been taken over by ne'er-do-wells in shoulder boards, and if they had been administered not by a dull Chekist but at least by someone like Anton Mikhailovich, but who wouldn't be afraid himself of the ignorant and all-powerful "bosses," then the fruits of their labor would have been much more significant and plentiful.

She nodded in agreement, even smiling. "Yes, you're right. Of course . . . perhaps . . ."

However, polite restraint crept into her friendly voice, and shadows of the familiar, old distrust flickered in her eyes. And I didn't try to explain anymore just how dangerous the kind son of the old Chekist was.

This nostalgia is noticeable in recent years in our fellow citizens, old and young, high-ranking and workers. In the corridors of closed Party meetings and in lines at grocery stores, where exhausted, irritable women argue and pensioners and talkative winos hold forth, you can hear very similar reasoning: "At least there was order under Stalin. No, don't tell me—the prices went down every year. And there was lots of everything in the stores and marketplaces. And think of the discipline in industry. People were drunk less and stole less. That's for sure—outrages were not allowed. They grabbed you by the scruff of the neck right away . . . Well, well, they did overdo it sometimes, but the family structure was tighter at least. And the young people weren't so wild—no beards, no miniskirts, none of this behavior. And there was a lot less hooliganism, too. They really watched then."

They don't usually listen to arguments. The older ones dismiss me: "Well, it did happen. But Nikita blew it out of proportion, exaggerated. And made up a lot, too."

Their children, their young listeners believe them and judge even more decisively. And they are even less capable of hearing the truth. And when you tell them of the nightmares of the GULag, about the millions of senseless deaths, about tens of millions of slaves, they simply refuse to listen. The more enlightened of them allude to Tupolev and Korolev*— "Now, they were incarcerated, but look how successfully they worked, how much they did for the development of aviation and technology."

Tupolev and Korolev also worked in sharashkas. They worked with the same passion with which Ivan Denisovich Shukhov laid bricks. Maintaining their "noble habit for work," they, just like my Marfino friends and comrades, were enthralled by their own ideas, projects, their calling. And were just as tightly bound to our country, its past and present, perhaps without always being aware of it.

*Sergei Pavlovich Korolev (1906–1966), a scientist who worked on liquid propellants for jet-assisted takeoff engines while in a sharashka. See footnote on p. 4 for Tupolev. (Translator's note.)

Someday the history of the sharashkas will be written. It will tell at length how people continued to think, work, and create in prisons, in slavery. This history, perhaps, will give a better understanding of the real miracles of our past and present life.

Viktor Andreevich was right. We left pieces of our souls in the sharashka.

On December 19, at morning roll call, the duty officer came in with a pile of standard files—"prison cases"—and didn't count us but called us by name. "So today pack up your things. Go to the office, fill out forms. And if you have personal things, bring them. You don't have to rush. Lunch as usual. And you'll have dinner at the other place."

By that time I had brought over almost all my archives from the laboratory to the yurt. My pals from the machine shop made me a large, sturdy plywood suitcase. I compiled lists and outlines of all the files, notebooks, pads, and lists of books. Everything in duplicate. Some of the "suspicious" texts—philosophy, history, and political thought—I had given to Gumer beforehand.

He and Ivan Emelianovich saw us off, "the last veterans of the acoustics lab." Gumer pulled out a bottle of vodka from his desk, poured it into glasses, measuring cups, and jars. Vanya and Valentina Ivanovna drank with us: "For the road."

"So that this is not our last time together. And that the next time will be out there."

Vanya and Valentina asked me to give their regards to Sergei Grigorievich, inviting us to visit them when we were out. Valentina wiped away tears.

The text of the dissertation had been typed and bound, only a few of the illustrations were needed. In my last hours I tried to explain something to her, but she waved me away—this wasn't the time.

Everyone was touched and agitated. However, it wasn't as upsetting or tense as the times when prisoners were "pulled out." And I had time to put together a rhymed epistle to the remaining ones. It began, "Farewell, the Marfino lindens, farewell, our phony institute." And it ended with a tender greeting to my friends and everyone who helped us in a difficult hour "with at least a kind word."

I dragged the extremely heavy suitcase from my yurt to the guardhouse before lunch.

"Please check these early. These are all my personal books, notes, creative and scientific materials."

The duty officer shrugged.

"What is there to check? You have a paper from the sharashka—certifying that you don't owe them anything. That means you're in order. You can take anything of your own that you want."

They took us away in the evening. We all fit in a single van. Another van carried our suitcases, bags, and backpacks.

Through the van's metal walls we could barely make out the creak of the gates, the voices of the guards. In the tiny, barred window the zone's bright streetlamp flashed. We hit a pothole. We were off.

Farewell, sharashka!

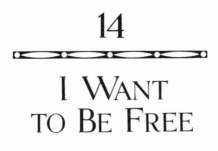

14

I WANT
TO BE FREE

Humanity lives by a single
Mutual guarantee of good.

—UNKNOWN NUN,
recorded by Marina Tsvetaeva

We greeted the New Year—1954—in prison. We spent three weeks there. Then the last eighteen Marfiners were taken to Kuchino, a settlement not far from Moscow, where several hundred prisoners and approximately the same number of free employed workers, engineers, and technicians prepared various kinds of radio equipment, electronic equipment, and measuring devices.

Vasilii and I worked in the technical library—translating and reviewing English, German, French, Italian, Czech articles, descriptions of equipment, and technical instructions and compiling a systematic catalog of books and journals. The quotas were the usual—a signature [twenty-four pages] of translation every four days, and a commensurate quota for reviewing and cataloging.

The overfulfillment of the quotas was rewarded with "credits." Depending on how much you overfulfilled, one workday could equal a day and a half, two and a half, and even three days of incarceration.

Another radical innovation was the fact that released prisoners simply walked out the gate. Back in Marfino, those whose term was almost up were taken away a month or six weeks before its end. From 1947 to 1953 everyone sentenced under Article 58 was sent to lifelong exile after prison or camp. But in 1954, the longtime residents of Kuchino, returning from family visits, said that their recently released comrades had already visited their homes, sent greetings, and were looking for work in Moscow.

Vasilii and I tried as hard as we could. We were sorry that overtime and work on Sundays were forbidden.

Our chief, an engineer major, an ox-eyed beauty with a braided crown, was more often generously benevolent than peevishly curt, and by the end of November, in the course of ten working months I had worked approximately one hundred fifty credit days. Instead of June 7, 1955—that was the date given at my last sentencing—I hoped to be set free before the end of 1954.*

On December 7 at morning prisoner count the duty officer called me. "You're being released today. Go fill out your forms."

About ten days before that I had dragged the same old suitcase to the local security officer—a dry, dreary captain—and asked him to check through it and fill out the permission form so that it could be taken out well ahead of time.

The last body search. Sitting undressed in the duty officer's room, I kept demanding my suitcase. The godfather came in, and looking off to the side, said that he hadn't had time to check it: "It's all in different languages. All kinds of scientific papers. I'm not required to understand that. We'll turn it over to the office."

Then I said calmly, even humbly, but firmly: "In that case I won't get dressed and I won't leave here until I get my things. You can carry me by force beyond the gates. These books and notes are the most important things I have. I won't leave without them."

The security officer and the duty officer were confused. The duty officer tried to shout and order me around. But I replied just as meekly: "From this day on I am a free citizen by law and I do not have to obey your orders. Without my books and notes I will not budge."

The captain left. I could hear him telephoning in the next room to his colleague—the security officer for the sharashka and head of the prison, who was out sick that day. Then he returned. And still looking to one side, he said irritably: "What are you doing sitting around as if you were in a bath? Get dressed, and take away your suitcase."

But he and the duty officer took their revenge. That fall almost every day somebody was released, and the former prisoners got perfectly decent clothing; engineers of "the first category" were issued felt hats and overcoats.

Back in Marfino I was issued an almost new winter coat. During the frisking it somehow disappeared, and the supply clerk brought me "a choice" of a greasy gray cotton padded jacket with burgundy patches or an older soldier's overcoat dyed black and with toggles instead of buttons. The duty officer said, laughing: "If you don't like it, you can throw it away beyond the gates. You're a free citizen now, and we are no longer responsible for your clothing or your health."

But I was looking through the contents of my suitcase, checking against the list. My heart was pounding in my throat. My ears burned. The main thing was to stay in control, not let them see how I was trembling.

Only minutes left. The young supervisor winked at me sympathetically.

The prison clerk came and handed me "the remainder from my personal

*How I lived that last year in prison is described in the first part of the memoirs I am writing together with Raisa Orlova.

account"—several tens of rubles. I held new money—issued since the reforms of 1947—for the first time in my life.

Wearing the short military coat—its fringed tails separated above my knees—I carried the heavy suitcase on my shoulder. At the gates the escort screw said: "Go on, and don't look back." And added: "Don't run, it's about two kilometers to the station, you'll be worn out."

Going outside, I tied a towel to the handle of the suitcase and dragged it in the snow. I walked along the empty street of the settlement. On one side was the sharashka wall, covered with green planks; on the other, occasional houses, gardens. It wasn't too cold. Soft, quiet snow fell . . .

FREEDOM!

Three boys passed me, hauling a sled with an aluminum jug on it. They looked around, had a whispered conference. Then they stopped and waited. "Mister—hey, mister, are you headed for the station?"

"Yes, boys. Is it far?"

"Uh-huh! Put your suitcase on the sled. It'll be easier."

They quickly arranged things; the jug went on top. We walked together. They glanced at me with merry curiosity. I asked them about school, their grades, what they were studying, if they went to Moscow often. They replied readily, interrupting one another. But they didn't ask me a single question.

We were walking along the embankment. There were about fifty paces to the station. The boys stopped and whispered among themselves.

"Mister, it's near now. We have to go back. Or the kerosene store will close, and we'll get it."

Those sweet Kuchino boys in their worn coats were the first kind greeting of freedom—liberty.

That December day—long-awaited, cherished, both the most ordinary and inexpressibly marvelous—it seemed to me that I had walked out of prison the same as I had come in.

In nine and a half years of prison I had experienced and learned no less, if not more, than in my years at the front. New experiences gave rise to new thoughts and to difficult, often indissoluble doubts. But I stubbornly believed, wanted to believe, that the cruel baseness and dull heartlessness of our organs of state security, procurators, judges, and prison and camp officers, as well as the shameless lies of our press, official propaganda, and official literature—all were merely unnatural, irregular perversions.

For I knew that despite all that there were people who, like me, unreservedly loved our country—tormented, sick, despoiled and at the same time great, the most righteous, and most wonderful country in the world. And I wanted to be with them and hoped that strengthened by my new experiences, I would return to the ranks of my former comrades, would once again be one of US.

. . .

More than ten years passed before I was convinced that I was incapable of marching in any ranks. I freed myself from my old idols and old ideals slowly, with difficulty, and inconsistently.

By the early sixties I began to realize that Stalin's policy was flawed not only in specific tactical "errors and extremes," but in its entirety from start to finish, and that both his tactics and his strategy contradicted not only the moral laws of humanity but also the principles of socialism and historical necessity itself.

However, even after that I still believed in the benefit and greatness of the October Revolution, in the immovable fairness of the basic propositions of Marxism-Leninism. And I still considered Stalin, albeit a cruel reactionary, an outstanding government leader; I didn't even want to compare him with those pygmies Hitler and Mussolini.

Khrushchev's exposé of the "cult of personality" agitated me, forced me to think not only of the past, and elicited the desire to participate in a new social life. But I felt his exposé was superficial, prejudiced, certainly not Marxist, and definitely not consistent. Blaming Stalin alone for all past disasters, catastrophes, and crimes, Khrushchev either extremely exaggerated Stalin's role or, on the contrary, diminished it to the point of caricature.

In those days I began reading the stenographic transcripts of Party congresses, the works of Plekhanov, Lenin, Bukharin, Stalin, Postyshev, and others. For the first time I read certain memoirs, old and new editions of documents. And I juxtaposed what I was reading and what I remembered with what I learned later, with what was going on in the world.

And thus I came to the conclusion that the leader who despotically had ruled our state for an entire quarter of a century—fawningly praised, endlessly sung, almost deified—was neither a genius nor a demonic titan like Caesar, Peter the Great, or Napoleon and had no superhuman qualities.

At first it was painfully shameful to admit that our idol had been no more than a clever scoundrel, a conscienceless, cruel power-lover, psychologically similar to the criminal gang leaders we encountered in the prisons and camps. (Panin, Solzhenitsyn, and several of my other zek pals realized this much sooner than I.)

Such despotic criminals are known in ancient history (Herod, Caligula, Prince Yuri Shemiaka). In our century they have been especially numerous and varied: Mussolini, Hitler, Al Capone, Stalin, Idi Amin, Pol Pot, Bokassa, Khomeini, the "Reverend" Jim Jones. You can say about each of them: "He wasn't great, he merely committed great evil." (Brecht had said that of Stalin.)

Of course, he did have some innate gifts: an excellent memory, a keen reason (reason, not intelligence), and acting ability that was better than the run of the mill. These are the very qualities that are indispensable for

professional criminals, *agents provocateurs*, and court intriguers. He knew
how to inspire trust, fool and even charm interlocutors who were quite
intelligent and perspicacious—Barbusse, Feuchtwanger, Churchill, Eisenstein; he knew how to pit against one another his actual and imagined
rivals. He thought quickly, knew how to maintain a "wise" silence, or say
a few apropos words when the topic was unfamiliar to him, and held special
briefings in order to impress specialists with his unexpected knowledge.

But spiritually he was sterile. He only managed to simplify—to coarsen
other people's thoughts, retell them in the bureaucratic and seminary-
catechismic language of his brochures and speeches. In plagiarism and
imitation, in playacting—not artistic but "real-life," practical—he was perhaps even talented. He successfully portrayed a straightforward, modest,
ordinary Party fighter—"the wonderful Georgian" that Lenin came to
love—or the crudely zealous and fierce apostle of the great Messiah, Ilyich.

Later he skillfully played the role of the democratic leader-apparatchik,
close to the rank-and-file Party members and thus far from the high-
faluting leaders and intellectuals; and so he reached the starring role as
zealous boss of the Party and government—the all-knowing, wise lover of
his people.

Like the dwarf Zaches in Hoffmann's tale, he obtained the magic power
to attribute other people's achievements and deeds to himself and to blame
his crimes and vile acts on others. Thus, by "postdating," he became a
leader and theoretician of the Revolution, a troop commander in the Civil
War, the author of those thoughts and manager of those events that at one
time created the popularity of Lenin, Trotsky, Bukharin, Tukhachevsky,
Kirov, and others. Killing his rivals, he pillaged—he plundered their
thoughts and projects. And for the disasters and defeats brought on by his
orders and ukases, his cowardice and ignorance, he punished his obedient
servants and executors: Postyshev, Kossior, Yagoda, Yezhov, Voz-
nesensky, the people's commissars, generals, Party bosses, and rank-and-
file apparatchiks. It was this way even in the early period of his despotic
rule, in 1929–1930, and it continued until the final weeks of his life, when,
totally paranoid and afraid of every shadow, he was ready to start a new
world war.

While convinced of the falsehood of my former perceptions of Stalin, I still
believed in the righteousness of Lenin and felt that the most dependable
means for the scientific comprehension of history was the critical method
developed by Marx, Engels, and the "real," nondogmatic, Marxists: Plekhanov, Eduard Bernstein, Rosa Luxemburg, György Lukács, and later
Milovan Djilas, Ernst Fischer, Robert Havemann, and Roger Garaudy.

However, I was beginning to understand that a decisive reevaluation
was necessary of the very bases of my views of the world and of man, and
of the laws of history, the interrelationship of life-style and consciousness,
politics, and morality.

The revolts in Poland and Hungary in 1956; the inexorable failure of our agriculture; the massacres of strikers in Novocherkassk and Dzhezkazgan (1960–1961); the end of the "thaw"—the era of "late rehabilitation"; the renaissance of Stalinist methods of ideological struggle: arrests, trials, arbitrary censorship; the Cultural Revolution in China, student revolts in the USA and France, the tragic fate of the Czech spring of "socialism with a human face," crushed by our tanks, the "socialist cults" of idols of varying caliber—Mao, Kim Il-sung, Fidel Castro, Enver Hoxha, and others—all this proved to me that the forecasts of Marx and Engels were utopian, the methods of their analyses were applicable only to certain problems of West European history, and the principles of their material dialectics apparently did not lead by accident from their foggy theories to the inhuman practices of Lenin and Trotsky and the totally unprincipled totalitarianism of Stalin, who killed millions of people, entire nations. (This was not unprecedented in history. Certain words of the Evangelists, the words and deeds of the Apostles led from the wholesome humanity of the New Testament to the wild fanaticism of the Crusaders and Inquisitors, to the cruel intolerance of the iconoclasts, the flagellants, the self-immolators.)

Freeing myself from the blinders of the Party, from severely two-dimensional criteria—"ours or alien, there is no middle course"—I was losing my fear of ideological taboos, my distrust of idealism and liberalism and the concepts of freedom of the personality and tolerance.

And I tried to overcome my inability to listen to people who disagreed with me, my inability to look from a point of view other than my own—that deafness and blindness that I used to think was ideological adherence to principle.

As a repentant prodigal son I returned to Leo Tolstoy, Korolenko, Schiller, Herzen. In a completely different way than before they were revealed to me and so were the limitless worlds—beloved since childhood—of the Bible, Pushkin, Goethe, Dostoevsky, which in my youth I had perceived in an impoverished, flat way. "May the highest joy of the children of the earth always be the personality" (Goethe).

For the first time I read Berdiaev, Teilhard de Chardin, Semyon Frank, Vernadsky, Camus, Sartre, Schweitzer, Martin Luther King, Jr., Robert Ardrey.

My discoveries astonished me. Probably the students of Galileo experienced the same joy as they escaped the cramped, tightly locked universe of Ptolemy.

Joy predominated despite many bitter feelings—pangs of conscience and attacks of shame. The world around and within me was becoming more spacious, kinder. Even though more clearly and persistently questions now appeared for which I couldn't find and no longer hoped to find answers, and knots of contradictions—social, tribal, religious, ideological—that are tragically long-lived and, at least in my time, are not to be untangled or cut.

Once I used to think that if I lost my faith in socialism I would immediately kill myself. And now I continue to stubbornly "squeeze out drop by drop the slave from myself" (Chekhov). I squeeze out from my mind and soul the servile dependence on that lost faith and on all ideologies that I had believed in, and on all the *we*'s with which I am eternally bound: *we* Soviets, *we* Russians, *we* intellectuals, *we* Jews, *we* frontline veterans, *we* former zeks, *we* former Communists, *we* dissidents, *we* parents, grandparents, old people.

I do not deny belonging to each and every one of those *we*'s, I don't forget or deny any of the obsolete ties or any of the ineradicable bonds that either grew out of deep roots or were intertwined by the whim of fate or by free choice.

But I want to be free of any sort of slavish dependence of the spirit. I will never bow to any idol, never submit to any higher powers in the name of which I must conceal the truth, fool others and myself, damn or persecute those who disagree.

Now I do not belong to any party, any "league of like-minded people." And I try to determine my relationship to history and the present through the lessons that I drew from everything that I had discovered or personally experienced.

I do not feel I have the right to teach anyone, and I can't imagine how much my lessons could influence anyone else; but I am certain that I must recount them as accurately as possible. This has become an inner need, acknowledged as a lifetime duty.

Tolerance is the main condition for preserving life on this planet, which is being filled every day with more numerous and more effective weapons of mass destruction. Arguments between nations and governments or parties, the growth of explosive hatred, can become at any moment a mortal threat to all of humanity.

Tolerance does not demand that disagreements and contradictions be hidden. On the contrary, understanding the impossibility of universal conformity and harmony, it demands that alien and contrary opinions be heard without hostility or hatred. Do not pretend to agree if you disagree. However, you must not suppress or persecute those who do not agree with you.

In the first century of our era it was said: "Blessed are the meek . . . Blessed are the merciful . . . Blessed are the peacemakers."

In the last two thousand years there has been no time when peacemakers were more necessary—real ones, not hypocrites, but selfless, tolerant peacemakers.

And in order for tolerance and actual peacemaking to be possible, we need *expression*. So that each and every person can express unhindered his thoughts, opinions, doubts, to report and learn about any event, wherever it may occur.

"Our work must not be done in the name of the future, but in the name of the eternal present, in which the future and past are one" (Berdiaev).

The meaning of my life is in working in the name of tolerance and expression. That is why I am recounting what I remember and know of the past and present.

Despite all the evil things to which I was privy—and realizing my guilt only much later and therefore even more strongly—despite all the misfortunes that befell me, I consider myself a lucky man:

because my first wife was Nadezhda Kolchinskaya—an actively kind, selfless friend without fear or reproach;

because Raisa Orlova-Kopelev became my second self;

because our daughters—Maya, Elena, Svetlana, and Maria—most of my relatives, and *all* of our friends generously give us their support, both in joy and in sorrow.

Various people have influenced and influence me now.

Some have already been mentioned—in dedications and in the text. I can't name them all here. Thinking of everyone, I here thank the following:

ANNA AKHMATOVA, whose poetry illuminated our lives in those years; enduring painful times, my wife and I read her poems, breathed them;

LIDIYA CHUKOVSKAYA, who devoted herself to the zealous service of Russian literature; a faithful and demanding friend, she is as solid as a diamond, defending the laws of morality and the laws of the Word;

MARION DOENHOFF, whose thought, clear and piercingly sharp, is a weapon of unfeigned tolerance ("my position is between all the chairs"); true to the noble traditions of the past, she is open to the present in a living unity of conservatism and liberalism, aristocracy and democracy;

FRIDA VIGDOROVA, an unforgettable friend, in word and deed she selflessly served good and truth, aided suffering people, unhesitatingly responding to every call for help;

MIKHAIL BAKHTIN, who leads me to the most profound, hidden sources of art and creative thought; his great wisdom, inseparable from a humility that is almost ascetic, is free of all bustle and is beneficial to the mind and the soul;

HEINRICH BÖLL, poet, human being, and friend; his statement "the word is the sanctuary of freedom," his thoughts and Christian heart, always capable of understanding and loving someone who thinks differently, helped me find the path to the religion of brotherhood that I will profess to the end of my days;

MAX FRISCH, a wise and sad writer, who reminded me of Korolenko's testament, warning against the creation of idols, and proved how current and timely that warning is in art and in the life of every person and every nation;

VYACHESLAV IVANOV, scholar and poet; I admire the genius, breadth, power, and inexhaustibility of his thought; I have been learning from him for many years and will continue to learn as long as I am able;

ANDREI SAKHAROV, the majesty of his spirit, the power of his intellect, and the purity of his soul, his chivalrous courage and selfless kindness feed my faith in the future of Russia and mankind;

I thank those who are no longer living—in my memory they are immortal.

I thank everyone named previously and now, and all my unnamed friends, teachers, and kind acquaintances whose deeds, thoughts, and words help me live.

INDEX

Freud, Sigmund, 122, 186, 187
Frisch, Max, 247–48
Fritz B., 117, 118, 203

Garaudy, Roger, 244
Gay-Lussac, Joseph Louis, 15
Genishta, E., 139
Georgii Dmitrievich, 235
Gestapo, 95–96
Glinka, Mikhail Ivanovich, 23
Goebbels, Joseph, 199, 228
Goethe, Johann Wolfgang von, 231,
  245
Gogol, Nikolai Vasilievich, 235
Good Soldier Schweik, The (Hašek),
  122
Göring, Hermann, 197, 198, 228
Gorky, Maksim, 14, 173, 186, 230
GPU, 48*n*, 96, 226
Griboedov, Aleksandr Sergeevich,
  150*n*, 166
Grigoriev, Lieutenant Colonel, 207
Grossman, Vasilii, 187
Gulliver's Travels (Swift), 101
Gumilev, Nikolai Stepanovich, 24,
  41
Gustav H., 123–24

Havemann, Robert, 244
Heine, Heinrich, 187, 201
Herzen, Aleksandr Ivanovich, 235,
  245
Hess, Rudolf, 197
Himmler, Heinrich, 197
Hitler, Adolf, 122, 135, 183, 185, 187,
  189, 193, 197–99, 208, 225, 227, 228,
  231–32
Hoffmann, Ernst, 244
Homer, 64
Horst R., 203, 204
"Horst Wessel Song," 122

I Chose Freedom (Kravchenko), 79
Ilf, Ilya Arnoldovich, 187
Inna Levidova, 23, 212, 218
Ivan IV Vasilievich (the Terrible),
  tsar of Russia, 224–25
Ivanov, Vyacheslav, 248

Ivan Yakovlevich (Vanya), 173,
  179–80, 182, 185, 194, 238
Izakov, Boris, 215
Izmailov, Gumer Akhatovich, 68, 92,
  139, 145, 146, 157, 160, 164, 178, 185,
  209, 211, 212, 216, 233, 234, 238
Izvestia, 8

Jalil, Musa, 92, 146
Jews:
  assimilation of, 187, 202
  in Bolshevik Revolution, 18, 41
  in Germany, 201–2
  persecution of, 182–89
  prejudice against, 83, 97, 133, 135,
    158, 173–76, 201–2
  in Rumania, 110–11
  torture of, 185
  Zionist, 182, 183
Journal of the Acoustical Society, 88

Kaganovich, Lazar Moiseevich, 14,
  175, 184, 205, 209
Kalinin, Mikhail Ivanovich, 232
Kamenev, Lev Borisovich, 223, 224,
  232
Kant, Immanuel, 17
Kapital, Das (Marx), 143
Kapitsa, Peter Leonidovich, 188
Katya, Auntie, 163–64
kaundka, 122
Kemnits, Anna Vladimirovna, 170,
  171
Kemnits, Viktor Andreevich, 170–72
Kerensky, Aleksandr Feodorovich,
  42, 232
KGB (Committee for State
  Security), 3*n*, 205
Khodasevich, Vladislav, 50
Khodynka Field, 195
Khromushina, Galina, 215
Khrushchev, Nikita Sergeevich, 56*n*,
  206, 210, 236
Kipling, Rudyard, 72
Kirov, Sergei Mironovich, 57, 58, 223,
  244
Kitaigorodsky, Professor, 117
Klubman, Mark, 213–14

About the Author

Lev Kopelev, who was born in Kiev in 1912, has been a leading figure in the Soviet human rights movement for almost two decades. A distinguished authority on German literature and linguistics, he established a reputation as one of the firmest opponents of Stalinism and arbitrary police power, defending many well-known dissidents, among them his friends Solzhenitsyn and Sakharov.

Ease My Sorrows is the third volume of his memoirs. *The Education of a True Believer* (1980) describes his early years as a Soviet loyalist. *To Be Preserved Forever* (1977) tells the story of Kopelev's experience in World War II, first as a Soviet officer, then as a *zek,* or prisoner. A major in Soviet intelligence, he was arrested for protesting the looting, murder, and rape of German civilians at the end of the war. Convicted of "bourgeois humanism," he spent seven years—the years described in *Ease My Sorrows*—in the GULag.

Kopelev, who was rehabilitated in the Khrushchev era, was instrumental in the publication of Solzhenitsyn's revolutionary novella, *One Day in the Life of Ivan Denisovich,* and, through his tireless activity on behalf of Russian writers and intellectuals, became acknowledged as "the white-bearded godfather of Moscow's disaffected literary elite." He and his wife, the writer Raisa Orlova, were stripped of their Soviet citizenship in 1981 and are now residents of the Federal Republic of Germany. Kopelev received the Peace Prize at the 1981 Frankfurt International Book Fair for his contributions to world peace.

About the Translator

Antonina W. Bouis's translations from the Russian include the memoirs of Dmitri Shostakovich and novels by Valentin Rasputin and Bulat Okudjava.